Microsoft® Press

Microsoft®
Flight Simulator 2000
inside moves

Bart Farkas

PUBLISHED BY
Microsoft Press
A Division of Microsoft Corporation
One Microsoft Way
Redmond, Washington 98052-6399

Library of Congress Cataloging-in-Publication Data
Farkas, Bart.
  Microsoft Flight Simulator 2000 : Inside Moves / Bart Farkas.
      p. cm.
  Includes index.
  ISBN 0-7356-0547-5
    1. Microsoft Flight Simulator (Computer file) 2. Computer flight games.   I. Title.

TL712.8 .F3696   1999
794.8'753--dc21   99-043751
                                                                         CIP

Printed and bound in the United States of America.

1 2 3 4 5 6 7 8 9 MLML 4 3 2 1 0 9

Distributed in Canada by Penguin Books Canada Limited.

A CIP catalogue record for this book is available from the British Library.

Microsoft Press books are available through booksellers and distributors worldwide. For further information about international editions, contact your local Microsoft Corporation office or contact Microsoft Press International directly at fax (425) 936-7329. Visit our Web site at mspress.microsoft.com.

Acquisitions Editors: Tamara D. Thorne, Christey Bahn
Project Editor: Sandra Haynes
Manuscript Editor: Jenny Moss Benson
Technical Editor: Jack Beaudry

Dedication

For Cori and Adam.
That says it all.

Bart Farkas

Contents

Microsoft
Flight Simulator 2000

Contents

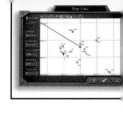

Contents

Microsoft

Flight Simulator 2000

Contents

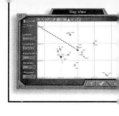

PART IV   APPENDIXES   231

Acknowledgments

I must begin by thanking the team at Microsoft Press: Christey, Sandra, Tamara, Jack, and Jenny. They were always there when I needed them to offer their support, expert skills, and experience. Thanks also to Rob Nance and Joel Panchot for the artwork, Carl Diltz and Dan Latimer for the layout, Shawn Peck and his proof team for keeping everyone on their toes, and Kevin Lane-Cummings and Dail Magee, Jr., for their additional review late in the project.

From the Flight Simulator 2000 team, I'd like to thank Bruce Williams and Kit Warfield, both of whom worked tirelessly to ensure technical accuracy. Also, thanks to Brent Conklin, who helped with getting the betas running and came through with some critical scenery details.

I also need to thank Ron Hunt, an experienced Boeing 767 airline pilot, for his many contributions throughout the book. To Jon Paul Hooie, Steve Barry, George Coy, and Mike Mullins, I must also give a big thanks for their expertise. Last, but certainly not least, I'd like to thank Doug Kiang for covering air rallies and aerobatics, and also for his critical help with the multiplayer section.

From my family, I want to thank my father, Glen Farkas, for understanding when plans fell through; and my one-year-old son, Adam, who always smiled at me when I emerged from long stretches of work in my office.

Bart Farkas

Introduction

The romantic idea of flying high above the Earth alone in an airplane has captivated human spirits since before powered flight was invented. But for many people, flight is only a dream. Aviation is expensive or inconvenient, and physical limitations such as bad vision, diabetes, or even a fear of heights keep some would-be pilots grounded.

These limitations in real-life flight are perhaps why Microsoft Flight Simulator has enjoyed such an unprecedented run as a top-selling game. With today's faster computers that are capable of bringing the simulated experience closer to reality, flight simulators allow everyone to taste the joy of flight in the comfort of their own home. Even for those of us who do hold pilot's licenses, Flight Simulator is an excellent tool for practicing everything from basic principles of flight and basic maneuvers to setting up elaborate "what-if" scenarios that would be unsafe in real aircraft.

We're lucky to live in a time when technology allows us to simulate so accurately something as complex as flight, and Microsoft Flight Simulator 2000 wins high marks among flight simulators for the personal computer. With its spectacular graphics, realistic flight models, and reams of background information on all aspects of flight, it provides everything you need to take your flight experience to a new level.

This Book

This book is not a glorified manual, but rather an extension of the Microsoft Flight Simulator 2000 *Pilot's Handbook*. Use this book in conjunction with the *Pilot's Handbook* to take your experience using Flight Simulator to a higher level. Flight Simulator offers a vast number of exciting, realistic, and entertaining scenarios, and this book is designed to get you involved in flight experiences that you have not even considered. Wherever possible, I've included anecdotes from real pilots (including myself) to bring the world of Flight Simulator 2000 even closer to reality.

I have left the basics of flight to the experts in those areas and concentrated instead on other aspects of flight. To get up to speed on flying or on Flight Simulator, I recommend the well-known aviation educator and humorist Rod Machado's excellent tutorials in the *Pilot's Handbook* or Flight Simulator's online Help.

Part I: Inside Flight Simulator

Chapter 1, "Making It Real," contains information on customizing Flight Simulator by adjusting windows, weather, and realism settings. Chapter 2, "The Aircraft," provides a closer look at each of the aircraft in Flight Simulator and details sample flights that highlight specific flight characteristics or special uses for each aircraft. Chapter 3, "Navigational Tools," deals with general navigation, including the use of the new Global Positioning System (GPS) receiver, while Chapter 4, "Adventures," takes you through the situations and supplies tips for several of the built-in adventures.

Part II: Exploring and Fun

This part of the book shows you fun and challenging flights that will take your piloting skills to the next level while still being entertaining. Chapter 5, "The Air Rally," offers a unique look at the air rally sport and contains a practice rally and four original rallies created especially for Flight Simulator 2000. Chapter 6, "Emergencies," takes you into the realm of emergencies, from two engines out in a Concorde to hydraulic failure in a Boeing 777-300; these emergencies will put your heart in your throat as you fight to get the aircraft safely on the ground.

Chapter 7, "Challenging Flights," contains some freshly devised challenging flights. These flights aren't emergencies, but they test your piloting abilities in various exciting situations. Chapter 8, "World Highlights," takes you on a tour of several graphically impressive and historically significant locations throughout the world. Chapter 9, "Flying with Others," shows how to get connected to the MSN Gaming Zone and suggests several novel multiplayer activities.

Part III: Flight Simulator Professional

This part of the book deals with aspects of Flight Simulator that are more pertinent to you if you have Flight Simulator 2000 Professional Edition; however, much of this section applies to both editions of Flight Simulator. Chapter 10, "The Aircraft Editor," covers this powerful tool, which allows you to customize aircraft in many ways, from the instrument panel to the intricacies of the flight dynamics. Chapter 11, "Advanced Flight Techniques," covers challenging skills including aerobatics and instrument flight rules (IFR) flight.

Part IV: Appendixes

Finally, the appendixes cover a host of topics including how to pick joysticks, rudder pedals, and flight yokes (Appendix A, "Controllers and Other Peripherals"), as well as how to get additional help (Appendix B, "Online Resources"). Of course, the appendixes apply to both editions of Flight Simulator.

The History of Microsoft Flight Simulator

Flight Simulator was first created by Bruce Artwick in 1978 for the then-popular Macintosh Apple II computer. As a pilot and programmer, Bruce had a unique vision that led him to produce popular versions of Flight Simulator for the Apple II and Commodore 64 computers. After Bruce founded the Bruce Artwick Organization (BAO), Ltd., Microsoft hired Artwick to complete a new flight simulator program for the IBM personal computer. The new 3-D graphics in this version made it a highly successful piece of software. The following is a timeline of the development of Flight Simulator and some of the features that each version incorporated.

- 1978: Apple II version of Flight Simulator released.
- 1979: Flight Simulator II for the Commodore 64 released.
- 1981–82: Flight Simulator 1.05 released for the IBM personal computer. Featured 3-D graphics.
- 1984: Bruce Artwick Organization, Ltd., officially formed.
- 1988: Flight Simulator 3.0 released. Featured multiple window support, new aircraft, and two-player mode.

- 1989: Flight Simulator 4.0 released. Featured 16-color scenery and new aircraft.
- 1993: Flight Simulator 5.0 released. Featured 256-color photo-realistic scenery, a new graphics engine, and flight models (how an aircraft is simulated).
- 1995: Microsoft purchases the Bruce Artwick Organization and relocates the company to Redmond, Washington.
- 1995: Flight Simulator 5.1 released. Featured navigational aids and worldwide scenery.
- 1996: Flight Simulator for Microsoft Windows 95 released. Featured multiplayer support.
- 1997: Flight Simulator 98 released. Featured 3-D acceleration support and more highly detailed cities. Software Development Kit (SDK) released early in 1998.
- 1999: Flight Simulator 2000 released. Read on to see what's new!

New Features in Microsoft Flight Simulator 2000

Not only are there a bevy of new features in Flight Simulator 2000, but there are also two different products to choose from: Flight Simulator 2000 and Flight Simulator 2000 Professional Edition. The Professional Edition differs from Flight Simulator 2000 in that it's geared toward Flight Simulator enthusiasts and real pilots who want more content and will use the simulator flight training. Here's just some of what's new in both editions of Flight Simulator 2000:

- Two new aircraft: the massive Boeing 777-300 and the only supersonic commercial jetliner in existence, the Concorde.
- New cockpits, instrument panels, and external 3-D models to make the simulator more realistic.
- 16-bit color scenery graphics and new true elevation and terrain data to make the view out of the cockpit highly realistic.
- Enhanced online Help and a detailed *Pilot's Handbook* featuring flight instruction from Rod Machado.

- A short video, "Getting Started," in which aviation legends John and Martha King explain how to start flying in Flight Simulator 2000.
- New realism options that affect the flight characteristics, engines, instruments, and flight controls of every aircraft.
- More than 21,000 airports (almost every public airport in the world).
- Real weather settings that allow you to download real-world weather information for the areas along your flight path, as well as highly detailed customizable weather settings including multiple cloud layers, precipitation, icing, and lightning.
- The ability to create flight plans for visual flight rules or instrument flight rules conditions using navigational aids such as very high frequency omnidirectional radio range transmitters and the Global Positioning System.
- Compatibility with Flight Simulator 98 adventures, aircraft, and scenery.
- Six new or improved high-detail cities with exceptional detail and 3-D modeling.

New Features in the Professional Edition

This is the first time that Microsoft has had two different versions of Flight Simulator, creating a new version for flight enthusiasts and pilots. Flight Simulator 2000 Professional Edition includes several exciting enhancements for the serious enthusiast who wants to take the flight simulator experience to the limit. The two biggest additions to the Professional Edition are the two additional aircraft and the powerful Aircraft Editor. Here's what you can expect:

- Extra-large high-resolution instrument flight rules (IFR) panels for the Cessna 182S and Mooney Bravo.
- Two new aircraft, the Mooney Bravo and the Beech/Raytheon (Beechcraft) King Air 350.
- Six new highly detailed cities: Washington, D.C., Seattle, Rome, Tokyo, Berlin, and Boston.
- The Aircraft Editor for customizing flight dynamics and instrument panels.
- Portions of a CD-ROM training package from Cessna.

Maximizing Performance and Realism

Flight Simulator 2000 places high demands on today's computers. There are, however, ways to get the most out of the software without sacrificing performance. Just adding a 3-D accelerator card can substantially increase the program's performance, and the installation option that you choose can also change the speed at which the simulator will run. This section addresses installation, 3-D acceleration, and joysticks/flight controllers.

Tip: *After you select an installation option, you'll see how much space it requires as well as the amount of space available on your hard disk. This is an easy way to tell if you have enough space to install the simulator fully.*

Installation

You have three options for installing Flight Simulator 2000: compact, typical, or custom, as shown in Figure I-1. In general, always choose the largest installation option that your hard disk has room for. If you have a large hard disk with 2 gigabytes (GB) or more of free disk space, I recommend that you choose the Custom install option to install the entire simulator and all scenery files on your hard disk. This will speed up performance and ensure that you won't be prompted to insert a different CD-ROM as you fly.

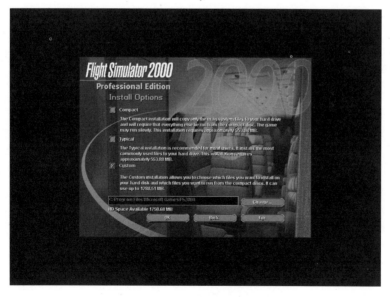

Figure I-1   *Choose the largest installation option that your hard disk has space for.*

3-D Accelerator Graphics Cards

Although adding random access memory (RAM), a faster CPU, dedicated flight controls, or a bigger monitor will all enhance the Flight Simulator experience, nothing will add as much value to your flight time as adding a 3-D graphics accelerator. Even an inexpensive 3-D card will make a major improvement to the quality of graphics displayed by Flight Simulator.

Graphics accelerators come in a wide variety of prices with a great range of features. Consider the following attributes of any 3-D card that you evaluate for use with Flight Simulator.

Memory Capacity

Most top-of-the-line 3-D cards come with 16 or 32 MB of RAM, which has two uses in the video card. The memory that is dedicated to holding the picture displayed on your monitor is called the *frame buffer*. A larger frame buffer means that the 3-D card can display a picture at a higher resolution (with more dots). A screen resolution of 640 × 480 pixels is generally considered the minimum acceptable resolution for modern graphical applications like games or simulators. Higher resolutions are preferable because they allow Flight Simulator 2000 to show more detail on the screen and to draw objects without jagged edges.

The second use for the RAM in the 3-D graphics card is to store the textures and other information necessary to draw each frame on the screen. By keeping textures and geometry data in the video card, the computer can allow the graphics accelerator to handle most of the work of drawing the image. This leaves the main system CPU free to keep track of more important things like how many buildings there are in downtown Chicago or how low the deck of the Golden Gate Bridge is when you zoom underneath it.

Color Depth

The number of colors that a 3-D graphics accelerator card is able to compute and display is called the *color depth*. This depth is usually measured in computer bits. Without delving into technical explanations, a picture that can have any of 32,768 colors has 16-bit color depth. The common color depths of 16-bit, 24-bit, and 32-bit are all quite good for 3-D simulations. Twenty-four-bit and 32-bit color depths are often referred to as "true color" modes because they can display 16 million colors at once.

What is important to know is that some 3-D cards can display only 16-bit color depth modes, while others can display 16-bit and true color modes. If you want to be able to run Flight Simulator 2000 in a true color screen mode, make sure that you have a 3-D accelerator card capable of such color depth. As you might expect, the more colors that the 3-D card uses, the more work that it has to do, and so the more slowly Flight Simulator 2000 will run. It is helpful to try your 3-D card at a variety of resolutions and color depths to see which ones provide the best experience.

AGP or PCI Interface?

Most home computers with a Pentium II processor or better feature an accelerated graphics port (AGP) slot for video cards. This is simply a specific kind of slot on the motherboard inside the computer into which you can fit an AGP video card. A video card that uses the AGP port is able to access the system RAM in the computer very quickly without interrupting the CPU. This fast memory access means that the video card can use the system RAM as if it were RAM on the video card. The upshot is that AGP video cards can use larger textures to create more realistic graphics. In short, if you have a computer with an AGP port, an AGP 3-D card is your best choice. If you don't have an AGP port, a PCI 3-D accelerator is the next best thing.

3-D Features

The market for 3-D graphics accelerator cards has become very competitive, so most 3-D cards are fully featured and perform as well as the other cards in their price range. However, it is still worthwhile to check the list of features of any 3-D card that you are considering. The 3-D card should have the following:

- **Anti-aliasing.** Anti-aliasing blends color and brightness along the edges of objects to blur the jagged lines created by the pixels on the screen.
- **Filtering.** Filtering removes the jagged, blocky appearance of textures on objects by blending colors of adjacent pixels. Bi-linear and Tri-linear filtering are slower methods of filtering that produce a better quality picture, but they require a fast and expensive video processor for acceptable performance.

- **Fogging.** Fogging, also called *alpha blending,* lets the video card produce fog effects in the picture on the screen. Cheaper cards "cheat" by adding fog to the picture two-dimensionally (meaning that the fog is "flat," not 3-D), but better cards produce a hazy mist that obscures objects in the distance more than those in the foreground. The quality of fogging effects can add a lot of realism to the simulation.
- **Lighting.** The quality of the lighting effects depends on the abilities of the 3-D accelerator. Good cards can calculate the color of a dot in the picture and the brightness with which that dot should be displayed in one step. Less expensive cards might require two steps to do the calculation or might skip the brightness calculation completely. Lighting has a dramatic effect on the quality of the image.
- **Geometry.** Most 3-D cards include a geometry engine that lets the video card calculate the perspective of the textures on an object and the relative shapes of the objects in the picture. This calculation takes a lot of load off the main system CPU and makes the game or simulation run faster.

Keep in mind that all of these 3-D effects have to be written into the simulation before the 3-D card can use them—they are not added automatically by the 3-D card.

Installing a 3-D Accelerator Graphics Card

Installing new hardware can be an intimidating task, even if you have previous experience doing it. Consult with sales staff where you buy your 3-D card for advice, and make sure to review and follow the manufacturer's instructions included with the new hardware. If the installation process goes correctly, the entire procedure can take as little as five minutes, but if the installation process goes incorrectly, it's another matter. Entire books have been written on solving the problems of misbdwlaving personal computers.

Flight Simulator 2000 uses the Direct3D API (application programming interface) to display 3-D graphics. You should choose a 3-D graphics accelerator that is compatible with all of the features of Direct3D. This does not mean that your 3-D card should not support other APIs, but full support of Direct3D is essential.

Joysticks and Flight Controllers

Although it's possible to fly using a mouse or your keyboard, it's much more realistic and fun to use a joystick or flight yoke. You can adjust the joystick settings as discussed below in the assignments section. See Appendix A, "Controllers and Other Peripherals," for details on some of the controllers that are currently on the market.

Calibrate Joystick

Point to Controls on the Options menu, and click Calibrate Joystick to open the Game Controllers dialog box. Here you can choose a new joystick or change settings for the current joystick by clicking the Properties button. (See Figure I-2.)

Assignments

Point to Controls on the Option menu, and click Assignments to open the Controls Assignments dialog box, which allows you to customize your controls specifically for the keyboard or for whatever joystick you are using. (See Figure I-3.) For example, if you want to use the L key to retract the landing gear, you can use this dialog box to match that key to the Landing Gear Up/Down action. This dialog box also shows what controls are currently set up

Figure I-2   *You can access joystick calibration by clicking the Properties button of the Game Controllers dialog box.*

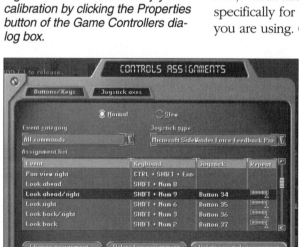

Figure I-3   *The Controls Assignments dialog box allows you to set which buttons on your joystick perform certain tasks.*

for your joystick. To change button or key assignments, click the Change Assignment button. For example, you might want your hat switch to pan the virtual cockpit rather than change viewpoints.

Sensitivities

Point to Controls on the Options menu, and click Sensitivities to display the sensitivities and null zone slider sets. (See Figure I-4.) Use this dialog box to set the sensitivities and null zones for each axis that your joystick controls. If you click the Simple button, you can set the sensitivities for all axes with just one slider, but if you want to get into the nitty-gritty, click the Advanced button. There are four axes: ailerons, elevator, throttle, and rudder. Each has a sensitivity slider. The further to the right the slider is, the more sensitive the controls will be. The Null Zone sliders dictate how much "play" there is in the controls. This means that a Null Zone slider set to the far right will take a more dramatic motion to get a response. An axis with the Sensitivity slider at the far left and the Null Zone slider at the far right will be very forgiving and slow to respond, while the opposite settings will require more skill to avoid overcontrolling.

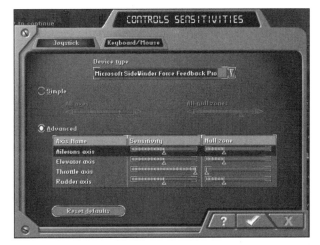

Figure I-4   *The Controls Sensitivities dialog box allows you to play with the virtual "feel" of the controls.*

Forces

If you have a force-feedback joystick or yoke, use the options in this section to control which events or effects result in forces. (See Figure I-5.) These forces

are Control Surface Forces (the feel of flight on the controls), Stick Shaker (a stall warning system on larger aircraft), Crash Effects, Ground Bumps, and Retractable Gear Thumps (when the gear lowers or raises). Clicking the check box beside these settings turns them on or off.

Figure I-5 *Use the Controls Forces dialog box to alter which events produce force-feedback reactions.*

PART 1

Inside
Flight Simulator

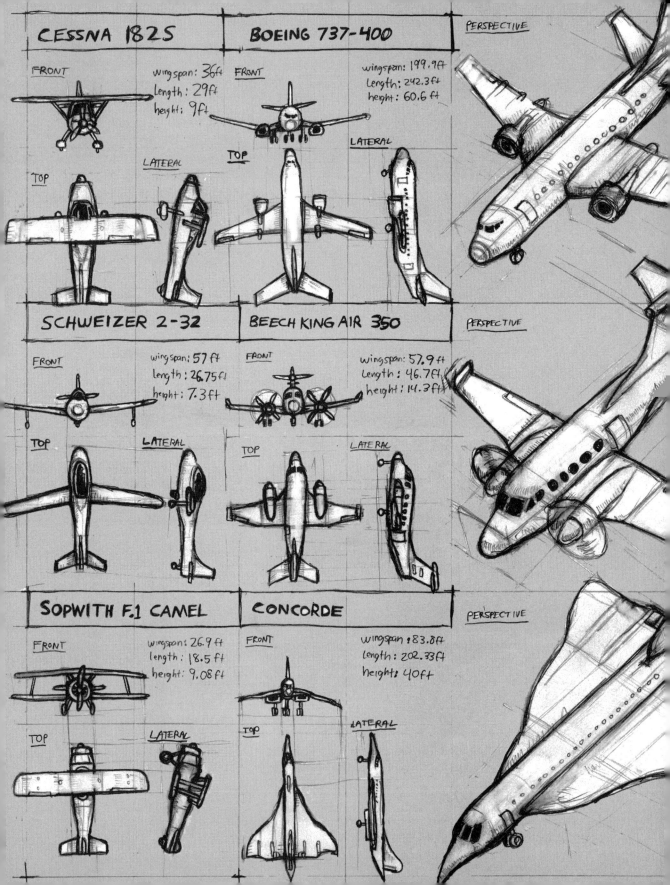

CESSNA 182S

FRONT

wingspan: 36ft
Length: 29ft
height: 9ft

TOP

LATERAL

BOEING 737-400

FRONT

wingspan: 199.9ft
Length: 242.3ft
height: 60.6ft

TOP

LATERAL

PERSPECTIVE

SCHWEIZER 2-32

FRONT

wingspan: 57 ft
length: 26.75ft
height: 7.3ft

TOP

LATERAL

BEECH KING AIR 350

FRONT

wingspan: 57.9 ft
Length: 46.7ft
height: 14.3ft

TOP

LATERAL

PERSPECTIVE

SOPWITH F.1 CAMEL

FRONT

wingspan: 26.9ft
length: 18.5 ft
height: 9.08ft

TOP

LATERAL

CONCORDE

FRONT

wingspan: 83.8ft
length: 202.33ft
height: 40ft

TOP

LATERAL

PERSPECTIVE

Chapter One

Making It Real

This chapter explores the variety of ways to personalize Microsoft Flight Simulator 2000. For example, you can:

- Set the realism settings to Hard and carry out all the tasks you would need to perform if you were sitting in a real airplane, or you can adjust the realism settings to Easy to automate the more repetitive tasks so that you can concentrate on flying.
- Use the Kneeboard to put frequently accessed information right at your fingertips, and you can customize the Kneeboard's Notes page to add your own flying and performance notes.
- Download real-time weather conditions from the Internet to duplicate the weather outside your very window.
- Arrange the windows in Flight Simulator 2000 to better represent the field of view that a pilot would have in a real airplane.
- Use the built-in navigation tools to plan, create, and print an actual flight plan for a route that you intend to fly.

In this chapter, you'll learn how to use all of these features to make your flights realistic and challenging, no matter what your level of experience is.

Realism Settings

Flight Simulator 2000 has a number of ways to customize the realism of the simulation itself. To access the realism settings, on the Aircraft menu, click Realism Settings. The Realism Settings dialog box appears. (See Figure 1-1.)

Current Realism Settings

At the top of the Realism Settings dialog box is the Current Realism Settings slider that represents the overall difficulty of the simulation based on the individual settings that you have configured. To get a general feel for how the various settings will affect the simulation, try moving the slider from Easy to

Figure 1-1 *These settings affect how accurately the simulated aircraft behaves.*

Medium and then to Hard. Watch how the individual settings are turned on or off automatically to suit the general difficulty of the simulation. This is the easiest way to set the overall difficulty of the simulation without having to manually adjust the settings.

Flight Model

You change the settings in the Flight Model section of the Realism Settings dialog box (as shown in Figure 1-2) to adjust how closely the simulated aircraft behaves like its real-life counterpart. By making the simulated aircraft behave more realistically, you can get a feel for what it would be like to fly the plane in real life. On the other hand, a more realistic aircraft is also generally less forgiving, and you'll need to be more attentive to the minimum and maximum operating speeds as specified in the Aircraft Information section of online Help.

Exactly how you choose to adjust these settings is mostly a matter of personal preference. Try changing them, and then click the check mark at the bottom of the dialog box to apply the changes and return to the simulation to see how the plane feels. If you're not satisfied, return to the Realism Settings dialog box and try changing the settings a little more until you find a combination that suits you. For specific information on what each of these settings does, consult online Help, or see the sections that follow.

P-Factor

The p-factor is the asymmetrical thrust that's generated by the spinning propeller. Increasing this will cause your aircraft to want to yaw nose-left when the engine is at high RPMs and low airspeed.

Torque

Torque is the tendency of the spinning engine and propeller to roll the aircraft left (counter-clockwise) about its longitudinal axis.

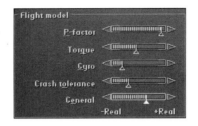

Figure 1-2   *The Realism Settings dialog box has a lot to offer those who dare to make their flight as real as possible.*

Gyroscopic Precession

Gyroscopic precession is a physical process that occurs with any spinning object. For instance, if you lean a bike to the right while riding straight ahead, the front wheel turns to the right. In an airplane, when you lift the nose off the runway, gyroscopic precession makes the plane yaw to the right. Also, when you are taking off in a taildragger airplane (such as the Extra 300S), the plane will yaw to the left when you lift the tail up as you accelerate down the runway.

Crash Tolerance

The farther to the right the crash tolerance slider is, the less tolerant (and more realistic) your aircraft's ability to handle impacts becomes. Thus, with the Crash Tolerance turned up, a hard landing that would be tolerated before might now cause a crash.

General

The General slider bar simply increases all the other realism factors that aren't otherwise in this list. If you want your flying to be as real as possible, slide this bar over to the right.

Other Settings

Manual Lights Control

If this check box is selected, you must manually turn on the instrument panel lights at night, which adds an extra sense of realism to the simulation. (This might seem like a small issue, but in real life, to be able to see the controls you must manually turn the lights on.) Otherwise, you can just leave the box unchecked, and the panel will automatically light up at night.

Gyro Drift

The heading indicator on the instrument panel is a gyroscopic instrument, which means it has a spinning gyroscope inside it that always points in the same direction despite how the plane moves around it. The result is that you can see what direction the plane is heading. Unfortunately, the gyroscope slowly precesses; over time, it drifts to point the wrong direction, and you need to reset it to the magnetic compass every 10 to 15 minutes. If you leave the gyro drift box unchecked, however, the heading indicator will not drift.

Engines and Propeller

These settings control whether you need to deal with enriching or leaning the fuel mixture as you change altitude, and whether you need to worry about refueling.

Crashes and Damage

This area of the Realism Settings dialog box is where you can make your plane invulnerable. Being invulnerable comes in handy if you're practicing some aerobatics or if you plan to buzz national monuments in Washington, D.C., and you don't want to worry about crashing and burning. For normal flight maneuvers such as practice landings, however, click the Detect Crash And Show Graph option. When you crash, you'll see a graph that shows what your descent rate was in the moments before the crash. This option button is controlled by the Crash Tolerance slider in the Flight Model area and can provide some compromise between the two. For example, if you want the aircraft to be somewhat more forgiving as you touch down on the runway but to crash you really set it down quite hard, select Detect Crash and Show Graph, but move the Crash Tolerance slider to the left toward –Real. For the most realistic flight experience, select all of the Crash and

Damage check boxes, click the Detect Crash And Show Graph option, and move the Crash Tolerance slider all the way to the right toward +Real.

Flight Controls

This area allows you to choose whether rudder movement is automatically coordinated with the ailerons. When the Auto-Rudder check box is selected, Flight Simulator 2000 automatically applies rudder when you roll the wings. If you want to

Coordinating the Rudder with the Yoke

At the bottom of the turn coordinator on the instrument panel is a small tube with a ball in it called the inclinometer, or slip-skid indicator. When you make a turn in a real airplane, you normally need to add a little bit of rudder in the direction of your turn. When the turn is properly coordinated, the ball stays centered in the tube. When the ball slides to the outside of the turn, the airplane is skidding. When it slides to the inside of the turn, the airplane is slipping.

practice landing in a crosswind or aerobatics, however, turn the Auto-Rudder feature off so that you can use the rudder in the opposite direction of the ailerons.

How to Use the Kneeboard

Pilots need to have all sorts of information right at their fingertips, such as radio frequencies, navigational charts, approach procedures for busy airports, and emergency procedures. In the most advanced jet aircraft, such as the Boeing 777, there are specific checklists for every imaginable situation, and all of these must be immediately accessible. One additional concern for Flight Simulator 2000 pilots is having all the keyboard commands handy—real pilots don't have to worry about whether the landing gear is triggered by the L key or the G key!

In a real aircraft, the cockpit is usually very cramped. There isn't much space to spread out maps or flight plans. To solve this problem, pilots often strap a small clipboard containing frequently accessed information right onto their thigh. This is what is known as a Kneeboard. In

Tip: You can also use the Kneeboard as an extra reference point for information you find in the online Help section. You can select, cut, and then paste any portion of information from online Help into the Notes section of the Kneeboard.

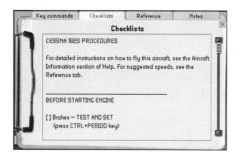

Figure 1-3   *The Kneeboard is a small window of helpful flight information that can be positioned anywhere in the cockpit.*

Flight Simulator 2000, all of this information is available on the Kneeboard in each aircraft. (See Figure 1-3.) To access the Kneeboard, on the Aircraft menu, point to Kneeboard, or press F10.

The Kneeboard in Flight Simulator presents information on four different tabs. On the first tab is a list of all the keyboard commands available for the aircraft you're flying. On the second tab is a series of checklists with specific instructions for operating procedures such as taking off, cruising, descending, and landing. These checklists are very detailed, with exact speeds given when appropriate. The third tab is a reference tab, with information that you would find in an aircraft handbook, such as minimum and maximum operating speeds and other performance specifications. Finally, and most importantly, the fourth tab is the customizable Notes tab, which you can use to store any information you want to have available during your flight.

Key Commands

On this tab, you'll find keyboard shortcuts for most aspects of the aircraft's operation. Some users of Flight Simulator find that this page is particularly useful when flying multiengine planes, when it's easier to use keyboard shortcuts instead of clicking on the screen (actually grabbing the knob by using the mouse) to control the power to each engine.

Checklists

It is often disconcerting to passengers on a commercial flight to see the pilot and copilot, both seasoned professionals with thousands of hours of flight experience, reading sheets of instructions while preparing to take off. "Shouldn't they know how to do this by now?" some passengers might ask. However, checklists are invaluable to pilots, who use them to remind themselves of the proper sequence of steps for various operating procedures. The checklists on the Kneeboard are adapted from the actual checklists recommended by the aircraft's manufacturers. You can use them simply as a guide to remind yourself of the proper flow of events, or you can follow them to the letter for the ultimate in flight realism. You can also set certain instruments to fail while in flight, and you can refer to the Reference tab or your Notes tab for the proper emergency procedures.

> **Tip:** *Drag the Kneeboard to a position on the instrument panel where it is most convenient for you to use.*

Reference

The Reference tab explains the various operating speeds for the aircraft you're flying. Even though the Reference tab provides the information at a glance, it's a better idea to memorize the most important airspeeds, such as V_{NE} (the "never-exceed" velocity) and the stall and approach speeds for the aircraft (both when it's heavily loaded and when it's light). Even with the Kneeboard, it might be difficult to find such vital information in time to take action.

Notes

You can type directly on this tab. It's a good place to store all kinds of information in one place so that you'll have it literally right at your fingertips. By cutting and pasting from sources such as online Help, the Windows Notepad, or even other tabs on the Kneeboard, you can gather all the information relevant to your flight on one page.

> **Tip:** *To cut and paste text, first select the text you want. Press Ctrl+C, click the Notes tab, and then press Ctrl+V.*

You might want to look up all the Automatic Terminal Information Service (ATIS) frequencies for current airport conditions and instrument landing system (ILS) frequencies for your flight navigation to your destination airport and paste them into the Notes page. You might also decide to keep track of specific notes and observations about each plane, such as its rotation airspeed (how fast you need to be going to take off) or a reminder to yourself not to overcontrol when landing the Mooney Bravo (because that was what made you crash and burn last time!).

Multiple Views

One of the most striking differences between flying on a computer and flying in a real plane is the increased visibility that a real airplane offers, particularly the peripheral view. Most cockpits offer a panoramic view of the world outside, so you can check out the side window and use your peripheral vision to keep track of what's going on ahead. This peripheral view is difficult to simulate on a computer because whenever you switch views, you lose whatever view you were previously looking at. However, Flight Simulator 2000 allows you to open multiple windows, each with a different view. By arranging these windows on your screen, you can give yourself a wider overall field of view, which makes it easier to keep track of what's going on outside the cockpit.

Figure 1-4   *Placing a small rear cockpit view in the upper center of the main view allows you to "check your six."*

The Rearview Mirror

Placing a small window with the rear view at the top of the main view (as shown in Figure 1-4) is helpful when you're flying with a lot of other airplanes in the vicinity. When dueling in a head-to-head game, such as Kamikaze Tag (see Chapter 9), the rearview mirror makes it much easier to tell if the other plane is trying to sneak up behind you.

You can also see the runway receding behind you in the rearview mirror as you take off, which might not be very realistic (few airplanes other than fighters sport rearview mirrors) but looks pretty neat.

How to Do It

On the Views menu, point to New View, and then click Cockpit. A second, smaller window pops up over the main view. Drag the lower-right corner of the window to shrink it to about half its original size, and then drag the window to place it in the middle of the main view, at the top of the screen. Now click View Options on the Views menu; you can select either COCKPIT – View 01 or COCKPIT – View 02 from the Window menu. Select COCKPIT – View 02, and then select Rear on the Direction menu. You now have a rear view in this new window.

The Panoramic View

If you place three small windows side by side, you can configure the left and right windows to be the forward-left view and forward-right view, respectively. (See Figure 1-5.) This arrangement simulates a much wider field of view. As you approach objects, be aware that they might "disappear" for an instant before re-appearing in the forward-side window, depending on how the windows are lined up. The panoramic view takes some getting used to, but many flight simulator enthusiasts swear by it.

How to Do It

Click anywhere on the main view, and press the closed bracket (]) key to close the main view. The entire screen will

Figure 1-5 *If you line up the three windows properly, you can see a forward view of nearly 135 degrees.*

go black. (For this reason, you should make these adjustments while the plane is on the ground or while the game is paused, not while you're flying.) On the Views menu, point to New View, and then click Cockpit. A smaller window pops up, showing the forward view. Drag the lower-right corner of the window to adjust its width to about one-third of the screen. Drag the window to position it in the middle of the screen. Then create another window the same size, this time selecting Right Front from the Direction menu for that window (in the View Options dialog box). Drag the window to position it to the right of the forward view. Finally, create a third window, selecting Left Front from the Direction menu for that window. Position this window to the left of the forward view. By adjusting the bottoms and sides of the windows as well as the corners, you can get the windows to line up almost perfectly.

The 225-Degree View

If you place three small windows side-by-side, you can configure the left and right windows to be the left-side view and the right-side view, respectively. This arrangement gives you a simultaneous view out of three of your windows (as shown in Figure 1-6), and it is very useful when you're flying very close to the runway before landing. It allows you to check out your side window to

judge when to turn from your base leg onto final approach without having to take your eyes off the front. There will definitely be two big blind spots, however, because you lose the forward diagonal views, but you can always glance out those views in the normal way by clicking a window and pressing 7 or 9 on the numeric keypad.

Figure 1-6   *This view takes some getting used to, but it offers a simultaneous view out of three sides of the plane.*

How to Do It

Follow the same sequence of steps in the previous section to create three separate side-by-side windows, but this time press 4 and 6 on the numeric keypad to switch the windows to the left and right views, respectively. As you arrange the windows, don't worry if the edges of the views don't line up; because of the perspective switch, the borders won't match exactly.

A Compromise

If you find the blind spots to be too disconcerting, you can use the two side views as smaller windows. The main cockpit view normally fills the screen (as shown in Figure 1-7), but you can overlay two smaller side views on top of it. You still won't see the forward diagonal views, but this arrangement is a little less disorienting than the 225-degree view or the panoramic view.

Figure 1-7   *This window arrangement still allows you a reference point on each side of the aircraft.*

Note: *Depending on the speed of your computer, opening multiple windows might make Flight Simulator 2000 run more slowly.*

Zooming and Panning

You can give yourself a wider field of view simply by zooming out of the main window. (See Figure 1-8.) Click the view out the cockpit, and then press the minus sign (–) key once or twice to zoom out. This allows you to see more of the terrain. It also tends to give you more of a fish-eye perspective, though, which might take some getting used to. Press the plus sign (+) key to zoom back in.

You can smoothly pan around the main window by pressing Shift+Enter, Shift+Backspace, Ctrl+Shift+Enter, and Ctrl+Shift+Backspace. These four key combinations effectively allow you to pan all around the main view and still keep the objects in front of you in sight. By holding down these keys, you can pan smoothly in a complete circle. To change the panning speed, modify the aircraft.cfg file in the Flight Simulator folder. If you have a joystick or control yoke with program-mable buttons or a hat switch (a smaller directional button on top of some joy-sticks), you can pro-gram the buttons to these keyboard com-binations for easy panning.

Figure 1-8 *This perspective uses the plus sign and minus sign keys to zoom in and out.*

Tip: *On final approach, your view of the runway might be blocked by the instrument panel. Press Shift+Enter to pan down so that you can see the runway.*

Real Weather, Real Life

In real life, there are many factors that a pilot can control to manage the level of risk affecting a given flight. The weather, however, is not one of them. We are limited in our ability to predict the weather, let alone change it. Weather is per-haps the single biggest factor that affects pilots. More often than not, the weather is the crucial factor in a pilot's decision to fly or not to fly, and the ramifications of that decision can have drastic results.

In Flight Simulator 2000, however, you have control over the weather. You can use any kind of weather that you can dream up to test your flying skills.

And if that isn't enough, you can even take a cue from Mother Nature and fly using the current weather conditions outside by downloading the weather data directly from the Internet. As pilots, we are humbled by the weather and learn to respect it. But that doesn't mean that we can't use Flight Simulator 2000 to have a little fun and tweak the weather to suit our liking!

Technology Benefits

Weather is a major factor for any pilot, but its impact on a given flight depends on several other factors: the experience of the pilot, the type of aircraft, and the on-board instrumentation. Captain Ron Hunt, a commercial pilot, explains that the largest planes, such as the Boeing 777, can fly in nearly any kind of weather because of their fly-by-wire control systems and advanced autopilot features, which can compensate for limited visibility and severe winds and can even land the plane.

Adjusting the Weather

To really get a feel for the different weather effects you can create, don't be afraid to experiment with all the weather settings.

You can opt to change the weather with just a few clicks, or you can fine-tune the weather down to the most specific detail. The following options can all be adjusted, either globally or locally. In some cases, you can customize these features in much greater detail by clicking the Advanced Weather button in the Weather dialog box. (See Figure 1-9.)

Figure 1-9 *The Weather dialog box allows you to make broad adjustments to the weather, either globally or locally.*

Keeping It Simple: Global Weather

The simplest way to adjust the weather is to change the weather affecting the entire planet—the global weather. This ensures that weather conditions remain consistent from the time you take off to the time you land.

Local Weather

A more realistic approach to weather is to create a specific weather condition in the local area in which you'll be flying. You can also change the weather as you travel along your intended route if you're traveling great distances. It's a bit more work than setting the weather conditions globally, but it will also create a more realistic flight because in real life weather conditions are rarely uniform along your entire flight route. By using local weather, you can simulate dramatic weather differences as you fly along your flight path. (Dramatic changes in weather are something that can happen in real life).

Real World Weather

By clicking the Real World Weather button, you can connect to the Flight Simulator 2000 server on the Internet and download a file that contains the current weather conditions for every area of the United States. The downloaded settings will override any settings that you have manually configured. If you have a laptop computer, try downloading the current weather conditions before taking a real cross-country flight. Then fly the same route in Flight Simulator route in real time and experience similar weather conditions!

Clouds

This slider adjusts the number and type of clouds in the sky. This is a very general setting; to alter the cloud conditions more specifically, click the Advanced Weather button at the bottom of the Weather dialog box. By using the Advanced Weather dialog box, you can customize the specific type of cloud cover and configure a specific type of precipitation. You can also set the rate and frequency of these atmospheric effects and set up different layers of clouds.

Precipitation

Precipitation can come in the form of rain or even snow. By adjusting this slider, you can vary the level of precipitation. Note that you can't adjust this slider unless the Clouds slider is set to Few or Greater. You can set the type of precipitation by clicking the Advanced Weather button and then clicking the

Clouds tab. (See Figure 1-10.) You'll see a Precipitation area, in which you can select the type of precipitation, the base altitude, and the rate.

Icing

Icing occurs when moisture adheres to the surface of the aircraft and turns to ice. This might not sound like much, but when ice builds up on the wing, it changes the wing's ability to create lift (which is what's keeping you in the air) and can cause the aircraft to quite literally cease flying. Icing is one of the biggest concerns for a single-engine aircraft pilot (or any pilot) because few single-engine aircraft are equipped with anti-icing equipment on their wings. Icing most often occurs when aircraft fly through visible moisture (rain or clouds) when the temperature is near or below freezing.

> **Tip:** *For more information about icing conditions and how to deal with them, see the article in the online Help by Thomas A. Horne called "The Worst Ice."*

You can simulate icing conditions in Microsoft Flight Simulator 2000 by selecting Weather from the World menu and then clicking the Advanced Weather button. In the dialog box that appears (as shown in Figure 1-10), there are four tabs. The Temp/Pressure tab will take you to the dialog box in which you can adjust temperature and dew point. Set the temperature and dew point to the same temperature (below freezing), and then fly through clouds to begin to see the effects of icing.

The effects of icing include ice buildup in the pitot tube and static system (which affects some of your instruments) and increases in drag on the aircraft as the wing and body take on ice. This buildup causes your aircraft to lose lift and increase drag and weight; the buildup also substantially raises the stall speed of the aircraft. Be especially careful when turning and landing with ice—the plane will stall at a much faster speed than usual.

Dew Point

Dew point is the temperature at which the air becomes saturated with moisture and the moisture starts to condense on objects. The warmer air is, the more moisture it can hold, and the colder it is, the less moisture it can hold. When a chilly winter morning comes along where the dew point is zero degrees Celsius and the temperature is zero degrees Celsius (that is, they meet), water vapor will start to condense on objects such as grass, cars, or whatever's around. In the above example, since the temperature is zero Celsius (freezing), the moisture will condense and form as frost, or ice. When flying in a similar situation (where the dew point and temperature meet near the freezing level), an airplane will start to build up ice all over its body.

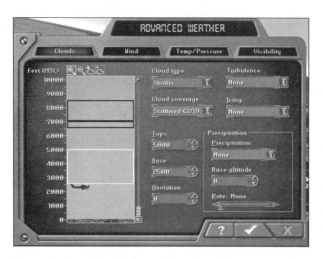

Figure 1-10 *The Advanced Weather dialog box allows you many more options for customizing the weather.*

Tip: *For more information on crosswind flight and landings, see the excellent article titled "Defeating the Crosswind," by Alton K. Marsh, in the Aviation Articles section of online Help.*

Visibility

By adjusting the visibility settings, you can simulate fog and reduced visual flight rules (VFR) flying conditions. Try using this slider to create a challenging landing in which you can barely see the runway. Click the Advanced Weather button, and then click the Visibility tab in the Advanced Weather dialog box to adjust the visibility layer for a more realistic effect. For example, you might try creating a 1000-foot layer of ground fog with 2000 feet of visibility, or a 6000-foot layer of stratus clouds with 4000 feet of visibility.

Wind Strength and Direction

Wind directly affects your ground speed and heading. The Wind Strength slider and the Wind Direction control allow you to specify the wind speed and direction. For a fun challenge, use these controls to configure a 15-knot wind blowing perpendicular to the runway heading, and then try to land. You'll have to adjust your heading and "crab" (turn the nose slightly into the wind) toward the runway to stay on course, or perform a side slip (lower a wing and add the opposite rudder to keep the aircraft straight despite the wind) to stay on course.

You can also customize the wind conditions in much greater detail by clicking the Advanced Weather button at the bottom of the Weather dialog box. After you become proficient at landing in a steady crosswind, try causing the wind to gust to a certain wind speed. You can also add turbulence and wind shear to the wind conditions to simulate very realistically a sudden storm. Consult online Help for more information on configuring wind conditions.

Realistic Navigation

Although it's fun to just hop into the Flight Simulator 2000 cockpit, take off from a busy airport, and fly anywhere you want, in real life you would never want to do this lest you become the new hood ornament for a jumbo jet. For a more realistic flight, try creating a flight plan using the Flight Planner in Flight Simulator 2000. After you click Flight Planner on the Flights menu, the Flight Planner dialog box appears. (See Figure 1-11.)

What Is Wind Shear?

Wind shear occurs whenever two regions of wind currents come together, creating large amounts of turbulence. Pilots flying into wind shear might experience sudden loss of lift, dramatic changes in airspeed, or downdrafts. If an airplane loses lift during takeoff or a landing approach, the result can be fatal. Wind shear is always associated with thunderstorms but also can be a significant problem within other types of clouds or even in clear sky. To deal with wind shear, carefully manage your airspeed and altitude ahead of time. Learn the conditions that lead to wind shear and how to recognize them. Keep the aircraft at or below maneuvering speed to avoid overstressing the aircraft in turbulence.

Figure 1-11   *The Flight Planner helps you plan a good flight route.*

Here you can specify a starting and destination airport and choose whether to fly direct using the Global Positioning System (GPS) or navigate using waypoints such as very high frequency omnidirectional radio range (VOR) stations. For a tutorial on how to create a flight plan, check out Chapter 3.

Why File a Flight Plan?

Visual flying is the process of controlling and navigating the aircraft using visual references and landmarks. Instrument flying uses the aircraft instruments and navigation equipment for the same purposes, allowing you to fly the aircraft in clouds or other conditions in which you have low visibility. Although pilots following the visual flight rules (VFR) are not required to file a flight plan within the United States, pilots flying using the instrument flight rules (IFR) are required to do so. In many other countries (such as in Canada), even VFR pilots must file a flight plan that details where they plan to fly, what route they will take, and at what altitudes they will be flying if they are straying more than 25 miles from their home airport. This information is then available to air traffic controllers, who can monitor the flight. It also provides a starting point for search and rescue teams should an aircraft fail to arrive at its destination. In Flight Simulator 2000, using the Flight Planner is a good way to take advantage of the built-in maps and automatic route generation features and come up with a good flight route. This flight route should include an alternate airport just in case your original choice is no longer available (because of inclement weather over the airport or an emergency situation on board, for example). You can find more information on creating a flight plan in online Help.

Chapter Two

THE AIRCRAFT

This chapter introduces each aircraft in Microsoft Flight Simulator 2000 by providing a background for the individual plane and leading you through a step-by-step example flight in the aircraft. The example flights are not intended to be comprehensive learning tools for each aircraft, but quick and basic tutorials that show you firsthand the characteristics of each aircraft, its strengths, and its practical applications. The chapter is organized by the type of aircraft that is included in Flight Simulator: propeller aircraft (including the Schweizer Sailplane glider), jet aircraft, and then the Bell JetRanger 206B, which is a helicopter. There are also sections on the Mooney Bravo and Raytheon/Beechcraft King Air aircraft, which are available only in Microsoft Flight Simulator 2000 Professional Edition.

Propeller and Glider Aircraft in Microsoft Flight Simulator 2000

Regardless of whether you begin your flight career in the Air Force or just by getting a private pilot's license, you start flying in a single-engine propeller-driven aircraft. These propeller planes (and the Schweizer Sailplane) are in a different realm of aviation from jet aircraft, largely because of their more modest operating speeds. Jet aircraft have higher takeoff, landing, and cruising speeds, and they require the pilot to be more proficient to safely handle the aircraft.

Cessna Skylane 182S

There's no better way to learn the nuances of flight than to start out as almost every pilot does, with a Cessna 152, Cessna 172, or Cessna 182. Flight Simulator allows you to start out with the Cadillac of Cessna single-engine aircraft, the Skylane 182S, which gives you a feel not only for flight, but for the simulator application as well. The Skylane 182S is great for cross-country trips; it is

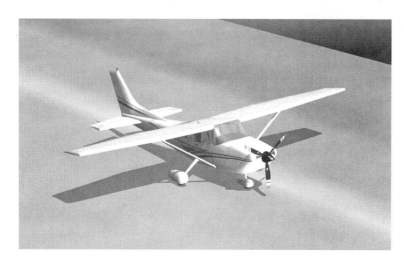

almost an extension of the family car or van because unlike smaller planes, it can carry a family of four plus their bags.

Flight Characteristics

The Skylane is a light aircraft that is simple to use when you're learning to fly, but it is also powerful and sophisticated enough for most flight enthusiasts. The Skylane's high-wing design provides excellent visibility of the ground out of the side windows, easy access and loading, and shade from the sun during flight. Like all of Cessna's high-wing single-engine aircraft, the Skylane is a good glider in the extremely rare case of engine failure.

The 182S's constant-speed propeller has many advantages over the fixed-pitch propeller of its sibling, the Cessna 172 Skyhawk. A fixed-pitch propeller uses a preset pitch angle for the best balance between takeoff power and efficient cruise power, but sometimes this preset angle is less than ideal. The controllable-pitch propeller of the Skylane acts like the transmission in a car. It gives you more "gears" to work with. An airplane with a fixed-pitch propeller is like a car with only one gear: there's always a compromise between the power required to accelerate from a stop and the efficient use of power at cruising speed. A constant-speed propeller, like a multigear transmission, makes more efficient use of the engine's power at a variety of speeds.

Real-world preflight planning for the Skylane is simple. After a quick walk-around preflight inspection, weight and balance calculations, and a fuel check, you're on your way. The simplicity of the Skylane and its great handling and flight characteristics provide a relatively light workload for the pilot and make it a great single-pilot aircraft. In short, the 182S Skylane is an extremely versatile and forgiving aircraft.

Note: *Although preflight planning on the Skylane is pretty simple, make sure you always go through your takeoff checklist. Press F10 to access the checklists on the kneeboard.*

Example Flight

This flight in the Cessna Skylane 182S is a standard one for new pilots. It involves simply taking off, flying around a little, and then landing. Licensed pilots have a chance to get acclimated to the simulator application, while novice pilots get a feel for flying one of the great civil aviation aircraft.

1. Show the cockpit view of Flight Simulator 2000 by clicking Fly Now on the opening screen.

   > **Tip:** *If you need to redisplay the opening screen, on the Flights menu, click Show Opening Screen.*

2. Step into the 182S by clicking Select Aircraft on the Aircraft menu. Then click Cessna Skylane 182S in the Aircraft drop-down list. Click the checkmark on the lower-right corner of the dialog box to apply your changes.

3. Start from Merrill C. Meigs Field in Chicago by clicking Go To Airport on the World menu. (See Figure 2-1.) Click Meigs in the Airport list, and then click the checkmark to apply your selection.

4. To open the takeoff checklist, point to Kneeboard on the Aircraft menu, and then click Checklists, or simply press F10. Complete the takeoff checklist.

5. Set the flaps to 10 degrees, add full power, and start a takeoff roll down the runway. After you hit about

Figure 2-1   *Setting up at Meigs Field.*

55 to 60 knots, gently pull the nose off the runway and let the plane climb.

6. After you're about 300 feet off of the runway, raise the flaps, and then climb at between 80 and 90 knots to an altitude of around 3000 feet (about 2500 feet above the ground).

7. Put the 182S through its paces: Bank from side to side, pull the nose up to see what happens when you stall the aircraft, and get a feel for the rudder controls (if you're not using the Auto-Rudder option in Realism Settings). To speed up, you should ease forward on the joystick to decrease the pitch attitude (lower the nose) slightly. To slow down, smoothly pull back on the joystick to increase the pitch attitude (raise the nose slightly).

8. After you've gotten your fill of flying around Chicago, turn back to the airport and prepare for landing.

9. Lower the speed to below 90 knots, and drop the flaps in stages until they are fully extended.

10. Descend at about 70 knots to the runway, adjusting the speed with pitch instead of with the throttle. If you think the plane is getting too low, add power with the throttle rather than pulling the nose up.

11. Pick a spot at the beginning of the runway and fly to it, keeping the speed at around 60 knots while you approach. Think of the aircraft as a dart, flying straight for the spot you picked at the beginning of the runway.

12. After you reach the spot and are about 10 feet off the ground, pull the power off, level out, and let the plane settle to the runway as you pull back on the yoke/stick. If all goes well, you'll touch down on the main landing gear first, and then the nose will gently settle onto the runway.

Cessna Skylane RG

The Skylane 182 RG is a Skylane 182S with retractable landing gear, although its dimensions are slightly different in several areas and its engine has five more horsepower. Retracting the landing gear reduces drag and enables the Skylane RG to achieve faster climb rates and cruising speeds, but the added weight of the retraction mechanism also lowers the service ceiling (the practical maximum altitude at which the aircraft can fly) by almost 4000 feet.

Flight Characteristics

You won't experience much difference in Flight Simulator between the Skylane RG and the Skylane 182S, except, of course, for the retractable landing gear in the former. Tucking the gear away delivers better performance, but you must remember to extend the wheels before landing. This

might seem obvious, but if you're used to flying an airplane with fixed landing gear, you might forget to lower the landing gear, especially during a particularly challenging crosswind landing. Like the Skylane 182S, the RG features the same forgiving nature and flight characteristics that make it such a great all-around aircraft.

Example Flight

As with the Cessna 182S example flight, this flight takes you around Chicago from Meigs Field. This time, however, you'll also retract the landing gear and adjust the propeller control after you reach cruising altitude.

1. Start from Merrill C. Meigs Field in Chicago.

2. Open the takeoff checklist by pointing to Kneeboard on the Aircraft menu and then clicking Checklists. Complete the takeoff checklist.

3. Set the flaps to 10 degrees, add full power smoothly, and start the take-off roll down the runway. After you hit about 55 to 60 knots, gently pull the nose off the runway and let the plane climb.

Figure 2-2   *Retractable landing gear is fun to watch as it's being retracted or deployed.*

4. After you're about 300 feet off of the runway, raise the landing gear (as shown in Figure 2-2) and flaps, and then climb at between 80 and 90 knots to an altitude of around 5000 feet (about 4500 feet above the ground).

Note: *As you climb, you might notice that the RG performs a bit better than the 182S because it lacks the drag created by the extended landing gear on the 182S.*

Tip: *For more information about propeller control, click Aviation Articles from the Help menu and then Aircraft Engines and Systems. The section titled "Using the Engine Controls" describes how the propeller control affects flight.*

5. After you reach an altitude of 5000 feet, pull back the throttle to about 22 inches (on the Manifold Pressure gauge).

6. Pull back the blue propeller control knob to change the "gearing" of the propeller blades so that they take a bigger bite of the air, which causes the RPMs to drop. I aim for 2000 RPM or so.

7. Experiment with how you can better manage power and fuel consumption by altering the pitch of the propeller along with the throttle.

8. Turn back toward Meigs Field, and prepare for landing.

9. Lower the speed to below 90 knots, and drop the flaps in stages until they are fully extended.

10. Descend toward the runway at about 70 knots. If the plane gets too low, add power rather than pulling up the nose of the RG.

> **Note:** *For more information on how pitch, power, and airspeed relate to landing, check out the "Tutorial 7: Landings" section in the* Microsoft Flight Simulator 2000 Pilot's Handbook.

11. Pick a spot at the beginning of the runway and fly to it, keeping the speed at around 70 knots while you approach. Again, think of the aircraft as a dart flying straight for the spot you picked at the beginning of the runway.

12. At an altitude of 1500 feet, lower the landing gear.

13. After you reach the spot you picked in step 11 and are still about 10 feet off the ground, pull the power off, level out, and let the plane settle to the runway as you pull back on the yoke/stick to land the aircraft.

Extra 300S

The Extra 300S, designed by Walter Extra, is made of a combination of metal and composite to deliver exceptional performance in aerobatic flight. The body and wings of an Extra 300S can withstand loading of plus or minus 10 Gs. The Extra was built with a specific type of flying in mind—gut-wrenching, heart-stopping, muscle-straining aerobatics! This machine is

not for those with fragile stomachs; certainly, its single-seat design and high-performance engine make it an aircraft that's capable of maneuvers that push the limits of flight. Putting an Extra 300S through its paces on a beautiful sunny

The Aerobatic Workout

It is possible to get a physical workout in an airplane. The workout in an aircraft like the Extra 300S comes from the G forces that are created when you perform aerobatics. When you sit in a chair at home, you experience a constant 1G load; in essence, you weigh what you weigh. However, when you fly in a standard loop, you experience about 4 Gs, which means that your hands and legs—in fact, every bit of you—will feel as if they weigh four times more than normal. This is only while you're in the initial and final pulls of the maneuver. Such a load requires extra muscle force to move or even to breathe. Negative Gs impact your body in the opposite way. For example, if you speed over a small rise in the road when you drive a car, you might get a funny or "light" feeling in your stomach. That feeling is magnified several times more in an outside loop as blood rushes toward your head. Your seat belt holds you down while you float off your seat and are pushed into the harness, and even your feet must be strapped to the rudder pedals to keep them in place. It's not unusual to burst a few blood vessels in your eyes in extreme negative G maneuvers, but fortunately you won't have that problem with Flight Simulator 2000.

Competitive aerobatics require very precise control of the aircraft along very rigid guidelines. While this precision makes aerobatics appear very graceful when viewed from the ground, performing aerobatics from the cockpit feels anything but graceful! Some aerobatic maneuvers require slight control movements, while others require drastic control movements that border on the violent. The pilot must be in great physical condition and be able to withstand a vigorous workout as he or she fights the effects of G forces during aerobatic flight.

afternoon matches any workout at the gym and provides thrills that rival those at any local amusement park.

Flight Characteristics

When you first see an Extra 300S, a few features will stand out. It's a single-pilot aircraft, it's a taildragger (meaning the pivot wheel is on the tail), and it's mostly an engine with wings. While the Extra's top speed is not necessarily impressive, the fact that it can withstand plus or minus 10 Gs is very impressive indeed. The ailerons are bigger than those on most general aviation aircraft and provide the Extra with an exceptional roll rate. The 300-hp engine gives the raw power to complement the responsiveness of the controls that helps the Extra 300 through any aerobatic maneuver.

This is not an aircraft for a novice pilot. It's a feat to master an aircraft like the Extra on the ground because it's a taildragger with such a large engine. As soon as you hop into the cockpit, you'll notice that there's very limited forward visibility. In the real world, the pilot of an Extra must weave from side to side and look out of the sides of the canopy to

see ahead while taxiing. During takeoff, a slow application of power helps maintain a straight path down the runway and makes compensating for engine torque more manageable. After you reach takeoff speed (about 70 knots), the tail of the aircraft will have already come up off the ground, helping you to see down the runway better. You'll probably notice that the controls are very responsive; during the climb, you use the rudder much more than in other general aviation aircraft to overcome the effects of engine torque and the large propeller.

Flying right side up is not what the Extra was built for; indeed, it will perform virtually any aerobatic air show maneuver. The wire triangles you see on the wing tips when you look out the left or right window provide reference lines for the pilot performing aerobatics.

Example Flight

This flight will simply show you the exceptional flight characteristics of the Extra 300S, and it will demonstrate an aileron roll. For more information on aerobatic maneuvers, click Aviation Articles from the Help menu, and select Aerobatics.

1. Choose a flight over lots of flat land. A good location is Henderson Airport in Las Vegas.

2. There's nothing special to set up for an Extra flight (there are no flaps), so just push the throttle to full open and start a takeoff roll.

3. Use a little right rudder, if necessary, to compensate for engine torque, which moves the nose to the left.

4. At around 75 knots, pull the Extra off the tarmac, but don't let the nose get too high. It can be difficult to see the horizon in front of you, so use side views or the attitude indicator to figure out the attitude. Keep the speed around 90 knots through the climb.

5. At 5500 feet, level out the Extra and let the speed build to about 140 to 160 knots.

6. To perform an aileron roll (as shown in Figure 2-3), from level flight pull the aircraft up to about a 20-degree pitch angle, and then, while holding some mild back pressure on the yoke/stick, move the yoke/stick to one side. You'll see just how quickly the Extra will roll.

7. After you roll through one rotation, move the yoke/stick back to center and notice how quickly the Extra's roll stops.

Figure 2-3 *The Extra in an aileron roll.*

As you can see, this is an aircraft that performs aerobatics well, so experiment!

Schweizer 2-32 Sailplane

Sailplanes look graceful whether they are just sitting still or circling lazily beneath a cumulus cloud on a warm sunny afternoon. The Schweizer 2-32 is a two-place tandem-seat sailplane (the two seats are positioned one behind the other, not side by side) with a single main wheel under its belly and small wheels or skids on the wingtips and tail section, as well as a skid on its nose. It has a glide ratio of about 32 to 1, which means that, assuming there is no wind, for every foot the aircraft sinks, it will travel forward 32 feet at its best glide speed (approximately 64 mph).

The most popular method of launching a sailplane is to be towed by another aircraft. Other methods of getting airborne are with a winch tow or auto tow. The tow rope is generally about 200 feet long and is attached to the nose of the sailplane or just in front of the wheel, depending on the type of launch and the individual aircraft. The rope can be released from either the towing aircraft or the sailplane. In Flight Simulator 2000, you don't have to bother with being towed by another aircraft; instead, you can simply press the Y key to begin slewing, and then the F4 key to move up several thousand feet; press Y again to stop slewing (a method in Flight Simulator to rapidly change the aircraft's position, direction, location, or altitude without flying), and begin soaring. Don't forget that you'll have to get the sailplane up to flight speed by pitching the nose forward before you can truly begin soaring. To avoid this condition, click Map View on the World menu, and enter a starting airspeed.

Flight Characteristics

Soaring is much like fishing; lift is where you find it, just as fish are where you find them. Lift is usually found in a *thermal*—a rising column of air created when the sun heats the earth's surface. Thermal soaring takes advantage of ground that heats up unevenly; a plowed dark field heats up

much more quickly than a grove of trees, for example. The physics that allow a sailplane to soar are simple: The air surrounding the sailplane is rising faster than the aircraft is descending, so the sailplane climbs. A special kind of soaring is *ridge soaring*. This occurs when a gust of wind hits a line of hills or cliffs and is forced upward; these updrafts can take a sailplane up in a jiffy. Another basic type of soaring is *wave soaring*. Wave soaring generally occurs at a high altitude. *Wave lift* usually occurs as a result of large-scale atmospheric phenomena, for example, fronts.

Sailplane pilots plot their course by the landscape, looking for locations with the best possibility of thermals while always keeping a landing spot in mind. In addition to the airspeed indicator, an important control in soaring is the variometer, a very sensitive vertical speed indicator that is calibrated to show the net climb or descent of the sailplane.

Thermal soaring is circling in the rising air of a thermal. To be successful at thermal soaring, the pilot needs a good knowledge of the stall characteristics and the feel of the sailplane at slow speeds and steep angles of bank.

Tip: *For more information on soaring, on the Help menu, click Aircraft Information and then Schweizer 2-32 Sailplane.*

Spoilers or speed brakes located on top of the sailplane's wings kill lift, thus increasing the descent rate. The spoilers are used in much the same way as the throttle control of an aircraft is used to control descent rate and speed in landing.

Captain Ron Hunt Speaks

Captain Ron Hunt is an accomplished aviator with over 17,000 hours of flight time. He currently pilots Boeing 767s. Here's what he had to say about soaring in a Schweizer Sailplane:

Soaring is probably some of the most enjoyable flying I have ever done. One of my best flights was a cross-country I flew into Iowa and back. The distance was over 190 miles and I was aloft for 6 hours and 10 minutes. I released from tow at 1800 feet AGL and never exceeded 4500 feet AGL the whole flight. Halfway out as the day was recycling (thermals reforming), I was being forced to think about landing, as there was little lift and I was getting low. I saw a hawk circling about a half a mile away, so I decided to see what he had going for him. It wasn't much but I was able to hold my altitude. Thankfully, the hawk didn't mind sharing the thermal, and he circled with me for close to 20 minutes, getting so close at times that I could see him turn his head as he looked my bird over. That thermal took me from 1600 feet AGL to eventually over 4000 feet after it got going again! And with that I was able to start for home. Great fun!

Note: *There are a couple of ways to get the aircraft back on the tarmac. You can circle in large descending turns and try to line up the runway, or you can put the spoilers on and dive steeply toward the far end of the runway. I suggest you dive because it will show you just how powerful the Sailplane's spoilers are. With a little practice, you'll be able to make landings just where you want.*

Example Flight

Flying the Schweizer 2-32 Sailplane requires finding the rising air so that you can stay in the air for the maximum amount of time. For this exercise, however, you'll try to lower the Sailplane onto a runway. The catch? You'll start directly above the runway with 4000 feet to bleed off before you touch down.

1. Set up a daytime flight in the Sailplane from San Francisco International Airport.

2. Press the Y key to enter slew mode, and then press F4 until you raise the Sailplane to 4000 feet.

3. Press the Y key to exit slew mode, and then tip the nose of the Sailplane downward to break the stall and begin the flight. (See Figure 2-4.)

4. Play around with the spoilers as you try to line up for a landing. If you misjudge the landing, simply go back into slew mode and give yourself a little extra altitude.

Landing the Sailplane should be soft; it's not the kind of aircraft that can absorb a hard landing like a Skylane. Fortunately, because of the great glide ratio of the 2-32, landing softly is a breeze.

Sopwith Camel

The Sopwith Camel is a biplane that was made famous by Canadian and British fighter aces in World War I. In fact, for many years it was reported that Canadian ace Roy Brown was flying a Sopwith Camel when he shot down Manfred von Richtofen, otherwise known as the Red Baron. However, recent research into the Red Baron's death shows that he was probably killed by a bullet fired from the ground. The *camel* part of this aircraft's name comes from the humplike structure on its nose, although it's hardly a defining

Figure 2-4   *Sailing over San Francisco in the Schweizer Sailplane.*

feature. The Sopwith Camel is reported to have claimed more enemy aircraft than any other Allied aircraft in WWI, although there have been reports that over 350 Sopwith Camel pilots died of non-combat crashes. This statistic alone should tell you something about the Camel: It's not an aircraft for the novice pilot. Fortunately for Flight Simulator enthusiasts, the flight dynamics of the Camel have been as faithfully reproduced as is possible with such an old aircraft so that you get an idea of just what flying this famous old airplane was like.

Figure 2-5 *Crashing on the ground before you even take to the air is common in the Sopwith Camel.*

Flight Characteristics

Compared to the other aircraft in Flight Simulator 2000, the Sopwith Camel is very unstable. If you don't stabilize the plane with right rudder control during the takeoff roll, it will do a ground loop and crash before you even take to the air, as you can see in Figure 2-5.

Once in the air the Camel is very touchy, and it requires calm, deliberate control. In short, this is a good aircraft in which to practice your basic skills in a very unforgiving environment; if you make a couple of mistakes back-to-back at low altitudes, you'll likely crash and burn. If you can master the Sopwith Camel, you'll be at an advantage with all of the other fixed-wing aircraft in Flight Simulator 2000.

Example Flight

This example flight gives you a basic feel for the Sopwith Camel. Even a simple task like taking off can be a challenge when you're used to flying more

stable and sophisticated aircraft, so this flight will concentrate on only the basics. Because of the Sopwith Camel's history, let's start our flight in France.

1. Select the Sopwith Camel as the aircraft for this flight.

2. On the World menu, click Go To Airport. Click Europe in the Global Region list and France in the Country list. Click Le Bourget in the Search Results list. Click the checkmark to apply your selection.

3. Push the throttle fully open, but do it slowly. As the aircraft starts to move, you'll notice a tendency for it to turn and lean to the left. Use the right rudder to control this turning action.

4. Once the speed starts to climb, you might also notice that the left wing is low, so very gently add correction to the right with the yoke/stick.

> **Note:** *Before pushing the throttle forward to start your ground roll, be sure to know to which keys/controls your rudder is set (the default keys are numeric keypad 0, keypad 5 [center rudder], and keypad Enter) because if you're flying with the Auto-Rudder option turned off, you'll need to use the rudder.*

5. At a speed of around 55 knots, pull the aircraft off the runway, but be very gentle as you pull back on the controls.

6. After the plane is airborne, climb to about 2000 feet above the ground.

7. At 2000 feet AGL, level the Camel out and increase the speed to at least 80 knots.

8. Roll the aircraft from side to side. Notice how much less responsive the Camel feels compared to the Extra or even the Skylane.

9. There is one thing the Sopwith Camel is famous for: tight left turns. Pull the Camel through a hard left turn to see why the Camel has a reputation as a tight left turner.

> **Note:** *The Camel tends to become uncontrollable when it stalls. The stall speed is around 50 knots, so if you are in a tight turn and notice the speed dropping, beware. A stall in this aircraft will bite you quickly and send the plane to the ground in a hurry. If you're at low altitudes, it's very difficult to recover from such a stall.*

Jet Aircraft in Microsoft Flight Simulator 2000

Even those of us with the privilege of being able to hop into an aircraft and go for a flight are usually not lucky enough to be able to fly a jet aircraft (at least I'm not). Flight Simulator gives us all the chance to get behind the controls of four very impressive jets, including the new Boeing 777-300 wide-body and one of the most intriguing aircraft ever built, the Concorde.

Learjet 45

The Learjet was the brainchild of William Lear, an engineer and inventor. In the late 1950s and early 1960s, Lear had a dream to create a small jet airplane that could be used for business purposes but still offer the performance of a commercial jetliner. The Learjet caught on quickly and became a symbol of success to those individuals and corporations that could afford it. The Learjet has been

revised several times and continues to be the business jet of choice.

It can be argued that the Learjet is one of those airplanes that has built its reputation more on visual appeal than on comfort or performance (although Lears are decent performers). Lears are indeed status symbols, but in reality they are a tad cramped, and some people say that the early versions of the Learjet were outright uncomfortable for anyone over 6 feet tall. Fortunately, many improvements to comfort and performance have been made in recent versions, including the Learjet 45.

Flight Characteristics

The Lear builds speed very quickly, so staying ahead of the aircraft—being organized so that you can concentrate on flying rather than handling peripheral tasks—is very important. By far the most dramatic thing that you will notice when you fly the Lear 45 is that everything happens much faster than in propeller-driven aircraft, and you will have much less time to sort things out on landing approaches. The Lear is a lot of fun to fly after you get used to its speed and touchy controls. The aircraft is very responsive and flies just like it looks it would, quickly and sleekly.

The Lear is not for flying into short or unimproved airfields, and as a rule it needs a lot of runway when carrying a load of passengers. Lear pilots must be aware of aircraft performance for every takeoff. The Lear is extremely quick and unforgiving of overcontrol by its pilot, but compared to the Sopwith Camel, it seems like a very stable aircraft. The Lear is also the first aircraft discussed thus far that has a digital cockpit. At first the cockpit can seem a tad overwhelming, but the information conveyed in a digital cockpit is actually easier to read and follow after you get used to each of the panel displays.

Example Flight

The Lear is a business jet that's used for a wide variety of purposes, from ferrying business executives between cities to long-haul flights that cross entire countries. For this exercise, pretend that you're the pilot for an oil executive who needs to get from the Calgary International Airport to Springbank Airport, nestled in the foothills of the Rocky Mountains. This short flight will give you a feeling for the Lear 45's handling and controls, as well as its speed.

1. Select Calgary International as the starting airport. Make sure it's summer. If you need to change the season, click Time & Season on the World menu, and then select summer.

2. To open the takeoff checklist on the kneeboard, on the Aircraft menu, point to Kneeboard, and then click Checklists.

3. Complete the takeoff checklist, and get that bird in the air!

4. Once airborne, raise the landing gear (if you haven't already), and take up a heading of 250 degrees (magnetic).

Note: *If you want, spend some time putting the Lear through its paces before you land.*

5. As you approach the Rocky Mountains, you'll see Springbank Airport. (See Figure 2-6.)

6. Land at Springbank Airport. The runways are only 3000 feet long, so you'll have a good opportunity to try to stay ahead of your aircraft on landing. Indeed, 3000 feet of runway can go by quickly if you come in too high and fast.

Figure 2-6   *The Springbank Airport, nestled in the foothills of the Canadian Rockies.*

Boeing 737-400

The Boeing 737 had its genesis in the early to mid-1960s, when Boeing decided to create an aircraft for the short-haul market. The 737-400 shares little in common with many of the previous incarnations of the 737 (the 737-100 or the 737-200). But the 737-300 and 737-400 aircraft are similar; the 737-400 is really a stretched version of the 737-300. In fact, the 737-300 and 737-400 are so similar that pilots can be cross-qualified to fly both. The first 737-400 was delivered on September 15, 1988, and since then more than 600 of these fine jet aircraft have been delivered all over the world. In fact, with over 3500 produced by Boeing so far, the 737 line of jets is the most popular ever created.

Flight Characteristics

The 737-400 is a very stable and forgiving aircraft, but flying one certainly isn't like flying a Cessna Skylane— that is, the Skylane has only one engine, and it's propeller-driven. As with the Learjet, the action in the 737 happens at a much faster rate than in a single-engine general aviation aircraft, so you need to stay ahead of the air-

craft—that is, having your landing gear down, flaps set, and the runway lined up in advance. If you don't, your chances of making a crucial mistake go up considerably. It's always better to make the aircraft react than to react to the aircraft.

Planning is everything, however. For example, to slow down you must allow about 1 mile for every 10 knots of airspeed you want to lose. To plan the distance needed for a descent, use this formula: Divide your altitude by 1000, and then multiply by 3 to get the number of miles for descent. Add 2 miles for every 10 knots of tailwind, or subtract 2 miles for every 10 knots of headwind.

The flight controls of most transport jets (including the 737-400) are hydraulically operated, so, except for some mild fluctuations, control pressures remain relatively constant throughout the flight, regardless of speed. However, a generous use of *trim,* an adjustment to relieve pressure on the flight controls, is needed as the airplane accelerates or decelerates. The varying control pressures are not as apparent in Flight Simulator 2000 as in real flight, because a simulation application (so far) cannot duplicate the feel of sloppy controls during slow flight. However, the feel of the controls is only half of the equation.

Tips on Flying the 737

Don't feel overwhelmed by the number of dials and gauges on the instrument panel. Much of the crucial information you need for flying, such as the altitude, airspeed, and heading, is simply repeated in several different places on the panel. Also keep in mind that it takes much longer for changes that you make to the throttle to take effect. This means that when you fly one of the big jets, you need to anticipate what you need to do and when you need to do it. Climbs, descents, and turns all take significantly longer to accomplish. Think ahead.

Example Flight

The Boeing 737-400 is a popular passenger aircraft—perfect for flights between a group of islands. In this example flight, you'll pilot a short flight from Kahului, Maui, to Honolulu International Airport on the main island of Oahu.

The islands that make up the state of Hawaii are very close to each other; an inter-island flight usually lasts only 30 to 45 minutes. In Flight Simulator 2000, you can fly the following picturesque flight in real time as you marvel at the beauty of the islands of Hawaii. The flight path will go northwest along the chain of islands; you'll pass over the island of Molokai before crossing Waikiki and Pearl Harbor on the way to the reef runway at Honolulu International Airport.

1. For the starting airport, select Kahului, Maui, runway 2.

2. Set unlimited visibility by clicking Weather on the World menu and then sliding the Visibility slider to the far right (Unlimited). Make sure that this is a daytime flight.

3. Set the flaps to 5 degrees, push the throttle up, and at 150 knots pull back gently on the yoke/stick.

4. After takeoff, retract the landing gear and the flaps, and climb to a cruising altitude of 10,000 feet.

5. As you cross the beach, turn left to a heading of 300 degrees, and look for Molokai, which is the island to the north.

6. Look directly to the west to the smaller island of Lanai. Both Molokai and Lanai (seen in Figure 2-7) are primarily small farming communities. Although there is an airport on Molokai, its runway is far too small for a 737.

You might be able to see the island of Kahoolawe behind Lanai, to the south. For many years the U.S. Navy used the tiny island of Kahoolawe to practice bombing runs and shelling.

7. As you cross Molokai, look straight ahead, and soon you will see the coastline of Oahu coming into view. The bulk of Hawaii's residents live there.

8. As you cross the southeastern tip of Oahu, you'll pass right over Diamond Head, a huge extinct volcano. Ahead of Diamond Head, look out for the famous Waikiki Beach, as seen in Figure 2-8.

Figure 2-7   *The islands of Molokai and Lanai.*

Figure 2-8   *Waikiki and the reef runway.*

9. As you pass over the skyscrapers of Waikiki and downtown Honolulu, look ahead for runway 26L, otherwise known as the reef runway because it was constructed on a 12,000-foot artificial reef.

As you make your approach to runway 26L, remember to adjust the throttle to maintain a good rate of descent (about 700 feet per minute), extend 30 degrees of flaps, and don't forget to lower your gear. Keep your speed between 130 and 150 knots. See you on the beach!

Boeing 777-300

The 777-300 is a new wide-body jet that was designed to fly the same routes once dominated by the 747 line of jetliners. It's also the largest twin-engine air-

craft ever built. The 777-300 is capable of flying over 6000 statute miles (about 10,000 kilometers). Flight Simulator 2000 pilots can now fly those long San Francisco-to-Hong Kong flights. The 777 is also capable of carrying a passenger load comparable to that of the 747 (although because of seat spacing, the 777 usually carries fewer passengers), but it actually burns one-third less fuel than its older cousin. The Boeing 777 is an example of the cutting edge in commercial airliners. It has one of the most advanced cockpits ever created, with flat-screen LCD displays and an integrated Airplane Information Management System (AIMS).

Flight Characteristics

While the 737 is big compared to any general aviation aircraft, the 777 is absolutely huge; the engine of the 777 is nearly as big around as the fuselage of the 737! In fact, because of the aircraft's size, it's often hard to see objects that are close to the plane; remember that the bottom of the fuselage of the 777 is several feet above your head if you stand underneath it. This jet feels big, and like many large jets, you can't see any part of the wing from the cockpit.

The 777 handles in much the same way that the 737 does, but you will notice a difference in the plane's size and its reaction to power. You handle power gingerly on these birds; pilots talk about making power adjustments by squeezing the throttles to get what they want and then waiting for the response to happen. It's very easy to overreact to power changes in these jets, and doing so will make it hard to maintain a consistent airspeed. The engines' position under the wings causes the 777 to react differently from aircraft with engines on the tail (Learjet) or in the nose (Cessna, Extra, Sopwith, and Mooney). As a rule, there is more of a pitching motion when the engines are under the wings. For example, adding full power in flight will require a great deal of forward pressure on the yoke/stick to keep the same pitch attitude. Of course, the reverse is true for pulling the power to idle, as the nose of the aircraft becomes extremely heavy, requiring backpressure on the yoke/stick.

Example Flight

The 777-300 is a very large aircraft, so it feels different from the other aircraft in Flight Simulator 2000. The 777-300's size makes the plane fly differently from other aircraft, too. When this much mass is moving in any one direction, it's that much more important to stay ahead of the aircraft and not fall behind on the task at hand (flying, landing, taking off). In this example flight, you complete a landing in the 777-300, which is one of the best ways to get a feel for the size and handling of the aircraft.

1. On the Flights menu, click Select Flight, and then click Learjet Cruise To O'Hare Int'l in the Available Flights list.

Large Jet Landing Technique

Other than the quick speed at which things happen in a 737-400, the landing technique is probably the one thing that confuses the general aviation pilot the most. General aviation pilots are used to pulling the power off and gliding to touchdown, but that is not how you land a large jet. As you slow a 737 or 777 for approach, pitch changes are large and very noticeable in the cockpit as the airspeed changes and flaps and slats are lowered. You should be configured for landing, with gear down and landing flaps extended, at around 1000 feet AGL.

In real life, landings for these jets are almost always planned with touchdown no sooner than the 1000-foot runway mark. A stabilized approach from 1000 feet to touchdown is extremely important. Landing weights can vary from around 100,000 pounds to several hundred thousand pounds, and this kind of mass does not react quickly to any input. To add to this problem, jet engines do not spin up from idle to full power instantly like reciprocating engines do, so planning and staying ahead of the jet are critical.

A high rate of descent or having your speed too fast (or too slow) can spell trouble in a hurry. For instance, if the aircraft's speed is slow and it has a high rate of descent prior to touchdown, just flaring the aircraft (applying back pressure to the yoke/stick to level off and establish correct landing attitude) might not be enough to stop the descent rate for touchdown; the only thing you could do is change the angle at which you hit the ground because the mass of the plane is not arrested by the flare alone. To make a good landing, a stabilized powered descent to the runway at the appropriate speed for the aircraft weight is extremely important.

Another big landing difference in large jets is the flare and body angle. Most large jets begin the flare when they are around 30 feet (30 feet in the 737 and 50 feet in the 777) above the runway. The nose of the aircraft is already pitched up 5 degrees or more on the final approach (as shown in Figure 2-9), which makes the view out of the window much different from the one most general aviation pilots are used to. An aircraft over 100 feet long with a body angle of 5 degrees or more puts the pilot quite a bit higher than the lowest part of the plane. For the touchdown you must keep in mind the size of the aircraft; the main wheels on the 777 are far behind the pilot seat.

2. After the flight starts, select the 777-300 as the aircraft. You will be roughly on course to land on runway 14R at O'Hare International Airport (which will be in visual range).

3. To open the landing checklist on the kneeboard, on the Aircraft menu, point to Kneeboard, and then click Checklists. Land that puppy!

Figure 2-9   *Note how high off the ground the nose of the 777-300 is when it's pitched up only a few degrees.*

Concorde

The Concorde is a supersonic jet aircraft that was designed and produced in a collaborative effort between Air France and British Airways. It's hard to believe that it's been nearly 25 years since the Concorde first broke onto the scene with a 3½-hour trip from New York to Paris! In fact, the Concorde's first (test) flight was in March 1969, which makes it a 30-year-old aircraft that still looks pretty snazzy. As the only commercial passenger supersonic aircraft, the Concorde never really caught on, but it still serves its niche market, traversing the Atlantic Ocean many times every day for Air France and British Airways. There are only 10 Concordes in active use today (four for Air France and six for British Airways), but the fact that they are still in use shows the robust nature of the Concorde's construction and design. The Concorde is still the pinnacle of air travel (at least where speed is concerned).

Flight Characteristics

At first glance, the Concorde seems small for an airliner. Despite its size, it looks ominous sitting on the ramp and is really a beautiful aircraft. The Concorde has a movable hook nose that is lowered for landings, taxiing, and takeoffs. Because of the angles at which the Concorde takes off and flares, the crew cannot see the runway. The movable nose cone solves this problem and adds to the unique look of the Concorde when it's on the ground. Even with the nose section lowered, visibility is very limited for the pilots, and the passenger windows are tiny because of the structural requirements of flying highly pressurized at 60,000 feet. (See the sidebar on cabin pressurization.) Watching the Concorde take off is impressive; the engines thunder and vibrate your entire body. It climbs out quickly at an airspeed just below the speed of sound and then is cleared for supersonic flight.

Cabin Pressurization

The cabin of any airplane that flies above 12,000 feet is usually pressurized. Air pressure decreases substantially as your altitude increases, so cabin pressurization allows the pilots and passengers to enjoy the same level of oxygen and pressure that they would if they were on the ground. If the pressure outside is lower than the pressure inside the aircraft, any problem in the aircraft's structure could cause the aircraft to explode. The situation is basically the reverse of that of the mini-submarines that went down to the Titanic; if the structures gave out, the intense pressure from the water would crush the mini-subs. Therefore, smaller windows are needed to ensure strength in the structure of the Concorde, just as in a mini-submarine.

Example Flight

The Concorde is unique in many ways: It can fly at very high speeds, at very high altitudes, and its delta-wing design gives it unique handling characteristics. This flight takes you from Boeing Field on a tour of the Cascade mountain range in western Washington, which will show off the Concorde's blinding speed.

1. Select Boeing Field/King Co Intl as the starting airport. You will start out on runway 13R, facing the spectacular Mount Rainier. (See Figure 2-10.)

2. After you're on the runway, select the Concorde as the aircraft.

Figure 2-10   *Mount Rainier looms ahead of you.*

3. To open the takeoff checklist on the kneeboard, on the Aircraft menu, point to Kneeboard, and then click Checklists.

4. Take off and head for Mount Rainier. Note the climbing power and speed of the Concorde.

5. After you pass over Mount Rainier, fly south. You will quickly see Mount Adams and Mount St. Helens before you.

6. Experiment with the Concorde. Take it up to 60,000 feet and enjoy the view!

Flight Simulator 2000

The Helicopter in Microsoft Flight Simulator 2000

Flight Simulator 2000 isn't limited to only fixed-wing aircraft. The Bell 206B JetRanger helicopter has again been included as one of the aircraft that you can take to the heavens, and with a new flight model, it's an entirely new experience.

Bell 206B JetRanger III

The development of the Bell JetRanger helicopter dates back to an army competition in 1965, but the 206B JetRanger III has been produced in quantity since 1977. There are over 8000 of these helicopters in service, making them the most widely used helicopters in the civil aviation world. All U.S. military helicopter pilots learn to fly on the Bell 206B. The JetRanger III is also used as an air ambulance, television news aircraft, and, of course, as basic transportation.

Flight Characteristics

The only similarity between helicopters and airplanes is that they both fly. If you're a fixed-wing aircraft pilot making the transition to helicopters, leave most of your ideas about flying at home because this is truly new territory.

Before you learn to fly a helicopter you should first see if you can rub your stomach, pat your head, and chew gum at the same time! Seriously, this kind of flight requires a level of coordination that makes piloting the Cessna Skylane seem like a walk in the park, but that doesn't mean that it's impossible to master and enjoy flight in the JetRanger. The first thing you need is a good understanding of how a helicopter actually works, and I recommend that you take a close look at the Basic Helicopter Flying section in online Help before moving on. To access it, on the Help menu, click Aircraft Information, click Bell JetRanger III Helicopter, and then click Basic Helicopter Flying in the left pane. Reading this section takes only a few minutes, and it will help you to fly sooner and safer, especially if you've never before experimented with helicopter flight.

The JetRanger is responsive and fun to fly, but it takes some experience to find your comfort zone. The controls will probably feel looser than what you're used to in a fixed-wing airplane. You manipulate the controls more by applying pressure than by actually moving them. Although the helicopter is known for its ability to hover, hovering is like balancing on the head of a pin and is much harder than it looks on television or in the movies. It's often said that it's easier to fly a helicopter without hovering, but at some point, you must learn how to hover.

Example Flight

This flight demonstrates some of the differences in maneuverability between a helicopter and a fixed-wing aircraft. The JetRanger provides a very different kind of flying experience for a pilot used to flying a fixed-wing aircraft.

Helicopters are often used to get to or from areas that are inaccessible to fixed-wing aircraft. You might use a helicopter to deliver medical supplies to a mountainous region or to ferry passengers to a ship or oil rig in the middle of the ocean. Helicopters take off and land vertically, so they can use a very small space as a landing area. Helicopters are also very maneuverable. When you are traveling slowly or are holding in a hover, you can use the pedals to control the anti-torque rotor and turn to any heading. (In Flight Simulator 2000, the anti-torque pedals are controlled by the same keys or joystick controls as the rudder in the airplanes.) In this exercise, you take off into forward flight, transition into a hover, turn 180 degrees, and then speed back the way you came. Try doing that in a Cessna!

1. Select the Bell 206B JetRanger for this flight. Click Map View on the World menu, and set your latitude to N40* 43.00', longitude to W74* 0.90', and altitude to 4 feet. Click the green checkmark to get started.

2. Pitch the nose down to gain some forward speed. Remember to use the collective and rudder to maintain your altitude and heading.

3. After you pick up airspeed to 50 knots or so, try moving the cyclic (joystick) left and right. You'll see that you can perform a banking turn, much as you can in a fixed-wing aircraft.

4. Now try turning on a dime. Pitch the nose up by pulling back on the cyclic. At the same time, reduce the collective slightly to maintain your altitude in a hover. (See Figure 2-11.)

5. Use the anti-torque pedals to swivel the nose around 180 degrees, and then pitch the nose back down and increase the collective to pick up some forward airspeed.

6. From a hover, practice moving forward quickly and then returning to a hover over Manhattan by picking various buildings as reference points. If you're flying multiplayer, Manhattan is a great place to play hide-and-seek with a partner helicopter. Don't run into any buildings!

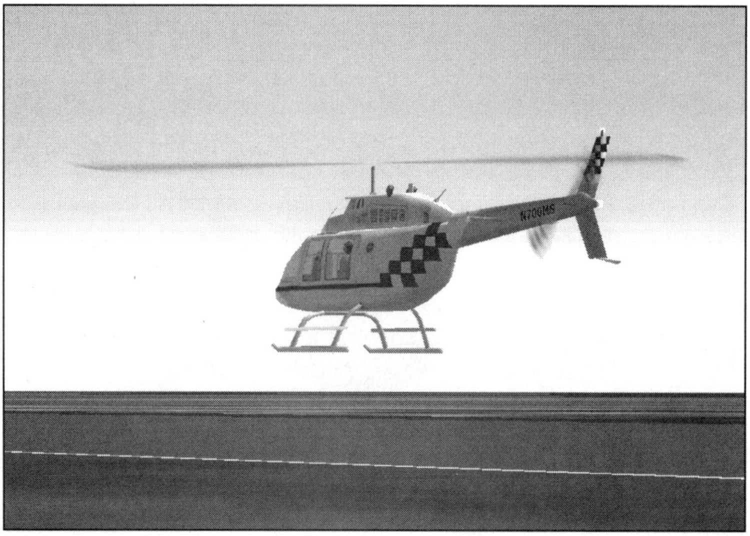

Figure 2-11   *Maintaining a hover is one of the most difficult parts of helicopter flight.*

Aircraft in Microsoft Flight Simulator Professional Edition

The Mooney Bravo and the Raytheon/Beechcraft King Air are aircraft that are available only in Microsoft Flight Simulator 2000 Professional Edition. Both are general aviation craft, but they have very different applications within the world of aviation.

Mooney Bravo

The Mooney Aircraft Corporation has produced single-engine civil aviation aircraft since the late 1940s. Perhaps the biggest selling point of the Mooney Bravo is its speed. The cabin of the Mooney is smaller than that in many other general aviation aircraft in its class, but its speed more than makes up for those lost inches of cabin space. The Bravo is capable of achieving altitudes of 25,000 feet, although it does not have a

pressurized cabin, so you'll need to use the four-mask oxygen system to climb to those altitudes (although you don't have to worry about that in Flight Simulator 2000).

Flight Characteristics

This is not an aircraft for a novice pilot. The Mooney is a complex aircraft with a constant-speed propeller and retractable gear, so the pilot's workload is a little more intensive than it would be in a Cessna Skyhawk or even a Skylane.

Of course, increased aircraft speed always adds to workload. The experienced pilot will find the Mooney Bravo to be a good airplane with a solid, responsive feel, and he or she will likely appreciate the speed at which it cruises to its destination. That said, the Mooney's flight characteristics require you to keep a close eye on the airspeed indicator when flying low and slow, such as when you're approaching to land the aircraft.

Example Flight

The best place to get a feel for the Mooney Bravo is the good old Meigs Field in Chicago. At this field you can take off, cruise around some spectacular scenery, and then come back for a landing. During the flight, compare the experience to your flight in the Cessna 182S. You'll quickly notice the differences in performance and overall speed of the aircraft as you fly around the Chicago area.

Tip: *If you need to redisplay the opening screen, on the Flights menu, click Show Opening Screen.*

1. To get started, click the Fly Now button on the opening screen of Flight Simulator 2000.

2. On the runway, you'll be in a Cessna 182S by default, so switch to the Mooney Bravo.

3. To open the takeoff checklist, on the Aircraft menu, point to Kneeboard, and then click Checklists.

4. Take off and fly around for a while, and then open the landing checklist on the kneeboard by pointing to Kneeboard on the Aircraft menu and then clicking Checklists. You might need to scroll down the list to see the landing checklist.

5. Land the Bravo at Meigs.

Raytheon/Beechcraft King Air

The Beechcraft King Air is a classic twin-engine turboprop aircraft, used for everything from hauling cargo, to transporting passengers for commercial airlines, to dropping skydivers. (A turboprop engine is a jet engine that drives a propeller to produce thrust.) The King Air is one of the most popular of the

turboprop aircraft, prized for its safety and reliability. Its pressurized cabin allows you to cruise in comfort at 30,000 feet at speeds of 280 knots, letting you make many short-haul flights in good time as well as in comfort.

Flight Characteristics

The King Air can do just about anything well; because of its great performance, you will find it just as comfortable on an unimproved gravel strip as it is on a runway 150 feet wide. Flying the King Air is a pleasure; it's extremely stable with lots of power and responsive controls. Its turbine engines provide ample power, and its reversible props can stop the airplane in a hurry. It can climb quickly to comfortable altitudes in the 35,000-foot range, making it very economical and giving it an extremely long range for its size. Even though its cruising speed is lower than that of corporate jets, the King Air can operate out of many airports that aren't suitable for jets. It can get passengers closer to their final destinations, which means shorter overall trip times. The King Air is very stable, especially for instrument flying, and can handle almost any weather condition.

Example Flight

One of the King Air's more unusual uses is dropping skydivers. King Air models such as the B90 and C90 are popular skydiving aircraft because they're sturdy, reliable, and can carry dozens of loads of skydivers quickly and efficiently every day. For a jump pilot, time is money, so the more quickly you can carry a load of skydivers to altitude, drop them, and return to pick up another load, the happier everyone is.

Although the King Air 350 isn't used much in skydiving operations because of its cost, with a rear cargo door modification there is no reason why it wouldn't make an excellent jump plane. In this exercise, you take off from a drop zone runway with a load of skydivers, circle to gain altitude, and simulate dropping them over the airport. Then you cut the power and descend rapidly at engine idle to pick up another load.

1. Select the Beech King Air 350 as the aircraft and Gardiner Airport in New York as the airport for this flight.

2. Fly about one-quarter mile east of the runway, with the nose of the aircraft pitched up about 15 degrees to maintain a good rate of climb.

3. Start a left turn, watching for air traffic.

4. Fly past the runway, and make another left turn.

5. Continue in this fashion until you have reached jump altitude, which is 3000 feet AGL to 14,000 feet AGL, depending on weather conditions. Remember that it's against Federal Aviation Administration (FAA) regulations to drop skydivers through clouds!

Tip: *The jump run that a plane flies is usually directly upwind, dropping the skydivers the right distance upwind of the target so that wind drift during free fall will blow them directly over the target by the time they open their parachutes at 3000 feet.*

Tip: *In Flight Simulator, after dropping the skydivers, it is possible to perform a half-roll to inverted, pull down to vertical, and swoop a formation of jumpers at terminal velocity before pulling out at V_{NE} ("never exceed" airspeed). To save time and fuel, it helps to get back down to the ground quickly—for a jump ship, you want to spend as little time as possible with an empty cabin and as much time as possible carrying skydivers. With each skydiver paying 20 dollars for a ride to altitude, time really is money.*

6. A King Air used in skydiving operations is equipped with a side door so that the jumpers can check where they are in relation to the landing area and then exit the plane. Try to hold the same heading and fly a nice, straight jump run so that the jumpers can land on target. While on the jump run, adjust the throttle and pitch attitude to climb at about 110 to 115 knots.

7. On the jump run, slow the plane down so that the jumpers can exit without being blown around too much. The airspeed as the jumpers are exiting varies, as it takes more airspeed to retain control of the aircraft with a large group of skydivers getting ready to launch than with a small group.

8. After the exit command is given, bring the throttles to idle, extend the flaps, and bring the nose up to reduce the speed. As the jumpers are climbing out, push the nose over to obtain the desired speed to maintain control of the aircraft. (See Figure 2-12.)

Figure 2-12   *The calm before the storm. The King Air will be diving in just a moment.*

9. As soon as the jumpers have cleared the aircraft, bank the plane hard to the left or the right, and dive for the ground. At this rate of descent, the King Air can match a skydiver's terminal velocity of 120 mph. In the Flight Simulator version of the maneuver, skydivers could expect to see the aircraft they have just jumped out of diving in free fall along with them!

Skydiving King Airs

Some King Airs are specially modified for skydiving operations. Mike Mullins' Super King Air, of West Tennessee Skydiving, is a B90 that is outfitted with 750-hp PT6 turbine engines and high-performance cowlings. This particular King Air can carry a full cabin of 12 skydivers to 14,000 feet, over 2½ miles, in seven minutes or less!

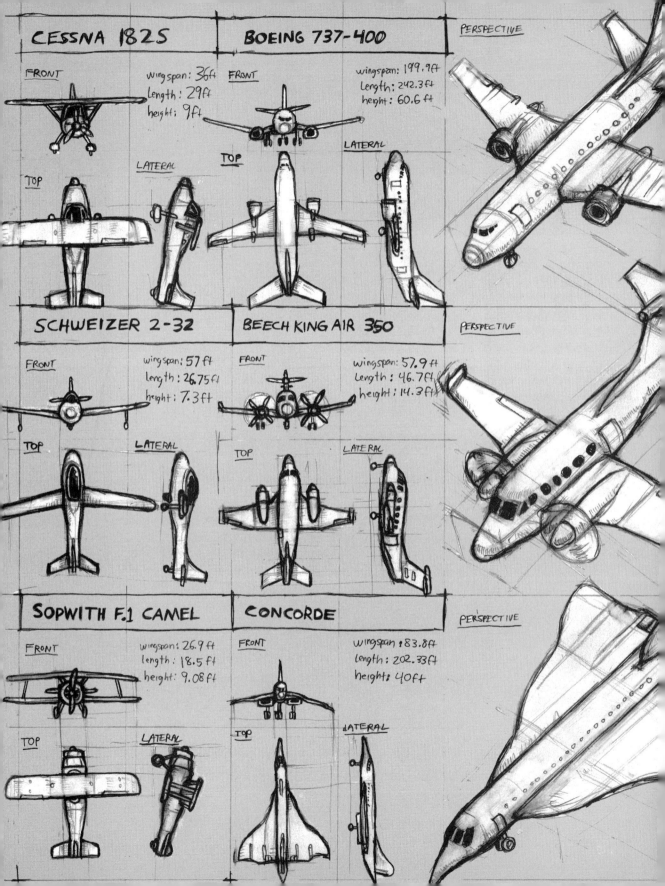

CESSNA 182S

FRONT

TOP

wingspan: 36ft
Length: 29ft
height: 9ft

BOEING 737-400

FRONT

LATERAL

TOP

wingspan: 199.9ft
Length: 242.3ft
height: 60.6ft

PERSPECTIVE

SCHWEIZER 2-32

FRONT

TOP

LATERAL

wingspan: 57ft
Length: 26.75ft
height: 7.3ft

BEECH KING AIR 350

FRONT

TOP

LATERAL

wingspan: 57.9ft
Length: 46.7ft
height: 14.3ft

PERSPECTIVE

SOPWITH F.1 CAMEL

FRONT

TOP

LATERAL

wingspan: 26.9ft
length: 18.5ft
height: 9.08ft

CONCORDE

FRONT

TOP

LATERAL

wingspan: 83.8ft
Length: 202.33ft
height: 40ft

PERSPECTIVE

Chapter Three

NAVIGATIONAL TOOLS

You often hear about the importance of the mechanics of flying an aircraft, but aircraft navigation is probably the most critical element in aviation because without proper navigation, getting lost would be the norm rather than the exception. You won't be very successful as a pilot if you can fly only within visual range of your home airport. You must know how to take advantage of the various navigational aids at your disposal to find your way from airport to airport.

This chapter explores the aspects of navigation in Microsoft Flight Simulator 2000 that aren't explained in detail in the *Pilot's Handbook*. These navigational aids include visual flight rule (VFR) principles, the Map View dialog box, slew mode, the Global Positioning System (GPS), and the flight planner.

Navigating takes up a large part of a pilot's training, but not everyone can take a flight training course. Fortunately for the novice flight simulator pilot, you can also learn a great deal about navigation from Rod Machado in Chapter 7 of the Microsoft Flight Simulator 2000 *Pilot's Handbook* or from online Help in Microsoft Flight Simulator 2000.

Navigating the Flight Simulator World

Navigation in the various incarnations of Flight Simulator has always been accurately modeled, but the newest version of Flight Simulator adds even more realistic and modern navigational tools like the GPS and advanced instrumentation like the horizontal situation indicator (HSI) in aircraft such as the Boeing 777-300. This section discusses the various ways to navigate the Flight Simulator 2000 world.

VFR Flight

Past versions of Flight Simulator lacked the kind of terrain detail that would allow you to fly VFR the way you would in real life. Flight Simulator 2000 now includes incredible visual detail. The view outside the Flight Simulator 2000 cockpit (with 3-D acceleration) is startlingly realistic. (See Figure 3-1.) You can fly via VFR from location to location if weather permits.

Figure 3-1   *The view out of the cockpit in Flight Simulator 2000 is lifelike.*

Generally speaking (because VFR rules vary from country to country), to fly VFR you must have a flight visibility of at least 3 miles and be able to stay away from clouds at least 500 feet below, 1000 feet above, and 2000

feet horizontally. Even if flight conditions are at VFR minimums, it can be a risky proposition to fly. Most VFR pilots I know won't fly unless they have at least 6 miles of visibility.

Instrument Flight Rules Navigation

Instrument flight rules (IFR) navigation is a complicated way to navigate using several radio navigational aids, which are explained exceptionally well by Rod

Flight Simulator vs. Real Life

With Flight Simulator 2000, the line between simulation and reality is increasingly blurred. Flight Simulator 2000 accurately simulates everything—from the view outside the windscreen to the feel of the aircraft and the instrumentation. As a Cessna pilot, I can tell you that this software is getting pretty darn close to reality. Whether you're flying following VFR or with navigational aids, this software is very much like real life.

The limitations of any simulator become evident when you start talking about physical sensations such as the feel of the controls, the popping of your ears as you descend, and the forces on your body when you pull a tight turn. These sensations are important to the flight experience, but they are not critical. Perhaps the most glaring problem with a computer flight simulator has to do with visual navigation. This problem arises because most people use Flight Simulator on a 15-inch or 17-inch flat monitor. This configuration leaves you without the peripheral vision that is so important in flight and the panoramic view that's important when navigating visually.

How do you solve the visual problems inherent in computer flight simulators? If you can, I recommend that you get three video cards and set up three monitors so that you have the front, left, and right views available all the time. Unfortunately, most people (including myself) don't have the means to support such a setup. An alternative solution is to set up several windows in the main viewing area that will give you this information. We discussed how to configure these views in Chapter 1, "Making it Real." This configuration greatly aids in VFR navigation because with it you can better and more quickly identify landmarks such as buildings, towns, and rivers.

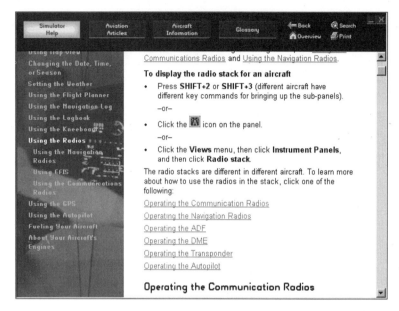

Figure 3-2   *All of the navigational tools are discussed in detail in on-line Help.*

Machado in Chapter 7 of the *Pilot's Handbook*. Many of the navigational aspects of IFR flight are covered in Flight Simulator's online Help. On the Help menu, click Simulator Help, and then click Getting From Here To There. (See Figure 3-2.) You can also read more about IFR flight certification along with some other thoughts on IFR from a longtime airline pilot in Chapter 11 of this book, "Advanced Flight Techniques."

Moving Without Flying: Slewing

Slewing is a mechanism provided by Flight Simulator 2000 that allows you to quickly change your aircraft's position without flying. When in slew mode, you can see all of the scenery that you would normally see if you were flying. To begin slewing, press the Y key. The coordinates, heading, and altitude are then displayed in red in the upper-left corner of the simulation view. (See Figure 3-3.)

Note: *If you enter slew mode from the runway and position the aircraft at a specific location, when you exit slew mode, the aircraft will have zero airspeed and will be stalled. You'll have to dive to break the stall before you can begin flying. To avoid this situation, set the position as well as the initial airspeed by using the Map View dialog box. (Click Map View on the World menu.)*

Depending on which controller you use, you can actually move the plane around while in slew mode by simply manipulating the controller in the direction that you want to move. But to really take advantage of slewing, I recommend using the keyboard. For a complete list of slewing key combinations, click Simulator Help on the Help menu, and then click Getting From Here To There. Read the section "Changing Your Position by Slewing." The following is a list of the common slewing key combinations:

Figure 3-3 *You'll see the coordinates, heading, and altitude while in slew mode.*

Key	Description
Y	Toggle slewing on or off
8 on the numeric keypad	Move forward
2 on the numeric keypad	Move backward
4 on the numeric keypad	Move left
6 on the numeric keypad	Move right
F4	Increase altitude quickly
Q	Increase altitude slowly
A	Decrease altitude slowly
F1	Decrease altitude quickly
F2	Freeze altitude

The Map View Dialog Box

The Map View dialog box in Flight Simulator 2000 is a new and powerful tool. It allows you to position your aircraft anywhere on the globe, displays your current position, displays airport information, and provides other useful navigation information. You access the Map View dialog box by clicking Map View on the World menu.

Tip: *The Map View dialog box is an invaluable tool for almost any situation in Flight Simulator 2000, but Flight Simulator's built-in adventures often disable the Map View dialog box.*

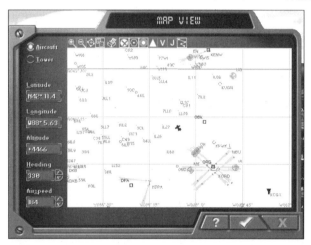

Figure 3-4 *You can place your aircraft anywhere in the world by using the Map View dialog box.*

Dropping In

You can position your aircraft anywhere in the world by using the Map View dialog box to enter the desired latitude, longitude, and altitude, as well as control the aircraft's initial course and speed by entering a heading and airspeed. (See Figure 3-4.) For example, you might use the Map View dialog box to place the aircraft at the summit of Mount Everest by obtaining the coordinates of the mountain and typing them in. You then just click the green checkmark, and wham, you're there.

Tip: *To learn more about the features of the Map View dialog box, on the Help menu, click Simulator Help, and then click Getting From Here To There. Then review the "Using Map View" section. (See Figure 3-5.)*

This method of placing the aircraft has an advantage over slewing: by using the Map View dialog box, you can configure your aircraft to be flying when you jump to the location, rather than just "showing up" stalled in mid-air. You'll notice that the Map View dialog box is used many times in this book to configure flight situations.

The Map

The map portion of the Map View dialog box supplies a variety of information, including your exact location, positions of airports, and locations of instrument landing system (ILS) localizers for the various runways. (See Figure 3-6.)

> **Note:** An ILS localizer beam is a radio beam that guides you horizontally by specifying if your aircraft's position is to the left or right of the runway.

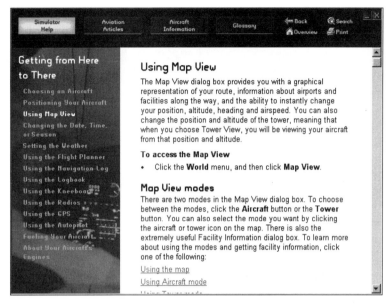

Figure 3-5 Online Help can give you much of the information that you need to know about using the Map View dialog box.

Figure 3-6 The localizers for airports with an ILS are clearly shown on the map.

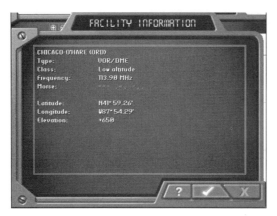

Figure 3-7   *The Facility Information dialog box supplies vital airport information.*

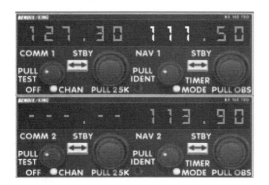

Figure 3-8   *Tune the NAV 1 radio to activate the ILS.*

The map can also provide information about nearby airports. To get detailed information on a particular airport, double-click the airport icon on the map to display the Facility Information dialog box. (See Figure 3-7.) This dialog box contains airport information such as the automatic terminal information service (ATIS) frequency, runway length and surface, and even ILS frequencies and headings. Map View is a powerful feature when you're flying into IFR conditions and need to find an ILS frequency at a nearby airport. Simply double-click the nearest airport to view the facility information. After closing the Facilities dialog box and the Map View dialog box, you can then point to Instrument Panel on the Views menu and click Radio Stack. Tune the ILS frequency supplied by the Map View dialog box on the NAV 1 radio to activate the ILS. (See Figure 3-8.)

Flight Planning

Flight Simulator 2000 includes an excellent flight-planning feature that makes it easy to construct simple or complex flight

plans. The Flight Planner lets you plan a flight in stages so that you can fly it in legs via waypoints to manage the navigation more easily. The data that you provide in Flight Planner is transferred to the GPS receiver, so you can then see and follow your preset flight path right in the GPS unit of your aircraft.

Let's plan a simple flight right now:

1. Click Flight Planner on the Flights menu to open the Flight Planner dialog box.

2. Click the Basic tab in the Flight Planner dialog box. (See Figure 3-9.)

3. Click the Select button in the Departure Airport area to open the Go To Airport dialog box. Select the departure airport of your choice, and then click the green checkmark.

4. Click the Select button in the Destination Airport area, and then select the destination airport of your choice.

ATIS

ATIS is a radio service that specifies weather conditions such as wind, cloud cover, dew point, and visibility, as well as other details such as which runways are active and current barometric pressure readings. Generally speaking, the ATIS message is updated hourly and is played continuously. Just tune your aircraft's radio to the specific ATIS frequency to get all this information.

Tip: *For more information on Flight Planner, check out "Using the Flight Planner" in the Simulator Help section of online Help.*

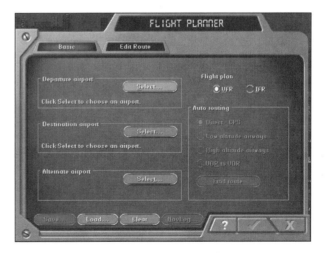

Figure 3-9   *The Flight Planner is a powerful tool for constructing flights of any duration.*

Tip: *You can also choose an alternate airport at this time. You might select an alternate airport as a safeguard in situations that require you to divert and land before you reach your destination. An alternate is also there in case you can't land at your primary destination (for example, when weather is poor). To select an alternate airport, click the Select button in the Alternate Airport area, and select the destination airport of your choice. Then click the checkmark to continue.*

5. In the Auto Routing area, click the Direct-GPS option. This will set the route into the GPS receiver. Display the GPS receiver after takeoff by pointing to Instrument Panel on the Views menu and then clicking GPS.

6. Click the Find Route button to have the planner calculate the route.

7. Click the Save button to write the flight plan to a file for later use.

GPS

The GPS is perhaps the most powerful navigational system in modern aviation. A GPS receiver in your aircraft can literally replace a map by telling you exactly where your aircraft is and what direction it's heading, as well as information about airspace, cities, roadways, and airport locations. Many GPS receivers (like the one in Flight Simulator 2000) have a built-in emergency feature that shows you the closest airports as well as the bearings or headings that you must fly to find them. Features like this make a GPS receiver an indispensable navigational tool.

What Is GPS?

The GPS is a navigational system based on a vast satellite network that can be used to pinpoint any spot on Earth by triangulating signals received from a group of satellites. The GPS is accurate enough to identify a location within about 60 feet of the receiver's location. The inclusion of GPS receivers in aircraft has changed general aviation for the better by eliminating potentially hazardous navigational errors.

You use the various views of the GPS receiver to get at the information that you need. Click the Mode button to cycle between the map view, Waypoint Info view, and Route Info view. The Direct To view and the Emergency view are accessed by clicking the D button with the arrow through it. (See Figure 3-10.)

The Map View in the GPS Receiver

The map view in the GPS receiver is a moving map display that shows the orientation from your aircraft (shown as a picture of an aircraft, always in the center of the map view) to the airports, *waypoints* that have been entered in the Flight Planner, and major road *intersections* that are displayed on the map. For the general aviator, probably the most important things that the map view displays are the airports and the ILS localizers (shown in green). (See Figure 3-10.)

Waypoint Info View in the GPS Receiver

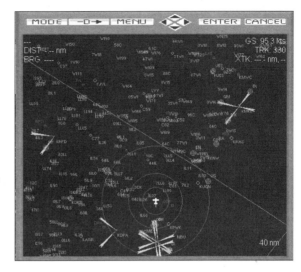

Figure 3-10   *The map view in the GPS receiver is updated constantly to represent the location of the aircraft in relation to surrounding airports, waypoints, and intersections.*

Note: *To access the GPS receiver in Flight Simulator 2000, point to Instrument Panel on the Views menu and then click GPS; or press Shift+2 or Shift+3 (depending on the aircraft you're flying).*

Waypoint Info view shows the name of the next waypoint, the distance to it, the heading you must fly to reach it, your current ground speed, and the time it should take you to reach the waypoint. (See Figure 3-11.) This view also includes the latitude and longitude of each waypoint. It's important to have this waypoint information if you're trying to stick to a specific flight plan.

Figure 3-11   *Waypoint Info view is full of important information.*

Figure 3-12   *Route Info view works in conjunction with the flight planner.*

Route Info View in the GPS Receiver

If you filed a flight plan by using the flight planner, this view shows you all the information of your planned route, including a list of waypoints, magnetic bearings between each waypoint, and estimated flying times. (See Figure 3-12.) This is useful because it gives you a quick glimpse of exactly how far you must travel between waypoints, as well as the headings you'll need to turn to once you reach each waypoint.

Direct To View in the GPS Receiver

Direct To view allows you to leave your current flight plan and instead fly directly to any airport, navigational aid, or intersection that you choose. This is a very useful view if you have a change of plans or even if you want to verify that you're on the correct heading to a selected landmark. Be careful when using the Direct To command, though. When you select a new airport, intersection or navigational aid to fly toward, the previous flight plan you entered is erased.

Emergency View in the GPS Receiver

Emergency view is very important because it helps you cancel your current flight plan and find the nearest airport. (See Figure 3-13.) This view displays a list of airports closest to your location. Select the airport you want as your destination or waypoint, and then click the Enter button. In the map view of the GPS receiver, you'll see your course to the airport that you chose (as shown in Figure 3-14), along with the information on the distance and bearing you'll need to fly to reach the airport.

Figure 3-13 *After you pick the nearest airport and click the Enter button in Emergency view, the map view displays your course to the airport.*

Sample Trip

This sample flight helps you practice using the flight planner to navigate via the GPS receiver through two waypoints to a final destination. After working through this brief tutorial, you'll be able to plan your own flights and use the flight planner and GPS to go wherever your heart desires.

Plan the Flight

This tutorial flight is between Merrill C. Meigs Field and Chicago O'Hare International Airport via the Chicago Midway Airport. Let's get started:

1. Click Flight Planner on the Flights menu to open the Flight Planner dialog box.

Figure 3-14 *The map view in the GPS shows the new waypoint that you entered in Emergency view.*

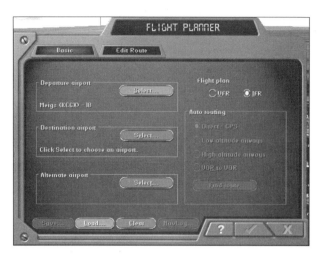

Figure 3-15   *Set up your flight to depart from Merrill C. Meigs Field in Chicago.*

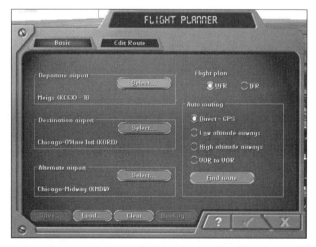

Figure 3-16   *After you supply the flight information in the Go To Airport dialog box, click the Find Route button.*

2. Click the Basic tab in the Flight Planner dialog box.

3. Click the Select button in the Departure Airport area to open the Go To Airport dialog box. Select Meigs as the departure airport (as shown in Figure 3-15), and then click the green checkmark.

4. Click the Select button in the Destination Airport area, and then select Chicago-O'Hare International as the destination airport and your first waypoint.

5. Click the Select button in the Alternate Airport area, and then select Chicago-Midway as the alternate airport. (We'll set this airport as one of your waypoints in step 7.)

6. In the Flight Plan area, click the VFR option. In the Auto Routing area, click the Direct-GPS option, and then click the Find Route button. (See Figure 3-16.) The Edit Route tab then opens, with the direct path from Meigs to O'Hare shown with a red line.

7. To place another waypoint or leg in your flight, click anywhere on the red line (the path from Meigs to O'Hare), and drag it down to KMDW, which is Chicago-Midway Airport. (See Figure 3-17.) A new red path line is drawn between Meigs and Chicago-Midway, and another new line is drawn between Chicago Midway and O'Hare (as shown in Figure 3-18), representing the two legs of your journey.

8. Click the green checkmark to open the Save Flight Plan dialog box.

9. Save the flight plan to your hard disk.

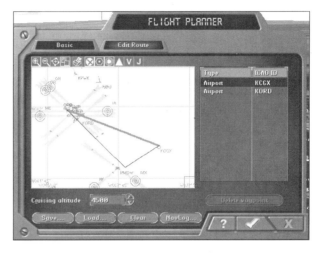

Figure 3-17   *Creating a new waypoint is as easy as clicking the path and dragging.*

Flying the Flight Plan

You will now fly the flight plan that you just created by using the GPS receiver as your navigational aid.

1. Before you take off, display the GPS receiver. On the Views menu, point to Instrument Panel, and then click GPS.

2. Click the Mode button to cycle between the three

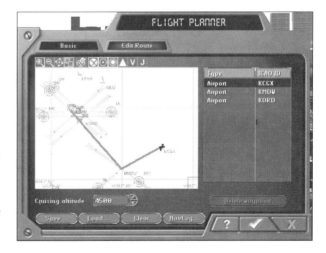

Figure 3-18   *This flight plan is ready to go. You can now save the flight plan and move on.*

Figure 3-19 *The map view of the GPS shows the paths (in green) to each waypoint. The box in the upper-left corner tells you the bearing and distance to KMDW (Chicago-Midway, your first waypoint).*

views: Waypoint Info view (which shows the distance and bearing to Chicago-Midway [KMDW]), Route Info view (which shows the two legs of your journey), and the map view (which pictorially shows you the route, as shown in Figure 3-19).

3. Take off from Meigs Field, and fly toward the first waypoint. The BRG (bearing) number in the upper-left corner will change as you fly, always telling you the heading that you need to get to the waypoint. The TRK (track) number in the upper-right corner of the map view shows you the actual track you're heading on. If you can match the TRK and BRG numbers, you'll be right on course. (See Figure 3-20.) The distance to the waypoint is displayed above the BRG, and your aircraft's ground speed (GS) is displayed above the TRK.

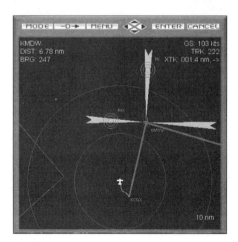

Figure 3-20 *Use all of the information that the GPS receiver provides, from the heading you need to be flying (BRG) to the heading you are flying (TRK).*

> **Note:** *On the GPS is a picture of an aircraft facing upward. This is* always *the direction in which your aircraft is heading.*

4. The graphic representations of the airports in relation to your aircraft make the GPS receiver an incredible navigational tool. Fly the pathway to the waypoint at Chicago-Midway, and then turn toward O'Hare (using the GPS receiver to follow the flight path). Your actual flight path will be represented by a yellow line.

5. When you reach Chicago-Midway (as shown in Figure 3-21), your waypoint will be reset automatically to O'Hare (KORD).

6. Turn to the new bearing (BRG) displayed in the upper-left corner of the GPS, and head for O'Hare.

7. As this tutorial shows, the Flight Planner and GPS are very easy to use. When they are used together, they can make flying between any two (or more) points

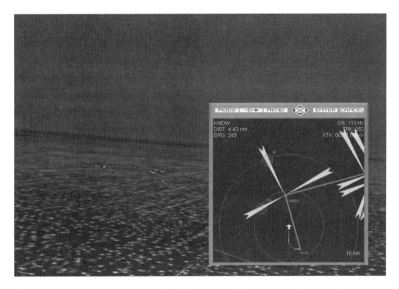

Figure 3-21   *Approaching the Chicago-Midway airport at night using a full-screen display with GPS.*

much easier than in the days prior to GPS; you simply follow a line on a moving map, and it doesn't get much easier than that.

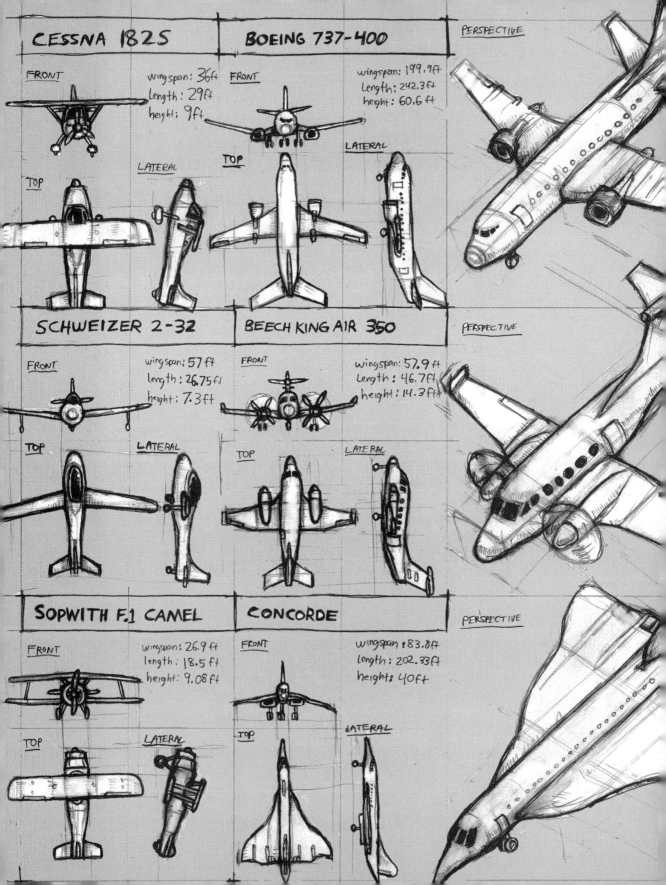

CESSNA 182S

FRONT

wingspan: 36ft
length: 29ft
height: 9ft

TOP

LATERAL

BOEING 737-400

FRONT

wingspan: 199.9ft
length: 242.3ft
height: 60.6ft

TOP

LATERAL

PERSPECTIVE

SCHWEIZER 2-32

FRONT

wingspan: 57ft
length: 26.75ft
height: 7.3ft

TOP

LATERAL

BEECH KING AIR 350

FRONT

wingspan: 57.9ft
length: 46.7ft
height: 14.3ft

TOP

LATERAL

PERSPECTIVE

SOPWITH F.1 CAMEL

FRONT

wingspan: 26.9ft
length: 18.5ft
height: 9.08ft

TOP

LATERAL

CONCORDE

FRONT

wingspan: 83.8ft
length: 202.33ft
height: 40ft

TOP

LATERAL

PERSPECTIVE

Chapter Four

ADVENTURES

Other chapters in this book will present challenging and adventurous situations that you can create, such as air rallies (Chapter 5), challenging flights (Chapter 7), and emergencies (Chapter 6). These "creations" allow you to experience Microsoft Flight Simulator 2000 in new and exciting ways, as well as show you possible ways to create your own interesting situations. However, Flight Simulator 2000 also comes with a number of built-in adventures that are already set up and ready to challenge you. This chapter deals with some of these adventures. I'll spell out the key objective(s) for each of the flights. I'll also include flight tips on how to successfully complete each adventure.

Flight Simulator's adventures are broken down into four skill levels: beginner, intermediate, advanced, and expert. To begin an adventure, on the Flights menu, click Adventures. Click a skill level, click a specific adventure, and then click the green checkmark to start.

Tip: *Flight Simulator also includes an option for converted adventures, which are adventures that you import from another source, such as add-on third-party adventure packs.*

Note: *Some adventures are available only in Flight Simulator 2000 Professional Edition. They will be clearly marked in this chapter.*

Beginner Adventure

This adventure is where you get your feet wet. It introduces you to the concept of adventures and eases you into the stressful situations that the more advanced adventures will place you in. You can complete the first adventure relatively quickly, whereas many of the later adventures (in the advanced section) involve long-haul flights over the oceans.

Moscow or Bust, 182S (Professional Edition)

In 1987, a young West German man named Mathias Rust flew a single-engine Cessna from Helsinki to Moscow, ultimately landing in Red Square. As you can imagine, it caused quite a furor, and a few high-ranking Soviet military officials were fired over the incident; after all, how could a simple single-engine general aviation aircraft penetrate the air defenses of a superpower?

This adventure puts you in the pilot's seat of a Cessna 182S charged with the same objective: to land safely in Red Square while flying in low to avoid the Soviet radar system. The adventure begins a few miles from Red Square, which is shown in Figure 4-1.

Figure 4-1 *Your goal in this adventure is to land inside the walls of Red Square.*

Flight Tips

- Red Square lies due east (your starting heading). Keep the altitude under 1500 feet MSL (height above mean sea level).
- Follow the river so that your approach to Red Square involves a tight turn on the square's south side. There are buildings around the square that will obstruct your path from other directions, so this makes for the best approach. (See Figure 4-2—landed inside Red Square.)

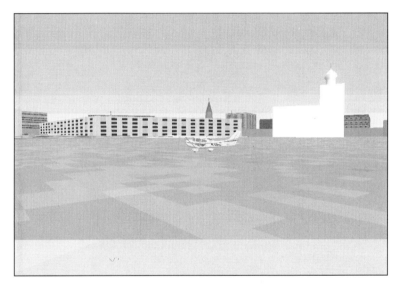

Figure 4-2   *It was difficult landing, but getting out poses another challenge. This is a shot of us inside Red Square.*

Intermediate Adventures

These adventures challenge your piloting skills a little more, but they shouldn't make you pull your hair out in frustration. If you've completed the beginner adventure, you're ready for the intermediate ones.

Keyhole, Cessna 182S

This flight puts you just outside the Los Angeles Coliseum, cruising at 140 knots. Your goal is to fly through the main archway of the Coliseum (as shown in Figure 4-3) and land on the playing field. The premise is that this is a half-time stunt, and the crowd is expecting your entrance. Let's just hope you don't disappoint them by pancaking on the side of the Coliseum.

Figure 4-3   *You must fly through this archway and then land on the playing field—no small task.*

Flight Tips

- First maneuver to line up with the archway, and then start to lower the speed as much as possible.
- To safely make it through the archway, it's preferable to be banked before the Cessna passes through the arch; this aircraft position increases your chances of clearing the archway walls. (See Figure 4-4.)
- Before you pass through the archway, kill the power because once you're inside the Coliseum, you'll have to put the Cessna on the turf and brake hard.

Figure 4-4   *Getting into the Coliseum is a tight squeeze.*

Figure 4-5 gives an aerial view of your landing. What a feat.

Figure 4-5   *It's a touchdown.*

Long Shot, Cessna Skylane 182 RG

This adventure puts you on approach to Block Island Airport. (See Figure 4-6.) As you approach the airport, you'll lose engine power and have to take the Cessna to the tarmac without any power. You'll need to make sure that you're not too low and too slow as you prepare for landing.

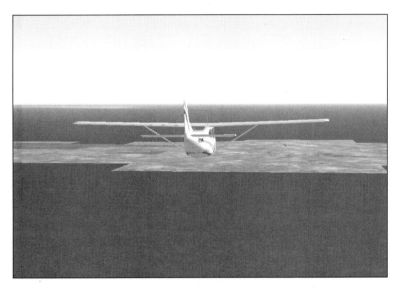

Figure 4-6   *Keep the altitude a little high on approach to Block Island Airport.*

Flight Tips

- Fly the approach higher than you normally would (keeping about 100 feet higher than normal) to provide a bigger margin of error when the engine fails.
- Even though you have power at first, remember that you will be without the engine in the final stages of this adventure. Try to maintain the best glide speed (80 knots) to get all the way to the runway.

- The runway at Block Island is not very long (as shown in Figure 4-7), so be careful not to overshoot the landing or else you'll run off the tarmac. If you think you will overshoot, try to slip down to the runway. A forward slip occurs when you use opposite rudder and ailerons to lose altitude quickly—for example, full right rudder and enough left aileron to keep you heading down to the runway. Don't forget to stop the slip before you land, or you'll land sideways!

Figure 4-7   *Making the runway is a great feeling.*

Advanced Adventures

The pressure knob has just been turned up another notch. These adventures take you to the next level of complexity by placing you in realistic situations in which your aircraft experiences mechanical failure. From a failure in the

vacuum system to an inability to lower your landing gear, these adventures will force you to act quickly, while using all your knowledge of flight and the aircraft to avert disaster.

From Bad to Worse, Mooney Bravo (Professional Edition)

You are in a Mooney Bravo approaching O'Hare International on a stormy night when the vacuum system fails your attitude indicator and heading indicator. You are still a few miles from the airport when this emergency happens, and you have not yet been vectored to an instrument landing system (ILS—see the *Pilot's Handbook* or online Help) approach. You must get the aircraft down to O'Hare in one piece—you might have to resort to using the GPS. (See Figure 4-8.)

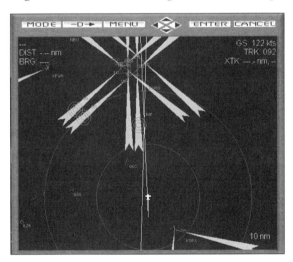

Figure 4-8   *Use the GPS to help find the ILS, the frequency of which is for runway 9R.*

Flight Tips

- The NAV 1 radio is tuned to ILS runway 9R, so you can fly this adventure by following the horizontal situation indicator (HSI) to the ILS localizers.
- If you don't make it onto the glideslope before the vacuum system fails, turn on the GPS and fly in using it.
- Remember that the elevation at O'Hare is around 700 feet ASL, so don't fly below 900 feet until you have the runway in sight and can land there safely!
- Because you lose your attitude indicator (AI) and heading indicator, you'll be flying with what's called a partial panel. This requires you to get your information from other sources. The attitude indicator can be replaced by looking at your altitude indicator, the vertical speed indicator (VSI), and the turn coordinator. Scanning these three instruments can give you the information you'll need to fly without the AI. For more information on partial panel flying, check out the excellent article in the Navigation area of online Help entitled "Partial Panel Emergencies" by Alton K. Marsh.

Emergency Landing, Schweizer 2-32

This adventure puts you in a dilemma that few pilots envy. The towrope on your Sailplane has broken just after takeoff, and, of course, the runway is behind you. (See Figure 4-9.) You must find a way to turn the aircraft around 180 degrees and land safely on the runway.

Figure 4-9 *The runway is behind you, and you have precious little altitude in which to maneuver.*

Flight Tips

- You start out on a heading of 240 degrees at about 60 knots. Make a tight left turn to a heading of about 60 degrees to take you on a course to the runway, which you'll see outside as shown in Figure 4-10.
- Once you're sure you've made the runway, open the spoilers to slow the aircraft down for landing.

- If you want to make this adventure tougher, make your first turn to the right rather than the left to leave you much farther away and out of position for landing.

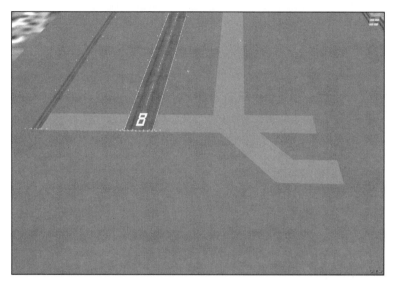

Figure 4-10 *The runway will appear when you reach about 60 degrees after you start your first left-hand turn.*

Short Stick, Beech King Air 350 (Professional Edition)

Your aircraft is leaking fuel (and to add insult to injury, your flaps won't go down), so you must get this bird on the ground as quickly as possible. You have a reasonable amount of altitude to start out with, but the Beech King Air

350 doesn't glide like the Cessna Skylane 182S, so you'll have to make decisions quickly and find the only airport that's nearby. (See Figure 4-11.)

Figure 4-11   *The airport you're looking for is by the body of water straight ahead of this view.*

Flight Tips

- Turn immediately to a heading of about 170 degrees to set the aircraft up to make it to the airport. Don't waste any time making this turn because you need all the altitude that you can get.
- After you lose power to your engines (which is almost right away), display the throttle quadrant by pointing to Instrument Panel on the Views

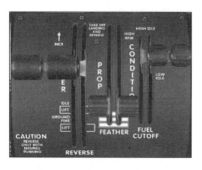

Figure 4-12   *Feather the propellers after you lose power.*

menu and then clicking Throttle Quadrant. Then feather both of the propellers by sliding the throttle controls into the red-and-white Feather area (in the Throttle instrument panel) to help your glide. (See Figure 4-12.)

- Don't lower the landing gear until the last minute. (See Figure 4-13.)

Figure 4-13   *Your best bet is to touch down early since the runway is short and you're landing without your flaps.*

Belly Dancing, Mooney Bravo (Professional Edition)

Flying in a Mooney Bravo, you discover that the landing gear won't deploy. You'll need to do a belly landing (a landing without landing gear), which is dangerous for obvious reasons. Trying to get the gear down will be fruitless— you'll have to put the plane down on its underside. (See Figure 4-14.)

Figure 4-14 *Fly the Bravo down to land as softly as possible on its belly.*

Flight Tips

- To find your way to the nearest airport, just have a look at the HSI, and fly a heading of about 120 degrees until you intercept the ILS localizer.

- When you intercept the localizer, fly along it (and start descending when you intercept the glideslope) for an ILS landing at the airport.
- For landing procedures and checklists for the Mooney Bravo, bring up the Kneeboard on the Aircraft menu, and select Checklists.

Expert Adventures

These are the adventures that separate the cats from the kittens. Most of these adventures are modeled after real-life commercial flights much like the flights that thousands of passengers take every day. These adventures take advantage of the new aircraft in Flight Simulator 2000 such as the Boeing 777-300, the Concorde, and the Beech King Air 350.

London to New York, Concorde

This adventure puts you in the pilot's seat of a Concorde on a revenue flight from Paris to John F. Kennedy International Airport in New York. A flight plan from Paris to JFK has already been filed for you when you start the flight. Your job is to make this flight as routine as possible. Because this is a transatlantic flight, you will have to be prepared to be at the controls for several hours.

Figure 4-15 *Turn off the afterburners after you hit cruising speed and altitude to save fuel.*

Flight Tips

- Keep the aircraft running smoothly. Don't make any wild control adjustments, and after you reach cruising speed and altitude, turn off the afterburners to save fuel. (See Figure 4-15.) To get the Concorde cruising at Mach 2, see the Concorde Flight Notes in the *Pilot's Handbook* for more information.
- Take advantage of the map view and GPS to ensure that you are on course.

• Don't begin your takeoff roll before you receive clearance from Air Traffic Control (ATC). Your call sign is Concorde One; you'll hear ATC refer to you in this manner when giving you instructions during your flight.

Chicago to London, Boeing 777-300

This adventure has you flying a Boeing 777-300 on an ETOPS flight from Chicago to London, England. ETOPS stands for Extended Range Twin-Engine Operations. ETOPS is a special FAA certification that allows airliners with two engines to operate over transoceanic flights by providing a flight pattern that is the most direct routing between transoceanic cities. You'll be taking off from Chicago O'Hare's runway 09R (as shown in Figure 4-16), and you'll need to listen to ATC in order to hear your instructions.

Figure 4-16   *Your Boeing 777-300 is ready to go on runway 09R at O'Hare.*

Flight Tips

- As the preflight briefing states, when you're over the Atlantic Ocean, you won't pick up VOR signals; this is where the GPS comes in. Use the GPS to ensure you're on track. (Your course will be mapped out on the GPS for you to follow.)

- ATC will address you as Travel One; listen for any instructions that come over the radio.

- After takeoff you will hear ATC tell you to turn to heading 060 and climb to flight level 290 (29,000 feet).

VIP to the Big Apple, Beech King Air 350 (Professional Edition)

Fly a group of government VIPs from Washington, D.C., to New York City in a Beech King Air 350. As the preflight briefing notes, you are a new pilot in command and you want to impress your boss by flying this route without any problems. The government VIPs are headed to a conference at the United Nations building in New York City, so you must get them there on time. The Beech King Air 350 will take off from runway 19R at Washington Dulles Airport for this approximately one-hour flight. (See Figure 4-17.)

Figure 4-17   *The Beech King Air is ready for takeoff.*

Flight Tips

- This flight takes place in the winter, so you have to get used to the snow-covered scenery that surrounds you.
- When climbing in the Beech King Air 350 at full throttle, the nose wants to pull up. Expect that action so that you don't end up over-controlling or battling the aircraft instead of concentrating on the flight plan.

CESSNA 182S

FRONT

wingspan: 36ft
Length: 29ft
height: 9ft

TOP

LATERAL

BOEING 737-400

FRONT

wingspan: 199.9ft
Length: 242.3ft
height: 60.6ft

TOP

LATERAL

PERSPECTIVE

SCHWEIZER 2-32

FRONT

wingspan: 57ft
length: 26.75ft
height: 7.3ft

TOP

LATERAL

BEECH KING AIR 350

FRONT

wingspan: 57.9ft
Length: 46.7ft
height: 14.3ft

TOP

LATERAL

PERSPECTIVE

SOPWITH F.1 CAMEL

FRONT

wingspan: 26.9ft
length: 18.5ft
height: 9.08ft

TOP

LATERAL

CONCORDE

FRONT

wingspan: 83.8ft
Length: 202.33ft
height: 40ft

TOP

LATERAL

PERSPECTIVE

PART II

Exploring and Fun

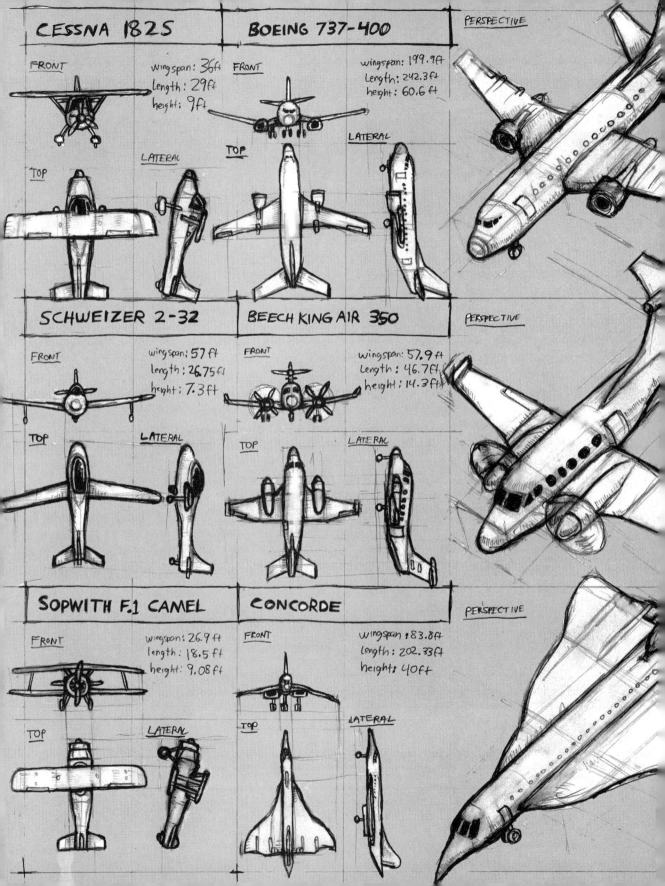

CESSNA 182S

FRONT

wingspan: 36ft
length: 29ft
height: 9ft

TOP

LATERAL

BOEING 737-400

FRONT

wingspan: 199.9ft
length: 242.3ft
height: 60.6ft

TOP

LATERAL

PERSPECTIVE

SCHWEIZER 2-32

FRONT

wingspan: 57ft
length: 26.75ft
height: 7.3ft

TOP

LATERAL

BEECH KING AIR 350

FRONT

wingspan: 57.9ft
length: 46.7ft
height: 14.3ft

TOP

LATERAL

PERSPECTIVE

SOPWITH F.1 CAMEL

FRONT

wingspan: 26.9ft
length: 18.5ft
height: 9.08ft

TOP

LATERAL

CONCORDE

FRONT

wingspan: 83.8ft
length: 202.33ft
height: 40ft

TOP

LATERAL

PERSPECTIVE

Chapter Five

THE AIR RALLY

One of the aviation sports that is gaining popularity is the air rally. This competition challenges teams to fly through a series of checkpoints, armed only with a map and navigation aids. This chapter first delves into the specifics of air rallies in the real world, including an inside peek into the U.S. air rally team's first foray into international competition. This chapter then suggests four complete and original air rallies to try with Microsoft Flight Simulator 2000. Flying air rallies is a heck of a lot of fun, and by flying the following four challenging rallies, you'll discover why air rallies are so popular throughout the world.

The Air Rally Experience

An air rally is a great test of flying and navigating skills. Each team, or *rally crew,* consists of a pilot and a navigator. Teams are challenged to find their way through a series of checkpoints, armed only with a map and a compass. They are given a specific time to arrive at the checkpoints and are penalized for arriving too early or too late. Along the way, teams might be asked to locate a specific landmark on a map or to orient or correctly identify a photograph of a landmark from the air. Points are deducted for mistakes in timing and accuracy. The team that is best able to estimate its ground speed and track and adjust its flight route to land safely and precisely on time at the correct airfield with the fewest penalty points is declared the winner. But besides just vying for first place, air rally participants invariably have a great time showing off their navigation skills and perhaps picking up a few exciting stories to swap with each other at day's end.

> **Note:** *When you fly an air rally in Flight Simulator 2000, penalty points won't be awarded automatically—you and your competitors will have to use the honor system—and a little creativity—to determine the winner.*

Official Air Rallies

In the real world, air rallies are conducted in accordance with the official rules published by the Fédération Aéronautique Internationale (FAI), which is the governing body for all world aerial competitions. According to the FAI, the purpose of an air rally is to "improve fundamental flying skills to enable a team (rally crew) to navigate and handle their aircraft under visual meteorological conditions (VMC) as independent of technical systems as possible." Becoming proficient in these skills enhances flight safety and builds piloting skills.

Although air rallies have long been popular in Europe and the rest of the world, they are just now emerging as a sport in North America. In the United States, air rallies are promoted by the U.S. Air Rally Association, which was founded in 1997. The U.S. Air Rally Association also represents the United States in international air rally competitions. A U.S. Air Rally Association team competed for the first time at the first World Air Games in 1997 in Turkey, where the United States placed a very respectable twentieth out of 32 countries.

Air Rally Techniques and Terminology

The idea of an air rally is to fly from the starting point to each successive checkpoint until you reach the last checkpoint, where you must land and come to a full stop on the runway. Rally checkpoints are numbered sequentially, starting at checkpoint 1 and continuing to checkpoint 2, checkpoint 3, and on to the last checkpoint, which is generally located at a runway or an airport. You must fly to the checkpoints in order, although if you're running late, you might find that you lose fewer points if you skip one checkpoint to recoup lost time, rather than arrive late at every checkpoint.

In real life, an air rally might consist of a dozen checkpoints, spaced out over a distance of 100 nautical miles (NM). Teams are given a list of the checkpoints about 15 minutes before the race is scheduled to begin, along with a map of the area. Directions to each checkpoint might contain:

- Coordinates (for example, "N47* 37.07', W36* 16.08'").
- The magnetic heading and distance from the previous checkpoint (for example, "120 degrees 12 NM from checkpoint 1").
- The time and ground speed from the previous checkpoint (for example, "Fly 120 knots for 12 minutes").
- A photograph, which might have been taken from an unusual angle or altitude.
- Descriptions (for example, "Look for the longest bridge").

In addition to finding your way to each checkpoint, you also need to arrive there at a specific time. For example, if the flight time between checkpoint 1 and checkpoint 2 is 7 minutes, or *7:00* in shorthand, the challenge is to arrive at checkpoint 2 exactly 7 minutes after leaving checkpoint 1. You lose 1 point for every 5 seconds early or late that you arrive at the checkpoint.

Air rally organizers generally stagger the starting times of air rally teams by a couple of minutes so that they don't get in each other's way at checkpoints. Still, there isn't enough time to double back or circle over a checkpoint if your team arrives early. Teams need to figure out exactly what their airspeed should be to arrive at the given checkpoint right on time. If there isn't any wind, a team's airspeed is essentially the same as its ground speed. But there's normally a bit of wind, and this can affect a team's actual ground speed as well as its track toward the target.

Airspeed vs. Ground Speed

Ground speed varies with wind conditions. For example, if the airspeed indicator reads 100 knots while you're flying into a 20-knot headwind, your ground speed is only 80 knots. This means that because of the headwind, you will cover only 80 NM in one hour, with all other conditions being equal. A tailwind increases your ground speed. If the airspeed indicator reads 100 knots with a 20-knot tailwind, your aircraft will actually cover 120 NM in one hour. One of the biggest challenges in an air rally is estimating what your ground speed will be given the current wind conditions. You might have to adjust your airspeed to account for the wind.

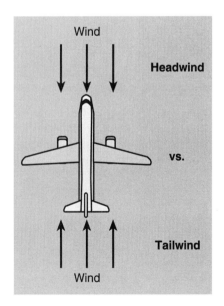

A headwind vs. a tailwind.

Courses

The rally steps express compass headings as magnetic courses. This means that if you were to plot an air rally course on a map, a point that lies 90 degrees from checkpoint 1 would lie directly east. If there were no wind, the reading on the heading indicator would always indicate the direction of your flight path. However, if you were trying to fly to a point due east of your position and there was a

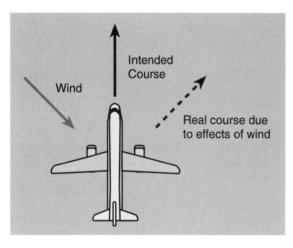

A crosswind can blow you off course even while you're maintaining a consistent heading.

20-knot wind from the south, you would end up north of your desired checkpoint, even though the heading indicator shows 90 degrees. If the winds are strong, you might have to adjust your heading significantly to maintain a course that takes you directly toward the next checkpoint.

Views in Flight Simulator 2000

When I'm flying an air rally in Flight Simulator, I add an extra view or two so that I know exactly where I am in relation to the ground. I use a map view and a cockpit view in addition to the main cockpit view. (See Figure 5-1.) The smaller cockpit view can be switched to a view of what's directly below the aircraft without losing sight of the instrument panel. I also like to open the compass by pointing to Instrument Panel on the Views menu and then clicking Compass. This helps me keep track of my heading. This arrangement of windows is a good way to compensate for the decreased visibility that you have in a simulation cockpit.

Figure 5-1 *Use this window arrangement for flying in air rallies.*

A Day in the Life of a Rally Crew

The following is an account by George Coy, a navigator with the U.S. Air Rally Association. He details his experience in an air rally in the World Air Games in Turkey.

Dateline: 0545 A.M., Tuesday, September 16, 1997—Antalya, Turkey

The phone beside the bed rings. I am half-asleep and roll over to answer it. It is the hotel front desk with my wake-up call. I haven't slept well, as I am both excited and worried about today. We, my pilot and I, will be flying not only our first air rally, but are the first crew of the team to represent the United States in the internationally recognized sport of air rallying.

My pilot, Gail Bevins, joins me for breakfast. Gail is a private pilot with about 350 hours total time. Like the rest of the U.S. team, this is her first air rally. We have made up and flown several practice rallies back home, but we did not know how they would correlate to the real thing. As it turns out, they bore little resemblance to the real thing.

> ## The U.S. Rally Association
>
> *The U.S. Rally Association, Inc., was formed as a non-profit organization to promote air rally flying in the United States. It is now a member of the National Aeronautics Association, which is the U.S. national air club that is recognized under international FAI rules.*

Air rally as conducted under the FAI rules has three components. The first is the ability to quickly plot a course from a printed set of instructions, and then fly it very precisely. The second involves observation of ground targets. The third is a spot landing [described later in this chapter].

Precision and Safety

When they say fly a course precisely, they mean precisely. This means flying the course within ¼ mile left or right of the center line while maintaining your ground speed exactly at the speed that we have told the organizers that we would fly. We need to come over the checkpoints between 500 and 1000 feet AGL [above ground level] at the correct time plus or minus two seconds. Every second beyond the two-second window costs you two penalty points.

Additionally, for safety reasons, if you are observed as flying more than 90 degrees from the course line, circling, or under 500 feet AGL, you may be disqualified from the competition altogether. You can imagine the possible safety problems if you are busy looking for ground targets, with only half an eye out for traffic, and someone who is lost or trying to lose time is circling at the same altitude on your course. This is why you must maintain the ground speed that you have declared to the organizers at the time of registration.

Observation

The second task is ground observation. The organizers have provided two sets of photographs. The first are photos of the checkpoints. They are in order and marked with the checkpoint number. The only hitch here is that the photos may be taken from any direction, not necessarily the direction of flight. Furthermore, the photos may be correct or incorrect [for the intended flight path]. If the photo is of an object that is incorrect, it may be a photo of an object more than 1/2 mile from the real checkpoint. Needless to say, if you are off course by over 1/2 mile, you may mark it as a correct photo when it is incorrect. This error will cost you 100 penalty points.

The second part of the checkpoint observation test is the ground target identification. The organizers provide 18 photographs of objects on the ground that you will only see if you are exactly on course. These photos are all taken from the direction of flight. The catch is that they are not in order. There are nine photos for the first half of the rally and nine for the second half. You need to look at and memorize these photos. They can be of a building, a tree in a field, a road bend, etc. They are carefully chosen by the organizers so that if you are more than 1/2 mile off course, you will probably not see them at all. You have to mark on your score sheet exactly where you saw the object and how many miles it was from the last checkpoint.

There are also large white letters on the ground at all of the timed checkpoints and some of the checkpoints that do not have ground observers recording your times. You have to mark down on the score sheet what letter you saw. Again the penalty for misidentification is 100 points, while the penalty for not observing at all is only 50 points.

Spot Landings

The third and last part of the rally consists of a spot landing. They really get serious about this. The aircraft tires are painted with white stripes, and all landings are videotaped. The white lines aid in determining when the wheel starts to turn, and thus the touchdown point is determined. The zero-penalty touchdown zone is 3 meters (not quite 10 feet) long. After that, you incur penalties for each 10 meters you land beyond the touchdown zone. If you land before the touchdown zone, it is 100, 120, or 200 points, depending on how short you were. The landing zone is only 36 feet wide, and if you are outside that area, it is 200 penalty points. Bounces, not putting the mains on before the nose wheel, and the mains not hitting simultaneously all cost more points.

Preflight

We know our launch time is 08:54, and it is our responsibility to start the engine and taxi onto the departure runway 35 minutes before launch time. The launch time is also known as zero time, as our printed instructions give us only the number of minutes and seconds that we are to cross each checkpoint after our launch time. The only navigation equipment allowed is the wet compass [a compass needle that floats in fluid—that is, an old-fashioned compass] and the gyrocompass [a compass that works by using a gyroscope].

Exactly 15 minutes before zero time, a crew comes around and gives you your packet. This packet has the course instructions, the checkpoint locations, the checkpoint photos, the en route photos, a scoring sheet for you to mark, and special departure instructions.

Now we are really busy. The butterflies in the stomach are unnoticed as Gail starts reading the instructions and I start plotting our course.

"Start point—N36* 55.18', E30* 35.45'. Described as a small sand airport." This is easy, as the airport is clearly marked on the map. "Got it," I say. Gail reads out "Checkpoint 1, magnetic course 94 degrees, 12.3 NM from start point. Looking for a road bend in a red road." I quickly estimate it and find several bends in a red-colored road on our map. I carefully draw N–S and E–W lines on the start point and carefully align my angle plotter. I carefully measure 12.3 NM. On the map, I see a bend similar to the one described and sketched for us in the instructions. I now figure a heading from the last point on our departure procedure to the start point to give Gail a rough course to follow to find the start point. I know that I will still be plotting checkpoints while she does the takeoff, flies the departure route, and hopefully finds the start point.

"Checkpoint 2, magnetic course 038 degrees from N37* 0.00', E30* 0.00' and magnetic course 306 degrees from N37* 0.00', E30* 30.00'. Looking for a village, and the little Moshe (Mosque) on the east side of the village," Gail tells me. I am madly trying to find the printed coordinates on the map for the latitudes and longitudes. I draw the lines and look at where they intersect. And so it goes until we start the plot for checkpoint 8 (there are 14 checkpoints plus the start and final point today).

Taking Flight

While I am plotting, Gail suddenly notices that we are to cross the start line in about one minute, and we have not even started the engine yet! The Cessna T-41 (the military version of a Cessna Hawk XP) that we have rented from the

Turkish military starts quickly, and Gail immediately pours the coals to it, and we cross the start line at almost flying speed. We are chastised later that night at the nightly team manager's meeting for unsafe operations. We were supposed to taxi up to the start line and then cross the start line at zero time (with up to 10 seconds leeway with no penalty points) by beginning our takeoff run at the start line.

We immediately realize we are already behind the eight ball. The next thing Gail notices as she is flying the departure procedure over the city is that we have failed to start our master clock at zero time. This is a big mistake. Now I have to figure an offset to each of the times at each checkpoint. This is a lot of extra work.

I am still trying to plot additional checkpoints when Gail says we are due at the start point and asks for help identifying it. We need to decide if it is the right place, if the photo is correct, and what the ground target letter is. Additionally we have to be here at just the right time. They allow 10 minutes for the departure procedure and allow circling before the start point so that you can cross the start point at the right time. We see the aircraft that is ahead of us as well as the aircraft behind us while waiting for the start time.

Ahead of us is a Greek team in a [Piper] Cherokee Six, while behind us is one of the Slovak teams also flying a rented T-41. Gail figures one more circle and we will cross on time. The circle took longer than she figured and we start 35 seconds late (66 penalty points at the start). We check the start point photo and it looks like the airfield. We mark it correct. This later turns out wrong. The photo was of a similar airport without some of the buildings.

Target Location

I give her the heading for the next checkpoint, and she slows to 80 knots indicated. We fly with 10 degrees of flaps to help lower the nose to better look for those pesky en route ground targets. Now I am trying to plot, look for ground targets, and tell Gail we are ahead or behind time as well as left or right of course. I am trying to do this by observing the terrain, villages, roads, etc., and correlating them with the map. The map is of very poor quality. As we found out the previous week during our three practice rallies, there were many roads, villages, and even entire lakes that did not appear on the map. It was also very difficult to determine elevations from the map. Later we learn that the other really good teams use two maps: one for the pilot and one for the navigator. The navigator plots the first three checkpoints and gives the map to the pilot. The navigator then plots the rest of the checkpoints on the second map while

the pilot is studying and flying from the first map. This makes it easier for both pilot and navigator to do their jobs.

This is the way it went during the whole course. We later found that I had plotted to the wrong village for checkpoint 1. There was an intermediate touch and go landing at a remote airport that had a spot landing point. This was in addition to the spot landing at the final airport. After the final landing, we had 10 minutes to mark and hand over our score sheet without incurring further penalties.

The Wrap-Up

After taxiing to parking, a crew met us and escorted us to the holding area where we were debriefed and our score sheets were reviewed by the judges. We had an opportunity to settle any disputes concerning the marking of our score sheet.

We were fed lunch and then bussed back to our hotel. We were able to see our other team members depart and knew just what they were in for.

I found myself unprepared for the timing accuracy as well as the ground observation. I have over 8000 hours flying around the United States in small aircraft. I have even flown across the United States and back in a 1935 open-cockpit biplane with nothing more than a hand-held radio and a pile of sectional maps, but it was nothing like the intensity that we experienced here in the air rally.

To give an indication as to how unprepared we were, on the previous day, we flew an official practice rally. This was done with timing and spot landings. It was to give the crews a chance to experience the real thing as well as test the judges and timing systems by the organizers. Our score in the official practice was 2350 penalty points. The Polish team had 2 penalty points! We did not come in last, but there was certainly room for improvement. We later found out that the Polish team had been doing rally flying for over 30 years. They used to be government-sponsored and came up through a farm system.

We decided after that day that we would be satisfied if we didn't get lost, didn't wreck an aircraft, and didn't embarrass ourselves by coming in dead last. We did accomplish those goals.

We heard from many teams that they were happy that the United States had finally put up a team for air rally. As the Chilean team said, "The U.S. was conspicuous by its absence in this sport."

Your First Air Rally

Now that you have learned a little bit about real-life air rally techniques, jump into the cockpit for a Flight Simulator 2000 air rally. For your first time out, I'll provide substantial details on each of the checkpoints. This should help you complete the rally fairly successfully and give you an introduction to the skills you'll need to fly the rest of the air rallies in this chapter. For a more realistic air rally, try flying it on your own, with no information other than the compass headings, photos, and flight times.

Note: *Because these are just simulated air rallies, it's only fair to throw in some improbable situations that would never occur in real life. For example, in some cases, you will have to change aircraft during the air rally. (Obviously, this can't be done in real life!) For example, you might need to land somewhere that's accessible only to a helicopter, or you might have an assigned flight time between two checkpoints that will be impossible to make in a Cessna. The best way to do this is to pause the simulation by pressing P, and then on the Aircraft menu, click Select Aircraft. You can also view the performance specifications for different aircraft by reviewing the Aircraft Information section in online Help.*

Note: *I suggest that you use a Cessna 182S to start these flights, but feel free to choose whatever aircraft you want. If you're asked to land on top of a building or some such odd place, you might consider switching to a helicopter!*

New York City: Escape From New York

Here's your chance to take a bite out of the Big Apple. Make sure that the graphic detail is set as high as possible for your computer; you can then see the checkpoints when you fly over them. To set graphic detail to maximum, on the Options menu, point to Settings, and then click Display. In the Display Settings dialog box, click the Image Quality tab. Adjust the Image Quality slider or individual settings that best suit your hardware. For more information on Flight Simulator 2000 image quality and performance, see the section "Making Flight Simulator 2000 Really Fly" in the Microsoft Flight Simulator 2000 *Pilot's Handbook,* or review Settings under the Simulator Help section in online Help.

Here's a copy of the instruction sheet:

1. Start: Brooklyn CGAS. Set your latitude to N40* 34.85', longitude to W73* 53.72', and altitude to +19.
   Flight Time: 00:00. Departure Time: 12:00:00 P.M.

2. Checkpoint 1: Follow a 9 NM magnetic course 327 degrees from Start. Find the landmark shown.
   Flight Time: 5:30. Arrival Time: 12:05:30 P.M.

3. Checkpoint 2: Follow a 2 NM magnetic course 60 degrees from checkpoint 1. Land on the tallest point in New York City.
   Flight Time: 1:30. Arrival Time: 12:07:00 P.M.

4. Checkpoint 3: Follow an 8 NM magnetic course 40 degrees from checkpoint 2. Find the landmark shown.
   Flight Time: 2:30. Arrival Time: 12:09:30 P.M.

5. Checkpoint 4: Fly at 90 knots ground speed 236 degrees from checkpoint 3. Look for the bridge shown.
   Flight Time: 8:00. Arrival Time: 12:17:30 P.M.

6. Checkpoint 5: Follow a 7 NM magnetic course 245 degrees from checkpoint 4. Land at the airfield shown.
   Flight Time: 4:30. Arrival Time: 12:22:00 P.M.

After you get the list, it's a good idea to plot your course on a map before you take to the air. You might recognize some of the landmarks shown in the photos already. If so, you're ahead of the game. Still, you should plan your airspeed, taking the wind into account, so that you don't arrive too early. The first time you try an air rally, configure the weather conditions for no wind to make your calculations a little simpler. In the instructions that follow, it's assumed that there is no wind at all because variable wind conditions require different compass headings and airspeeds.

By reviewing the checkpoint times, you can estimate the speed at which you'll need to travel. Remember that at 60 knots, you'll cover 1 NM in 1 minute.

A more realistic airspeed for the Cessna is 90 to 100 knots. If there is no wind at all, at an airspeed of 90 knots, you will cover 1.5 nautical miles in 1 minute. To travel from checkpoint 4 to checkpoint 5 in 4 minutes and 30 seconds, you would need to travel just a bit faster than 90 knots, because at 90 knots it would take you about 4 minutes and 40 seconds. So plan on passing over checkpoint 4 and heading for checkpoint 5 at just over 90 knots.

There is a simple formula that you can use to figure out what your ground speed needs to be to reach a checkpoint at the appointed time. *Multiply the distance in nautical miles between the checkpoints by 60 minutes, and divide the product by the time in which you must cover that distance.* This will give you your required ground speed in knots.

For example, consider the first checkpoint. You need to cover 9 NM in 5 minutes and 30 seconds.

1. Multiply 9 NM by 60 minutes to get 540.

2. Convert the time from hours and seconds into a decimal number: 5 minutes and 30 seconds is the same as 5.5 minutes.

3. Divide 540 by 5.5 minutes to get a rate of approximately 98 nautical miles per hour, or 98 knots.

It's a good idea to figure out your ground speed for the rest of the checkpoints in the same manner. Remember that if there is any wind, you also need to take the wind speed and direction into account.

After you've gotten a basic idea of your flight plan, it's time to start flying. The list specifies an exact starting location in Brooklyn, so let's begin there. On the World menu, click Map View and then set your latitude to N40* 34.85', longitude to W73* 53.72', and altitude to +19. Then click the checkmark to start.

1. Start: Brooklyn CGAS. (See Figure 5-2.)
   • Flight Time: 00:00. Departure Time: 12:00:00 P.M.

2. Checkpoint 1: Follow a 9 NM magnetic course 327 degrees from Start. Find the landmark shown in Figure 5-3.
   • Flight Time: 5:30. Arrival Time: 12:05:30 P.M.

The Brooklyn Coast Guard Air Station is closed, but don't let that stop you from hopping the fence and starting up the engine in the Cessna 182S. Click the clock in the upper-left section of the instrument panel, and click the digits to change the time to 11:59:40 so that the clock will read 12:00 just as you take

off. To find out how to use the clock, right-click the clock, and then click What's This? on the context menu to access online Help. Starting with your clock at 12:00 is a good way to keep track of your elapsed time. For this first leg, you'll need to average 98 knots as you fly, so go to full throttle in the Cessna for takeoff, and then manage your airspeed by making small adjustments to the throttle and the pitch of the aircraft. Remember that during an air rally, you generally stay below 1000 feet.

As soon as you take off, check the heading on the heading indicator or the magnetic compass, and turn to a heading of 327 degrees. Review Figure 5-3 so that you know what to look for, and keep your eye on the clock and the airspeed. If you maintain the planned airspeed and watch carefully, you

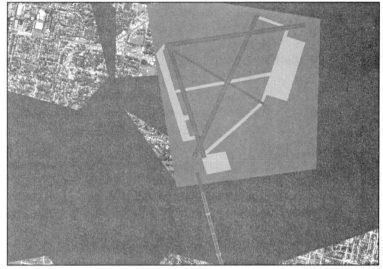

Figure 5-2   *Start this air rally at the Brooklyn Coast Guard Station.*

Figure 5-3   *Find this landmark at checkpoint 1.*

Tip: *Press the P key to pause the simulation so that you can mark the time and read ahead to the next checkpoint.*

should see checkpoint 2 approximately 5 minutes after you take off. Study the photo for clues about where this checkpoint might be located. Watch the time as you approach, and try to estimate exactly when you'll pass over checkpoint.

2. You might have to use the throttle or pitch to manage the airspeed. Press 5 on the numeric keypad to switch to the view below the plane, and note the time as you pass over the checkpoint.

3. Checkpoint 2: Follow a 2 NM magnetic course 60 degrees from checkpoint 1. Land on the tallest point in New York City. (See Figure 5-4.)
   • Flight Time: 1:30. Arrival Time: 12:07:00 P.M.

Figure 5-4   *Land on the tallest point in New York City.*

Can you do it? Reading the instructions for this checkpoint, it's clear that you need to pull off a landing that you would never be able to do in the Cessna. It's time to switch aircraft, this time to the Bell 206B JetRanger helicopter. (Obviously, in a real air rally, you stay in the same plane at all times unless you have a parachute.) You have exactly 90 seconds to make a perfect landing on the top of the tallest building that you can find in New York City, and that's your next checkpoint. See you there.

4. Checkpoint 3: Follow an 8 NM magnetic course 40 degrees from checkpoint 2. Find the landmark shown in Figure 5-5.
   • Flight Time: 2:30. Arrival Time: 12:09:30 P.M.

Check the clock. Are you on time? If you're running behind schedule, you might need to fly a little faster to make the arrival time at checkpoint 3. If you're right on time, from checkpoint 2, you need to average ((8 NM * 60) / 4.5 min.), or approximately 107 knots, which is at the upper range of the JetRanger's operating speed. Depending on your ground speed estimates, you can continue to use the JetRanger or you can switch to a different aircraft, such as the Cessna Skylane 182S. One advantage of the helicopter is that it can slow down or even hover in mid-air if you find that you are a little early. Air rally purists, however, probably wouldn't want to hover at a checkpoint because hovering makes it too easy.

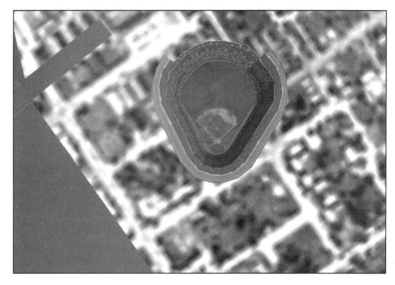

Figure 5-5   *Find this landmark at checkpoint 3.*

Tip: *If you decide to switch to another aircraft, gain some altitude in the helicopter first, because there are railings on the rooftop deck that will destroy your aircraft if you hit them.*

5. Checkpoint 4: Fly at 90 knots ground speed 236 degrees from checkpoint 3. Look for the bridge shown in Figure 5-6.
   • Flight Time: 8:00. Arrival Time: 12:17:30 P.M.

As you pass over checkpoint 3, pause the simulation by pressing the P key. The instructions in step 5 are a little different from the previous ones because they don't tell you how far away the next checkpoint is. If you maintain the given ground speed for the given amount of time, you will be close enough to the landmark that you can spot it from the air. If there is no wind, your airspeed is the same as your ground speed, so all you need to do is

Figure 5-6   *Look for this bridge. (It's blue.)*

watch the airspeed indicator. Otherwise, you'll need to estimate your ground speed with the effects of wind. Depending on how good your estimate is, you might find yourself at the right place at the right time, or you might have to search for the bridge a bit. There are a lot of bridges in this area, so study the picture carefully so that you can find the right one. (It's blue.) Remember that the picture of the bridge might have been taken from any direction, not necessarily from your direction of flight. Stay low (below 1000 feet) so that you can spot the landmark easily.

6. Checkpoint 5: Follow a 7 NM magnetic course 245 degrees from checkpoint 4. Land at the airfield shown in Figure 5-7.
   • Flight Time: 4:30. Arrival Time: 12:22:00 P.M.

Ah, the home stretch! After you pass over the bridge, turn to a heading of 245 degrees, and continue for 7 NM. You will need to come to a stop at precisely the appointed time, which means that you should maintain a ground speed that will bring you to the airfield with enough time left over to land and come to a full stop safely on any runway. Cratering into the runway doesn't count as a full stop in an air rally!

Total your "points." How did you do? An air rally is all about precise timing, good map skills (the ability to convert what's on the map into what you see out the window), and the ability to think under pressure. In real life, there's no Pause button! You can make air rallies in Flight Simulator more challenging by adding different wind effects. Try using Real World Weather, and fly the same course using the current wind conditions. See if you can better your point total now that you recognize the various checkpoints.

Figure 5-7   *Land at this airfield to complete the rally.*

Other Air Rallies

You can use your newfound air rally skills to race the following air rallies. Each rally is based on the world of Flight Simulator 2000 rather than on any real-life rallies, so you won't have to worry about violating any illegal airspace or updating your passport. Good luck!

Boston: Lost in Beantown

This air rally takes place in and around the greater Boston area. Because Boston is a fairly compact city, most of the distances are fairly short. But don't worry—you'll be doing a fair amount of backtracking just to keep things interesting!

1. Start: Beverly Municipal Airport.
   Flight Time: 00:00. Departure Time: 12:00:00 P.M.

2. Checkpoint 1: Follow a 13 NM course 248 degrees from Start.
   Locate the landmark shown.
   Flight Time: 5:00. Arrival Time: 12:05:00 P.M.

3. Checkpoint 2: Follow a 4 NM course 105 degrees from checkpoint 1.
   Circle the landmark shown.
   Flight Time: 3:00. Arrival Time: 12:08:00 P.M.

4. Checkpoint 3: Follow a 4 NM course 275 degrees from checkpoint 2.
   Find the structure shown.
   Flight Time: 3:00. Arrival Time: 12:11:00 P.M.

5. Checkpoint 4: Fly a 110-degree course from checkpoint 3. Look for the
   feauture shown.
   Flight Time: 3:30. Arrival Time: 12:14:30 P.M.

6. Checkpoint 5: Follow an 8 NM course 57 degrees from checkpoint 4.
   Look for the building shown.
   Flight Time: 5:30. Arrival Time: 12:20:00 P.M.

7. Checkpoint 6: Follow a 6 NM course 220 degrees from checkpoint 5.
   Land on the runway at the airport shown.
   Flight Time: 2:30. Arrival Time: 12:22:30 P.M.

For this air rally, try using Real World Weather to download actual weather conditions from the Internet. To enable this feature, click Weather on the World menu, and then click the Real World Weather button. Also set the image quality as high as your computer can manage so that you will see the landmarks when you fly over them (as explained earlier in the chapter).

1. Start: Beverly Municipal Airport. (See Figure 5-8.)
   - Flight Time: 00:00. Departure Time: 12:00:00 P.M.

The first leg of this course is the longest, but you have a very short amount of time in which to complete it. You will probably have to start out in the Extra 300S and maintain at least 160 knots indicated air speed (IAS) to come close to the flight time. After selecting your aircraft, on the World menu, click Go To

Airport. In the dialog box that appears, type **Beverly Mun** as the airport name, and click the green checkmark to place yourself on the runway.

Change the time on the digital clock in the lower-left corner of the instrument panel to 11:59:40, which should give you just enough time to throttle up and take off for checkpoint 1.

Figure 5-8   *The start.*

2. Checkpoint 1: Follow a 13 NM course 248 degrees from Start. Locate the landmark shown in Figure 5-9.
   • Flight Time: 5:00. Arrival Time: 12:05:00 P.M.

As you approach this area, look carefully at the photograph. There are a lot of antenna towers in this area, but there is only one cluster of

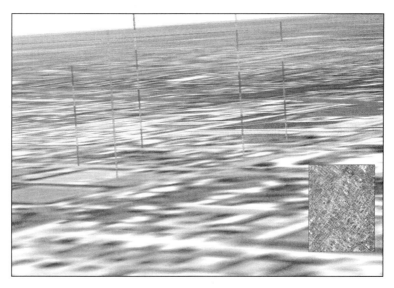

Figure 5-9   *Look for these antennae at checkpoint 1.*

Figure 5-10 *Look for this landmark at checkpoint 2. Find this object on the ground, and then fly in a 360-degree circle around it.*

Figure 5-11 *Look for this structure at checkpoint 3.*

four red-and-white antennae and one white antenna. You'll need to find the correct one to navigate to in order to find the next checkpoint. Because the next few checkpoints are so close to each other, the Extra 300S might be a little too fast. If you find that you're arriving at the checkpoints too early, try switching to the Cessna 182S.

3. Checkpoint 2: Follow a 4 NM course 105 degrees from checkpoint 1. Circle the landmark shown in Figure 5-10.
   - Flight Time: 3:00. Arrival Time: 12:08:00 P.M.

4. Checkpoint 3: Follow a 4 NM course 275 degrees from checkpoint 2. Find the structure shown in Figure 5-11.
   - Flight Time: 3:00. Arrival Time: 12:11:00 P.M.

   This checkpoint is only 4 NM from

the previous one, but you need to look carefully to find it. There is only one structure like this in the immediate area.

5. Checkpoint 4: Fly a 110-degree course from checkpoint 3. Look for the feature shown in Figure 5-12.
   - Flight Time: 3:30. Arrival Time: 12:14:30 P.M.

Figure 5-12   *Look for this feature at checkpoint 4.*

You won't need the exact distance to find this feature. Just fly at the assigned heading and keep your eyes out for it. When you find it, you're at checkpoint 4.

6. Checkpoint 5: Follow an 8 NM course 57 degrees from checkpoint 4. Look for the building shown in Figure 5-13.
   - Flight Time: 5:30. Arrival Time: 12:20:00 P.M.

Figure 5-13   *Look for this building at checkpoint 5.*

Just to the southeast you'll see Logan International Airport, which is the end of this air rally. There is one more detour, however, that will take you north. Study the picture carefully; there are many buildings on Boston's North Shore, but only one building that looks like the one in Figure 5-13.

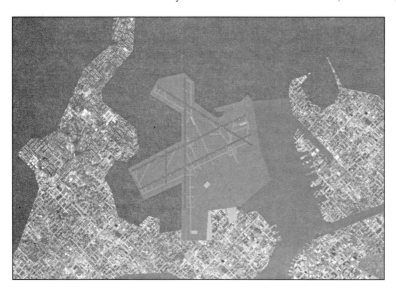

Figure 5-14   *Land on any runway.*

7. Checkpoint 6: Follow a 6 NM course 220 degrees from checkpoint 5. Land on any runway at the airport shown in Figure 5-14.
   • Flight Time: 2:30. Arrival Time: 12:22:30 P.M.

Just after you reach checkpoint 5, turn to a heading of 220 degrees and prepare for a landing at Logan International Airport, which is checkpoint 6. You will have 6 NM to set up an instrument approach. If you are using Microsoft Flight Simulator 2000 Professional Edition, try making an instrument landing in a more powerful plane like the KingAir or the Mooney Bravo for an extra challenge.

Paris: From One Grass Strip to the Next

This air rally takes place in the scenic countryside in and around Paris. You'll take off from one grass strip on the banks of the Seine River, locate five separate checkpoints, and come in for a challenging landing on another tiny grass strip somewhere inland. Grab your compass and map, and let's go!

1. Start: Les Mureaux Army.
    Flight Time: 00:00. Departure Time: 12:00:00 P.M.

2. Checkpoint 1: Fly at 90 knots ground speed 155 degrees from Start.
   Find the landmark shown.
    Flight Time: 8:00. Arrival Time: 12:08:00 P.M.

3. Checkpoint 2: Follow a 7 NM course 70 degrees from checkpoint 1.
   Land inside the landmark shown.
    Flight Time: 5:00. Arrival Time: 12:13:00 P.M.

4. Checkpoint 3: Follow a 7 NM course 83 degrees from checkpoint 2.
   Find the landmark shown.
    Flight Time: 4:00. Arrival Time: 12:17:00 P.M.

5. Checkpoint 4: Follow a 15 NM course 236 degrees from checkpoint 3
   Look for the landmark shown.
    Flight Time: 8:30. Arrival Time: 12:25:30 P.M.

6. Checkpoint 5: Follow a 9 NM course 90 degrees from checkpoint 4.
   Land on the grass strip at the airfield shown.
    Flight Time: 7:30. Arrival Time: 12:33:00 P.M.

For this air rally, you again set the weather to be wind-free. Check the wind direction and speed by clicking Weather on the World menu, and then slide the Wind Strength slider to the far left (no wind).

1. Start: Les Mureaux Army. (See Figure 5-15.)
   - Flight Time: 00:00. Departure Time: 12:00:00 P.M.

Figure 5-15   *This grass strip at Les Mureaux is small, so set flaps to 20 degrees during takeoff.*

Use the Cessna 182S for this air rally, with the exception of checkpoint 2, for which you'll need to use the Bell JetRanger helicopter to land. The Cessna 182S is the best choice to start with, although if you start falling behind, you can always switch to a faster plane to catch up. After you select the aircraft, on the World menu, click Go To Airport. In the dialog box that appears, type **Les Mureaux Army** as the airport name, and make sure 10 is selected in the Runway list. Click the green checkmark to place yourself on the grass strip at Les Mureaux.

Tip: *Set the time on the digital clock to 11:59:40.*

Figure 5-16   *Look for this landmark at checkpoint 1.*

2. Checkpoint 1: Fly at 90 knots ground speed 155 degrees from Start. Find the landmark shown in Figure 5-16.
   • Flight Time: 8:00. Arrival Time: 12:08:00 P.M.

   The checkpoint is directly in the middle of the area shown in the photograph. Press the P key to pause the simulation just as you pass overhead so that you can record your time and switch to the Bell JetRanger helicopter for the next segment.

3. Checkpoint 2: Follow a 7 NM course 70 degrees from checkpoint 1. Land inside the landmark shown in Figure 5-17.
   • Flight Time: 5:00. Arrival Time: 12:13:00 P.M.

Stay focused as you approach this famous landmark, the home of the French Open tennis tournament. You will need to make a perfect landing in-

side the walls. To see what's directly beneath your helicopter as you land, on the Views menu, point to New View, and click Cockpit. Then press 5 on the numeric keypad to switch to the view from the bottom of the helicopter. Give yourself a pat on the back if you can land the helicopter in the smaller tennis court next to the stadium! If you don't want to chance losing all your points by crashing and burning, skip the landing and just fly over checkpoint 2.

Figure 5-17   *Land inside this landmark.*

4. Checkpoint 3: Follow a 7 NM course 83 degrees from checkpoint 2. Find the landmark in Figure 5-18.
   • Flight Time: 4:00. Arrival Time: 12:17:00 P.M.

Take off from checkpoint 2, and follow this course exactly. You'll be heading

Figure 5-18   *Find this landmark at checkpoint 3.*

to a densely populated area of Paris, so stay low and look sharp. You don't have to worry about running into any skyscrapers in Paris. With very few exceptions, architects are forbidden to build any buildings more than three stories tall in downtown Paris. There are a couple of clusters of office buildings to the west, and the Montparnasse Tower in the center of Paris, but for the most part Paris has remained relatively skyscraper-free.

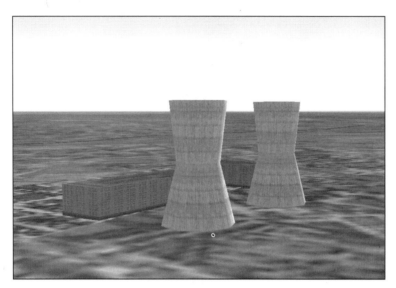

Figure 5-19   *Look for this landmark at checkpoint 4.*

5. Checkpoint 4: Follow a 15 NM course 236 degrees from checkpoint 3. Look for the landmark shown in Figure 5-19.
   • Flight Time: 8:30.
   Arrival Time: 12:25:30 P.M.

Look carefully for this nuclear reactor. For an extra challenge, try flying between the two towers. There is some risk involved, though. Even after completing 4 out of 5 checkpoints, if you crash into the reactor and cause a nuclear meltdown, you'll have to give yourself a zero for this air rally, and you'll probably be deported.

6. Checkpoint 5: Follow a 9 NM course 90 degrees from checkpoint 4. Land on the grass strip at the airfield shown in Figure 5-20.
   • Flight Time: 7:30. Arrival Time: 12:33:00 P.M.

Directly to the east of the reactor is an airport with a small grass landing strip. Make sure to watch the compass heading because there are a number of airports in the Paris area. Press Shift+left bracket ([) to display the map view, and use the plus sign (+) and minus sign (–) keys to zoom in and out until you can find the right airport. This airport has several concrete runways, but to finish the air rally you need to make a landing on the

Figure 5-20   *Land on the grass strip here.*

grass strip at the southern end of the airport. You must come to a full stop with all wheels still on the grass part of the runway. The trick is to come in at a very low approach speed; use full flaps, and start lining the plane up with the runway early. You have a little bit of extra time to make a good approach.

Bonne chance!

Tokyo: *Lost in the Rising Sun*

There are many beautiful landmarks in the Tokyo metropolitan area. This air rally takes you past picturesque monuments and sights as you work your way from checkpoint to checkpoint. Don't forget to

> **Tip:** *If you are using Microsoft Flight Simulator 2000 Professional Edition, you will see even more detailed scenery in Tokyo.*

look carefully for the specific checkpoints; some of them are small and are easy to miss.

1. Start: Yokota AB.
    Flight Time: 00:00. Departure Time: 12:00:00 P.M.

2. Checkpoint 1: Follow a 15 NM course 130 degrees from Start. Locate the vehicle shown.
    Flight Time: 9:00. Arrival Time: 12:09:00 P.M.

3. Checkpoint 2: Follow a 7 NM course 25 degrees from checkpoint 1. Find the landmark shown.
    Flight Time: 4:00. Arrival Time: 12:13:00 P.M.

4. Checkpoint 3: Follow a 115-degree heading from checkpoint 2. Find the symbol shown.
    Flight Time: 1:00. Arrival Time: 12:14:00 P.M.

5. Checkpoint 4: Fly a 105-degree course 11 NM from checkpoint 3. Locate the building shown.
    Flight Time: 5:30. Arrival Time: 12:19:30 P.M.

6. Checkpoint 5: Follow a 8 NM course 25 degrees from checkpoint 4. Land on any runway at the airport shown.
    Flight Time: 4:00. Arrival Time: 12:23:30 P.M.

You can make this air rally more difficult by using Real World Weather as described in the other air rallies. Also ensure that the image quality is set as high as suitable for your hardware, as described earlier, so that you will see the landmarks when you fly over them.

1. Start: Yokota AB. (See Figure 5-21.)
    • Flight Time: 00:00. Departure Time: 12:00:00 P.M.

This course is best flown in the Cessna 182S if you are keeping track of your time, but you are always free to choose whichever aircraft you like. After selecting the aircraft, on the World menu, click Go To Airport. In the Go To Airport dialog box, type **Yokota AB**, and click the green checkmark to place yourself on the runway.

The digital clock is in the lower-left section of the instrument panel. Click the hours and minutes to change them to 11:59:40, which should give you just enough time to throttle up and take off for checkpoint 1.

2. Checkpoint 1: Follow a 15 NM course 130 degrees from Start. Locate the vehicle shown in Figure 5-22.
   - Flight Time: 9:00. Arrival Time: 12:09:00 P.M.

This checkpoint is actually a small red truck parked outside a cluster of buildings. You won't see this truck unless you're flying below 800 feet mean sea level (MSL), so stay low and decrease the airspeed as you approach. It also helps to maximize the cockpit view by pressing W. You might also want to add another window by pointing to New View on the Views menu and then clicking Cockpit. Then press 5 on the numeric keypad to give you a view of the terrain directly beneath the aircraft.

Figure 5-21   *The starting point at Yokota AB.*

Figure 5-22   *Locate the vehicle seen here at checkpoint 1.*

Figure 5-23   *Find this landmark at checkpoint 2.*

Figure 5-24   *Find this symbol at checkpoint 3.*

3. Checkpoint 2: Follow a 7 NM course 25 degrees from checkpoint 1. Find the landmark shown in Figure 5-23.
   - Flight Time: 4:00.
   Arrival Time: 12:13:00 P.M.

   You shouldn't need the exact distance to find this feature. If you follow a 25-degree course for 4 minutes at 100 knots indicated airspeed (IAS), you should find the National Stadium. Built for the 1964 Olympic Games in Tokyo, the National Stadium seats 60,000 and is a distinctive landmark from the air.

4. Checkpoint 3: Follow a 115-degree heading from checkpoint 2. Find the symbol shown in Figure 5-24.
   - Flight Time: 1:00.
   Arrival Time: 12:14:00 P.M.

This checkpoint is very close to checkpoint 2. Nearby is the Imperial Palace, which has housed members of Japan's royal family for generations and is open to the public on only two days each year. Look for this mysterious red and white symbol, which could be anywhere in the immediate area. When you locate it, fly directly above it and note your time.

Figure 5-25   *Locate this building at checkpoint 4.*

5. Checkpoint 4: Fly a 105-degree course 11 NM from checkpoint 3. Locate the building shown in Figure 5-25.
   • Flight Time: 5:30. Arrival Time: 12:19:30 P.M.

This low building has a distinctive shape that can be spotted from the air fairly easily. It might be hidden by other structures, however. Just to the west of this building is the beautiful Shinagawa-Tatsumi bridge.

6. Checkpoint 5: Follow an 8 NM course 25 degrees from checkpoint 4. Land on any runway at the airport shown in Figure 5-26.
   • Flight Time: 4:00. Arrival Time: 12:23:30 P.M.

Checkpoint 5 is a small airfield with a single runway. If you maintain a 25-degree course heading as you approach, you will need to make only a small adjustment to line up for a landing on runway 36.

There is a lot of other scenery to admire in the Tokyo area, such as the Tokyo Tower and the Meiji Shrine. After you complete the air rally, take a flight on your own through the area, and see what you can discover!

Figure 5-26 *Land on any runway at this airport at checkpoint 5.*

Chapter Six

EMERGENCIES

Whether you're a commercial airline pilot or a private pilot flying a Cessna Skylane 182S, a large portion of your pilot training is focused on dealing with emergencies. This emphasis is not surprising considering the direct consequences of mid-air mishaps.

Emergencies, from ominous engine or hydraulic failures to seemingly minor failures of radios and instruments, test a pilot's mettle. This chapter re-creates emergencies for Microsoft Flight Simulator 2000, complete with background information and setup instructions. It also gives limited flight tips, but the onus is on you and your piloting skills to extricate yourself and your aircraft from these emergencies. I'm not going to tell you how to do it; instead you must use whatever skills you have and references such as the Microsoft Flight Simulator 2000 *Pilot's Handbook,* online Help, and most important, the Kneeboard's checklists to help you find your way to safety.

Terror in the Andes

On Friday, October 13, 1972, a Fairchild F-227 (a twin-engine turboprop aircraft) carrying 40 passengers as well as a crew of two pilots, a navigator, a steward, and a mechanic left Mendoza, Argentina, for Santiago, Chile. The plane had been chartered to transport an Uruguayan rugby team from Montevideo, Uruguay, to Santiago, but bad weather held up the plane in Mendoza, on the east side of the Andes. After a one-day delay, the Fairchild F-227 took off from Mendoza on a flight plan that would take it across a corridor in the Andes to Curicó, Chile, and then north to Santiago.

During the flight over the Andes, a tailwind turned into a headwind and slowed the Fairchild by as much as 30 knots. For some reason—unexplained to this day—the pilot turned north, deeper into the Andes, instead of heading west toward Curicó. The pilot could not confirm his position, probably because thick cloud cover obscured the mountains and ATC could not observe him on radar, and he started his descent near the Tinguirica volcano instead of in the safety of the valley.

As the pilot took the Fairchild down from 18,000 feet mean sea level (MSL) to 15,000 feet, there was no reason for him to be concerned; air traffic control had agreed with his decision to descend, although controllers were taking his word for the Fairchild's location. He continued the descent, and the aircraft entered the clouds and began to experience turbulence, which is typical in clouds. Sadly, as the aircraft came under 11,000 feet, it cleared a cloudbank and the pilot found himself flying straight for a mountain. Despite the pilot's best efforts, the Fairchild hit an outcrop with the right wing, causing the wing to rip off and flip over the top of the aircraft, ripping off the tail section of the Fairchild. Amazingly, the fuselage (the main body) of the aircraft didn't impact the rock face but instead slid like a giant toboggan down the side of the mountain, finally coming to rest some 11,500 feet MSL in deep snow. Incredibly, 16 of the passengers managed to survive in the incredibly harsh environment of the Andes for nearly ten weeks. They were finally rescued after two of the rugby players managed to climb out of the Andes on their own and got help.

This emergency puts you at an altitude and location similar to that of the Fairchild. Your job is to extricate yourself from the situation and safely land at any of the nearest airports: Mendoza, Argentina; or Curicó, Chile.

Setup

1. Select as the aircraft the Cessna Skylane 182 RG or, if you're using Flight Simulator Professional Edition, the Beech King Air 350, which more closely approximates the Fairchild's performance.

2. Set up the weather. On the World menu, click Weather to open the Weather dialog box. Click Global and adjust the Clouds slider to Overcast.

3. Click the Advanced Weather button and set a cloud layer between 17,500 and 15,000 feet MSL. Specify the Cloud Type as Cumulus and Cloud Coverage as Overcast (8/8). Set Turbulence to Moderate and Icing to None.

4. Click the Add Cloud Layer button and set a second cloud layer between 15,000 and 7500 feet MSL. Specify the Cloud Type as Cumulus and Cloud Coverage as Scattered (4/8). Set Turbulence to Moderate and Icing to None (see Figure 6-1). Click the green checkmark in both the Advanced Weather dialog box and the Weather dialog box to apply the changes.

5. On the World menu, click Map View.

6. Enter **S35* 18.22'** in the Latitude edit box and **W70* 4.86'** in the Longitude edit box. Enter +11,600 in the Altitude edit box, **140** in the Heading edit box, and **90** in the Airspeed text box (for the Cessna) or **120** (for the King Air).

7. Unpause the simulator and go to it.

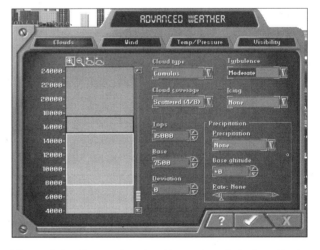

Figure 6-1   *Set up the cloud layers to mimic the actual conditions on October 13, 1972.*

Flight Tips

- There are several large mountains all around you (see Figure 6-2). If you start out in a cloud (and you likely will), prepare for the unexpected.
- If there's a mountain in your path and you can't get out of the way, try a tight turn to fly along a valley.
- Don't let the turbulence throw you off; just "ride the wave."

Figure 6-2   *The first thing you need to do is get back some of the lost altitude before you end up decorating the side of a mountain with your aircraft.*

- Fly due east or west to weave your way out of the mountains. To the east lies Argentina, and to the west, the green valleys of Chile. Flying east or west means you'll have to dodge mountains to get out, but flying north or south leads you deeper into the mountains.

Engine Out in San Fran

One of the scariest emergencies is an engine failure in a twin-engine jet (like the 777-300) just after takeoff. This is actually one of the times when an engine failure is most likely to occur because during takeoff, the engines operate at full power and experience the most stress.

The Bay Area is famous for fog, so SFO (see Figure 6-3) is the best place to practice an engine failure in low visibility. This emergency starts soon after takeoff in the Boeing 777-300. You're already in the air, so you can't just plop back onto the runway.

Figure 6-3   *San Francisco in fog is a challenge to any pilot.*

Potential Problems

Many emergencies can occur when an engine has problems on takeoff, as Ron Hunt, a captain for a commercial airline, points out:

> *Having an engine failure at V_1 (decision speed for takeoff) is very realistic and something I dread more than a single-engine landing! V_1 puts you at a very critical stage; you are at a high speed on the ground with limited directional control and on the edge of flying speed. There are several ways that a pilot trains for this. First would be to have a catastrophic failure (the engine explodes); the sudden failure at high engine speeds creates an immediate yaw factor (a tendency to turn either right or left), making directional control very hard, not to mention an almost instantaneous loss of half of your power.*

> *Then there's the possibility of having an engine fire warning on takeoff while the engine is still producing power; they don't always just quit! Now the pilot must decide how long to let the fire burn before shutting down the engine and dealing with the resulting control problems. Many pilots with low experience have actually created a much bigger problem for themselves by rushing into a shutdown checklist before they were really ready or safe to do so. There are few if any emergencies that need immediate action without consideration of what your actions will do to the performance of the aircraft at that moment. Always fly the aircraft, and then deal with your problems!*

Setup

1. Select the Boeing 777-300 as the aircraft for this emergency.

2. On the Aircraft menu, click Realism Settings, and make sure that the Auto-rudder check box is clear. (Dealing with engine-failure-induced yaw is part of the drill.)

3. Select San Francisco International as the airport. The default runway, runway 10L, is fine.

4. Set up the weather. On the World menu, click Weather, and in the dialog box that appears adjust the Clouds slider to Overcast.

Figure 6-4 *Using a black fuel control switch in the Boeing 777-300 is an excellent way to stop one of the engines, even though it isn't exactly something that any pilot would do under normal circumstances.*

5. Click the Advanced Weather button and set a cloud layer between 300 and 7500 feet MSL. Specify the Cloud Type as Cumulus and the Cloud Coverage as Overcast (8/8). Set the Turbulence to Light and Icing to None.

6. On the Aircraft menu, point to Kneeboard and then click Checklists, or simply press F10. Then complete the takeoff checklist to take off from San Francisco International airport.

7. After the plane is 500 feet off the ground (give or take a hundred feet), press the P key to pause the simulator. Then on the Views menu, point to Instrument Panel, and click Throttle Quadrant.

8. After the throttle quadrant appears, click one of the two black fuel control switches below the throttle to the cutoff position (see Figure 6-4). This will stop one of the two engines by starving it of fuel. The engine will stop almost immediately.

9. Press the P key to restart the simulator, and find a way to solve your new one-engine problem.

Flight Tips

- The 777-300 is a massive aircraft, and you won't have a heck of a lot of speed after the engine fails. You'll be surprised at just how slowly the 777 will climb when it has no power. Don't pull back too aggressively on the control stick or else you'll stall it for sure.
- As foolish as this might seem, it's best to turn left out toward the water (across the bay), which is anywhere between compass headings 330 and 060. This move will give you a nice flat area underneath to allow you time to gain altitude (and avoid crashing into a building or hill.)

Caught Speeding

One of the primary controls in a sailplane is the spoilers, which help the aircraft lose altitude quickly without flying apart from being overstressed by high speeds. Spoilers or speed brakes reduce the wing's efficiency, making it impossible to continue soaring. If they jam open, you have to find a place to land—quickly.

This scenario puts you over Seattle (a detailed city in the Professional Edition) at 9000 feet, with the speed brakes jammed open. You must find a way to land safely at one of the many airports in the Seattle-Tacoma area, even though the speed brakes are open the entire time. Fortunately, you've already been soaring for over an hour and have managed to get your altitude up to 9000 feet, so you've got some room to maneuver. Good luck!

Setup

1. Select the Schweizer 2-32 Sailplane for this emergency.

2. On the World menu, click Weather. Set the Wind Strength slider to Moderate. Set the Wind Direction to 70 degrees and click the green checkmark to save your changes.

3. On the World menu, click Map View.

Figure 6-5 *Open the speed brakes to simulate this emergency.*

4. Set the latitude to N47* 20.89', the longitude to W122* 26.45', the altitude to +9000, the heading to 120 degrees, and the airspeed to 60 knots. Click the green checkmark to start. You'll begin facing Mount Rainier with the Seattle area beneath you.

5. Open the speed brakes (on the left side of the instrument panel). (See Figure 6-5.)

Flight Tips

- First, take a second or two to enjoy the view of Mount Rainier before you start looking for places to land.
- As soon as you have had your fill of the scenery, pick out a place to land. There are several airports in the area, and one of these should be your goal (rather than an off-field landing).
- Fly directly to the field of your choice to make sure that you have enough altitude to maneuver into position once you are overhead. Use the en route time to get a feel for the winds.

- The speed brakes make it easy to lose altitude (as shown in Figure 6-6), but it's very difficult to get the altitude back once it's gone, so don't dive for the runway until you're sure you can make it.

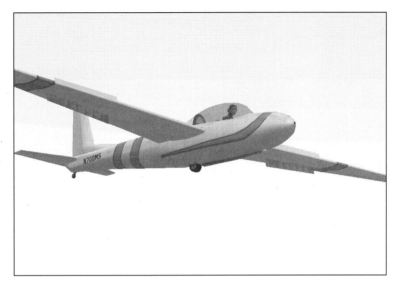

Figure 6-6   *Here is a Sailplane with its speed brakes jammed open.*

Engines Only

Flight Simulator pilots have an advantage over real-life pilots; they can "safely" practice responding to even the rarest of emergencies. The odds of the following emergency happening are next to zilch, but in 1989, it did. You might find it impossible to resolve this emergency even after several tries, yet a real pilot did crash-land a jet liner in just this situation, saving 185 lives, which makes the simulation even more compelling.

On July 19, 1989, a large passenger jet was flying over Iowa en route from Denver to Chicago at an altitude of 37,000 feet MSL when parts of the tail engine disintegrated, causing all three of the hydraulic systems in the aircraft to lose fluid and fail. (This was a large jet with three engines, one on each wing and a third mounted in the tail section.) Commercial airliners are technical wonders, with multiple redundancies built in for every possible emergency, so the likelihood of having a total hydraulic failure on an aircraft with three hydraulic systems seemed impossible. Still, it happened, leaving the passengers and crew in serious trouble.

The engine disintegration and subsequent hydraulic failure left the large jet with almost no control of the ailerons, rudder, elevator, or even flaps! The pilots found that they could set the aircraft into large sweeping right turns (and only right turns) by varying the power of the two remaining engines (one on each wing). After a lengthy descent and the luck of being able to line up with a small airport near Sioux City, Iowa, the aircraft crash-landed on the runway. Just getting the aircraft anywhere near a runway, let alone lining it up for a landing, was an incredible feat.

This emergency puts you in command of a 737 near Sioux City, Iowa. To simulate the hydraulics failure, you'll adjust the sensitivity settings of the controls and avoid using the ailerons. You'll use the Throttle Quadrant window to manage the power between the two engines, and you can use elevator control, but no rudder. This is an extremely difficult task to complete, but it makes you marvel at the pilot's skill in landing a large jet with only the use of varying engine power. This will be a true test of your piloting skills.

Setup

1. Select the Boeing 737-400 as the aircraft for this emergency.

2. On the World menu, click Weather. Set the Clouds slider to Clear, and the Visibility slider to at least 30 miles. Leave the Wind Strength slider at None and click the green checkmark.

3. On the World menu, click Map View.

4. Set the latitude to N42* 55.32', the longitude to W96* 4.20', the altitude to +37,000, the heading to 90 degrees, and the airspeed to 225 knots. This will put you near Sioux City, Iowa, with altitude and weather conditions similar to those that the plane encountered on July 19, 1989. Click the green checkmark to start.

5. On the Options menu, point to Controls, and then click Sensitivities. On the Joystick tab of the Controls Sensitivities dialog box, set the All Axes slider to the left and set the All Null Zones slider to the right (see Figure 6-7). If you use the keyboard-mouse combination to fly, click the Keyboard/Mouse tab and drag all of the sliders to the left. This will make your controls very sluggish. Click the green checkmark to accept the settings.

Figure 6-7   *Set the control sensitivity to the lowest setting for this emergency.*

6. On the Views menu, point to Instrument Panel, and then click Throttle Quadrant. The throttle controls appear, which you'll use to alter the thrust between the two engines.

7. Use a small amount of elevator to control the aircraft, but don't use rudder or ailerons—these controls will work even though their sensitivities are reduced. A great way to avoid using the ailerons is to use the keyboard for control. Because you simply have to avoid touching the aileron keys, the joystick is a different matter.

8. Maneuver the aircraft only by adjusting the engine thrusts (along with using a little elevator to keep your pitch right), and get it safely landed at an airport. Good luck.

Flight Tips

Figure 6-8 *Use the throttle controls to manage your turns in this emergency.*

- Take your time—you have lots of altitude in which to manage the situation. You also have lots of fuel and full power of the two engines, so get a feel for flying with just the engines.
- To turn with just the engines, increase the thrust of one engine while dropping the thrust of the other. (See Figure 6-8.) For example, if the left engine is at full thrust, and the right engine is at idle, the aircraft turns right, toward the idling engine. Be aware that turns made using only differential power are very gradual.
- In the actual emergency, all hydraulic power was lost, so the pilot had to manually lower the landing gear. In this simulated emergency, go ahead and lower the landing gear normally because you can't lower it manually.

Icing in a Cessna

Icing is a major concern in small aircraft that don't have built-in anti-icing equipment on their wings and control surfaces. When ice builds up on a wing, it changes the wing's ability to create lift, thereby reducing the ability of the aircraft to fly. The following emergency has been played out hundreds of times before in a multitude of aircraft, often with disastrous results.

This emergency uses a Cessna Skylane 182 RG, not only because this aircraft lacks anti-icing equipment on its wings but also because its fuel flow is regulated by a carburetor rather than by fuel injection (as in the Cessna Skylane 182S). The downside of carburetors is that they are susceptible to icing not only in standard icing conditions but much of the time.

Carburetor Icing

Under moist atmospheric conditions, and within a temperature range between –5 degrees Celsius and 30 degrees Celsius, ice can form in the intake of the carburetor, blocking the flow of fuel and air into the engine. Carburetor icing usually manifests itself as a gradual loss of power. It's insidious and can creep up on you; as ice builds up in the throat of the carburetor, the fuel flow is slowly cut off. To prevent this from happening, you can turn on the carburetor heat, which recirculates hot air into the carburetor, melts any built-up ice, and prevents ice from forming in the first place. My flight instructor taught me to put the carb heat on every 15 to 20 minutes for about 10 seconds at a time while in cruise flight to prevent any carburetor icing. It might seem like overkill, but I've never had a carburetor ice up on me.

The first indication of carburetor ice is a drop in manifold pressure (in an airplane equipped with a constant speed prop) or a drop in RPM if the airplane has a fixed-pitch propeller. Pull out the carburetor heat knob right away. It might make the difference between watching the engine sputtering and dying for good and getting it back up to full power. If there was carburetor ice present, thawing the ice out with carb heat will often cause the engine to run rough temporarily for a few seconds as the melted ice passes through the engine.

Setup

1. Select the Cessna Skylane 182 RG as the aircraft for this emergency, and place it at any airport.

2. On the World menu, click Weather, and then click the Advanced Weather button in the dialog that appears. Set a cloud layer between 500 and 7500 feet MSL. Specify the Cloud Type as Cumulus and the Cloud Coverage as Broken (7/8). Set Occasional Turbulence and Severe Icing. (See Figure 6-9.)

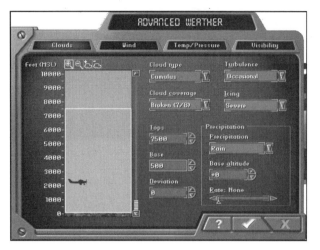

Figure 6-9 *Set up the weather so that your aircraft will be in a severe icing situation.*

3. On the Aircraft menu, point to Kneeboard and then click Checklists, or simply press F10. Then complete the takeoff checklist, and take off.

4. As you fly through the icing conditions, you will start to experience problems with the lift capabilities of the aircraft and possibly some instrument problems. After you experience problems, try to get back to an airport and safely land the aircraft.

Pitot Heat

The Cessna Skylane 182 RG has several important instruments that are attached to the pitot-static pressure system: the altimeter, the airspeed indicator, and the vertical speed indicator. The pitot tube is the air intake part of this system, and it sits underneath one of the wings on most small aircraft. The intake portion of this system can get clogged with ice. If this happens, the airspeed indicator will fail or give erratic readings. To avoid such problems, use the pitot heat switch on the main control panel. This switch simply turns on a heating system that keeps the pitot intake warm enough to avoid collecting ice, thus preventing instrument failures due to icing.

Flight Tips

- After takeoff, turn on the carburetor heat switch to prevent carburetor icing by pulling the Carburetor Heat knob on the instrument panel. For an extra challenge, leave the carburetor heat off until you start to experience some problems with the engine.

- Icing can raise the stall speed of an aircraft. For example, if the aircraft normally stalls at 50 knots (with flaps up), icing could raise that stall speed to 65 knots or more. This can mean that the aircraft can stall while

executing a tight turn that would normally be acceptable at 65 knots. If the airplane stalls, it can be hard to recover, because every time you pull the aircraft out of the stall, it'll restall and dive again. Eventually, you'll run out of altitude in which to manage multiple stalls.

Attitude Problems

The attitude indicator is a critical instrument, an instrument that some pilots rely on far too much. A failure of the attitude indicator doesn't necessarily mean the end of the world. As Captain Ron Hunt says, "When the attitude indicator fails, controlling the aircraft becomes more work. It's amazing how many pilots focus most of their instrument flying on the attitude indicator, when there is so much more information available to them. When the attitude indicator fails in instrument flight rules (IFR) conditions, the horizontal situation indicator (HSI) becomes the main wing leveler (the instrument used to help the pilot keep the wings level), power controls the vertical speed, and pitch controls airspeed. When flying IFR with the attitude indicator out, *never* make any big changes to the aircraft attitude; small controlled changes will make controlling the aircraft a snap."

This situation puts you on final approach to the San Francisco International airport in IFR conditions with an attitude indicator failure in a Mooney Bravo (with the IFR instrument panel), as seen in Figure 6-10.

IFR

IFR stands for instrument flight rules, which is a set of rules for flying when the conditions do not meet the criteria for visual flight rules (flying by sight alone). For more information on IFR and a detailed description, check out the Glossary in online Help.

Setup

1. Select the Mooney Bravo IFR as the aircraft for this emergency.

2. On the World menu, click Weather. Set the clouds to overcast and the visibility to no better than ¼ mile. Set the winds to light at 325 degrees.

3. On the World menu, click Map View.

Figure 6-10   *With no attitude indicator, you'll have to rely on other instruments to bring this bird in safely.*

Note: *For more information on IFR flight and the techniques for flying IFR, see "Tutorial 13: Understanding Instrument Approaches" in the Microsoft Flight Simulator 2000* Pilot's Handbook. *Also, Flight Simulator's online Help contains several articles such as On Instruments and IFR Departures that provide more information on IFR flight.*

4. Set the latitude to N37* 32.84', the longitude to W122* 12.24', the altitude to +3200, the heading to 286 degrees, and the airspeed to 125 knots, and then click the green checkmark. This will put you on approach for runway 28L at San Francisco International.

5. On the Aircraft menu, click System Failures. On the Instruments tab, select the Attitude Indicator Failed check box, and then click the green checkmark to start the emergency.

Flight Tip

• This is a similar approach to that of the preset San Francisco 28L ILS Approach flight. If you want to practice this approach visually, click Select Flight on the Flight menu, and then select San Francisco 28L ILS Approach from the Select Flight dialog box. Click the green checkmark, fail your attitude indicator, and you're ready to go.

Concorde Engine Failure

The Concorde is an amazing aircraft. As the world's only supersonic jetliner, it has commanded respect and inspired a sense of awe since it started flying commercially in the mid 1970s. I remember when the Concorde flew into my hometown airport in Calgary in 1977 to commemorate the opening of the new airport. The Concorde floating across the sky was an awesome sight, its delta-wing design and sleek nose cone looking more like an alien spaceship than a commercial jet.

Amazingly, the few Concordes that have continued in service for Air France and British Airways have had an exemplary safety record. For this reason it's impossible to make reference to a real-life Concorde emergency. Having both engines on one wing fail poses a substantial problem (as it would in any aircraft), but on the Concorde the problem is magnified because of its unique design. This emergency will place you high above the ocean near Easter Island (see Figure 6-11) when two engines on one wing fail; you'll have to manage the aircraft carefully to put it down safely on land.

> **Tip:** *For more information on the Concorde, go to the Help menu, click Aircraft Information, and then click Concorde.*

Setup

1. Select the Concorde as the aircraft for this emergency.

2. On the World menu, click Weather. Set the clouds to clear and the visibility to at least 30 miles. Use no wind for this emergency.

3. On the World menu, click Map View.

4. Set the latitude to S27* 20.56', the longitude to W109* 36.94', the altitude to +55,000, the heading to 025 degrees, and the airspeed to 600 knots. Click on the green checkmark to begin.

5. On the Views menu, point to Instrument Panel, and then click Fuel Panel. On the fuel panel, turn off the Engine Ignition switches for engines 3 and 4. This will shut down the two engines on the right wing.

Figure 6-11 *Easter Island looms ahead as your only chance to land on solid ground anytime soon.*

Flight Tips

- A failing engine on one wing in any aircraft causes a yaw toward the side that's not powered. This yaw can make flight difficult, but the difficulty is magnified in the Concorde, which is not a particularly responsive aircraft. So when the engines are turned off (fail), be ready for this effect.
- To avoid the yaw displacement caused by two failed engines (while the other two are at high throttle), drop the power to the remaining engines and instead start a descent to maintain your airspeed. This effectively turns your Concorde into a glider (with a little power coming from the left side).

- If you have trouble visually acquiring the runway on Easter Island (or the island itself), use the GPS. Also, you can tune the NAV 1 radio to 110.30 to tune in the ILS frequency (Figure 6-12).

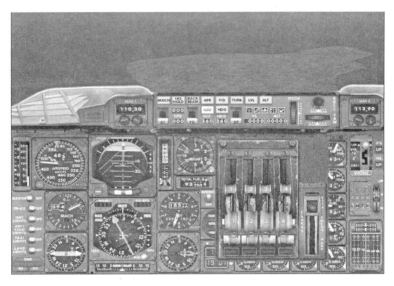

Figure 6-12   *If you want to use the ILS at Easter Island, tune in 110.30 on the Nav 1 radio.*

Bell JetRanger III Autorotation

The Bell JetRanger is the most popular general-purpose, turbine-powered helicopter in the world. It's a powerful, durable workhorse that can be used to ferry equipment and supplies to remote mountain areas in South America, or to carry business executives to a board meeting in the skyscraper jungle of Manhattan's Wall Street.

The JetRanger relies on its main rotor to provide lift and its tail rotor to counteract the torque produced by the rotation of the main rotor. Losing either one of these rotors puts you in a very difficult situation. A main rotor failure is most often caused by engine failure, and it is an emergency that all helicopter

Autorotation

Autorotation uses the helicopter's pitch and descent rate (as well as the unpowered rotation of the main rotor) to keep the main rotor spinning in the wind (created as the helicopter falls). Ideally, this creates just enough lift to slow the helicopter's descent rate. Just before landing, you "flare" the helicopter by pulling the nose up. If your timing is right, you can land the helicopter and walk away in one piece. Autorotations are required maneuvers during training. For more information about autorotation, go to the Help menu, click Aircraft Information, and then click Bell JetRanger III Helicopter. (See Figure 6-13.)

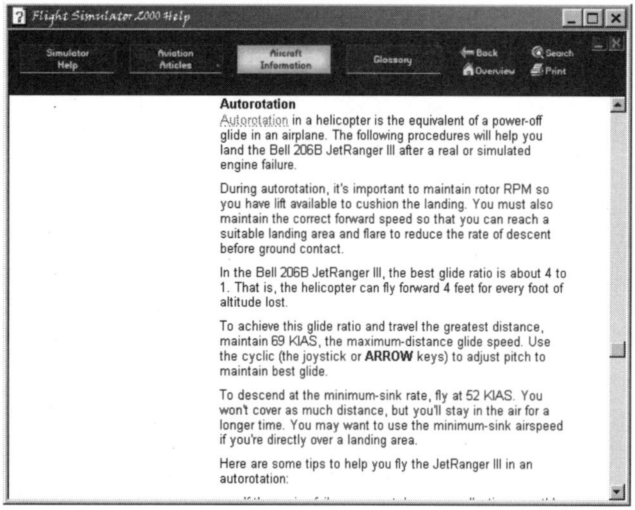

pilots must train for. When the engine fails, autorotation (described at left) is the only way to get on the ground safely.

Luckily, the JetRanger is a tough little aircraft, and your chances of survival are fairly good even if you lose power to the main rotor and are forced to land the helicopter by autorotation. This scenario puts you behind the stick of a Bell JetRanger III when the engine loses power 3000 feet off the ground.

Figure 6-13   *Online Help describes the intricacies of autorotation in a Bell JetRanger III.*

Setup

1. Select the Bell 206B JetRanger III as the aircraft for this emergency.

2. On the World menu, click Weather. Set the clouds to clear and the visibility to at least 30 miles, with the wind set to none.

3. On the World menu, click Map View.

4. Set the latitude to N30* 32.32', the longitude to W91* 9.51', the altitude to +3000, the heading to 180 degrees (although the heading doesn't matter in this emergency), and the airspeed to 70 knots. This will put you directly over the airport in Baton Rouge, Louisiana. Click the green checkmark to begin.

5. Level out the aircraft, and then make the main rotor inoperative by turning off the red fuel valve. This action stops the power to the engine immediately and forces you into autorotation.

Flight Tips

- Main rotor failures are usually preceded by certain clues, such as a change in the engine sound or excess vibration of the airframe. In any case, as soon as you see the engine rpm drop in the tachometer (and you will in this emergency because you turned off the fuel switch), immediately lower the collective by pressing F2. This action changes the angle of attack of the rotor blades and preserves rotor rpm for your descent. If the rotor stops spinning, you'll fall like a rock; game over.

- After you've decreased the collective, pitch the nose of the aircraft down, and maintain some forward airspeed while you look for a good place to land. One good thing about crash-landing the JetRanger is that the descent is much steeper than the descent in a fixed-wing aircraft, so you can land in a much tighter area.

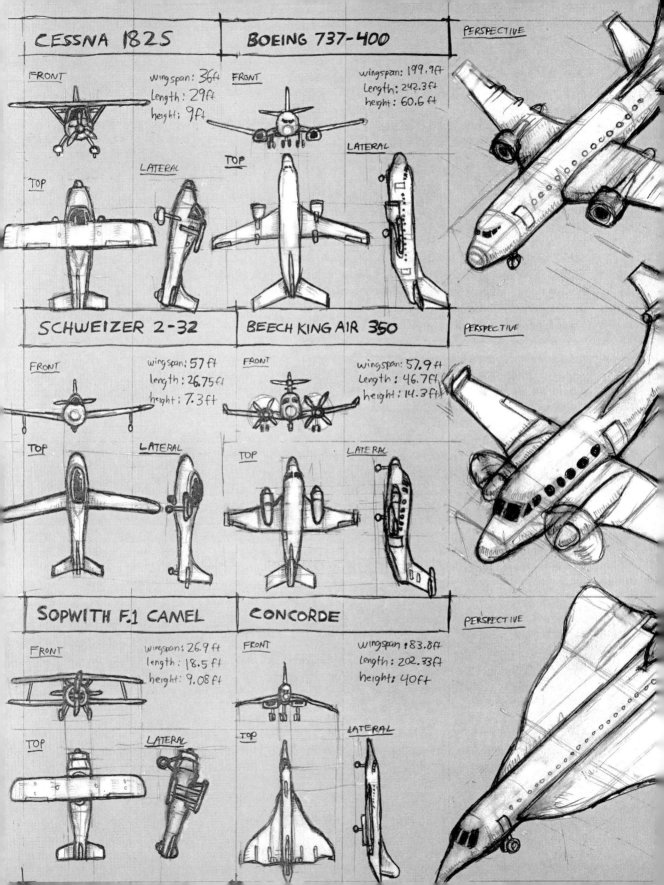

CESSNA 182S

FRONT

wingspan: 36ft
length: 29ft
height: 9ft

TOP

LATERAL

BOEING 737-400

FRONT

wingspan: 199.9ft
length: 242.3ft
height: 60.6ft

TOP

LATERAL

PERSPECTIVE

SCHWEIZER 2-32

FRONT

wingspan: 57ft
length: 26.75ft
height: 7.3ft

TOP

LATERAL

BEECH KING AIR 350

FRONT

wingspan: 57.9ft
length: 46.7ft
height: 14.3ft

TOP

LATERAL

PERSPECTIVE

SOPWITH F.1 CAMEL

FRONT

wingspan: 26.9ft
length: 18.5ft
height: 9.08ft

TOP

LATERAL

CONCORDE

FRONT

wingspan: 83.8ft
length: 202.33ft
height: 40ft

TOP

LATERAL

PERSPECTIVE

Chapter Seven

CHALLENGING FLIGHTS

Microsoft Flight Simulator 2000 provides many ways to challenge your flying skills. By devising your own flights, you can choose just what challenging situations are the most educational and fun. This chapter details eight realistic flights and provides some flight options you can choose to make your flying the most demanding it can be. Many of these challenging flights come straight from the minds of seasoned pilots who have personally experienced them. As you enjoy the following flights, let them push your piloting skills to the limit.

Flight Challenge 1: Nap of the Earth

Nap of the earth flight, or terrain flight, is a technique used by helicopter pilots in combat. It involves skimming over the terrain at altitudes of 100 feet or less to avoid detection and enemy fire. You'll need quick reflexes and excellent flying skills to master this type of flight.

The Bell JetRanger is better suited to this form of flying than any fixed-wing aircraft in Flight Simulator 2000 because its maneuverability and low flight speed capability make it easier to fly low and remain undetected by radar. Fixed-wing aircraft don't often make use of terrain flight, but if you're looking for a real thrill, try skimming over hills and into valleys in an Extra 300S.

In the following flight, you demonstrate terrain flight in simulated combat by flying in hilly terrain outside of Chelan, Washington. Your job is to impress a group of military brass watching on the ground by showing that the Bell JetRanger

Scud Running

One of the few times a civilian pilot might use terrain flight would be during scud running, *running beneath a low layer of clouds, hoping to get to an area of better weather. Unfortunately, the pilot usually ends up squeezed between rising terrain and lowering clouds, and the pilot chooses to go into the clouds. Unintentionally flying into instrument conditions causes some of the deadliest accidents for small aircraft. It's much safer to try scud running in a flight simulator!*

Figure 7-1   *The Bell JetRanger helicopter is one of the best aircraft to use to fly low to the ground.*

can successfully evade conventional radar when it is flown by a skilled pilot. (That's you.) As a rule, you should keep the helicopter below 50 feet AGL and follow the hilly terrain as closely as possible. (See Figure 7-1.) Although you should complete the course as swiftly as possible, accuracy is more important than speed. Avoid crashing to the ground—it tends to upset the spectators.

Note: *Flying a helicopter is very different from flying a fixed-wing aircraft. Consult the Bell JetRanger III Helicopter Flight Notes in the Aircraft Information section of online Help for the specifics of flying a helicopter; you might need to spend some time practicing before you attempt this challenge.*

Note: *To determine when you're less than 50 feet off the ground, check the perspective of the ground after takeoff (when you know the altitude of the airport) and maintain that perspective as you fly.*

Setup

1. Create a new flight using the Bell 206B JetRanger helicopter, and select Chelan Municipal Airport in Washington State as the starting airport.

2. Take off into a hover, and then transition to forward flight. Turn to a heading of 270 degrees to see the rolling hills of Chelan. Fly toward the hills, staying below 50 feet AGL.

3. After you've shown the generals all that the Bell JetRanger can do, return for a landing at the yellow helipad. Fly to impress!

Flight Tips

- Practice smoothly starting and stopping from a hover. You also need to manage the anti-torque pedals and the collective to maintain the heading and altitude. If you feel the aircraft drifting, pitch the nose down to pick up some forward speed, which can help to stabilize the helicopter.

- Pitch the nose down to move forward. Although the helicopter is easier to fly when it has some forward movement, it takes some time to gain altitude. If you find that you are getting too close to a mountain, pitch the nose up to slow down (as shown in Figure 7-2), and add a little collective. You can fly backwards by pitching the nose above the horizon.

Figure 7-2 *Pitch the nose of the helicopter up to slow down if you're heading straight for a hill.*

- To make quick turns, bring the helicopter into a hover, and then use the anti-torque pedals to swing the aircraft around. Try coming to a hover inside a valley, and then add collective to pop up over the next hill.

- When the helicopter hovers a few feet above the ground, it is subject to *ground effect* (the effect of the ground causing the rotor to produce lift more effectively), caused by the backwash of the rotor blades against the ground. Decrease the collective smoothly to settle the plane to the ground.

Tip: *Is this challenge not difficult enough for you? Try setting up a crosswind by clicking Weather on the World menu and then clicking the Advanced Weather button in the Weather dialog box. On the Wind tab, add a surface layer of wind of 15 knots at 210 degrees. You can also try flying the Extra 300S for this challenge. For the ultimate test, try flying it upside down, although you'd never do this in real life!*

Flight Challenge 2: Deadstick from 5000 Feet

Forced landings—spontaneous landings caused by engine failure or weather—are an essential part of a pilot's initial training. The flight instructor decreases the throttle to idle and makes the student go through the steps for an immediate landing. Forced landing drills teach pilots to be aware of available landing locations in the event of engine failure or other emergencies that require immediate landing.

Real-Life Deadstick

A deadstick landing in a large transport aircraft such as a Boeing 737-400 or 777-300 is a pilot's worst nightmare, but it has been done successfully. In 1983, a commercial airliner ran out of fuel over the province of Manitoba, Canada—the ground crew miscalculated the amount of fuel that the airliner was carrying, so the crew didn't add enough fuel for the trip. The pilot had to glide the jet onto a remote abandoned airstrip in Gimli, Manitoba. Remarkably, the jet landed safely without any power from the engines, leading the flight community to call this jet the Gimli Glider.

Perhaps the most difficult part of a forced landing is judging the altitude and the distance to the prospective landing site. Whether you can reach a prospective landing site is determined by the best glide ratio for the aircraft you're in. For example, if your aircraft can go 2 NM for every 1000 feet of altitude at a glide of 70 knots, you know that at 70 knots at 2500 feet AGL, you can glide for 5 NM. But judging altitude and distance when looking at the closest farmer's field, not a runway, can be tough. It's surprisingly difficult to "make" the field when you don't have power. Forced landings are nothing new in the world of flight simulator programs, but a *deadstick landing* (landing without engine power) from above an airport presents an interesting challenge.

Setup

You can perform this maneuver with any jet-powered aircraft over any airport, although there's certainly more challenge to making it work with a larger jet. Remember that you have only one chance to make the field, and most people lose it by turning to the final approach too high or flying too fast.

1. Select a jet aircraft such as the Learjet 45.

2. Choose an airport. Any airport will do for this challenge, but an airport with just one runway is the best choice because it limits your landing options. I suggest Mataveri International (Easter Island).

3. On the Aircraft menu, click Fuel to open the Fuel dialog box. Click Off in the Fuel Selector list (as shown in Figure 7-3); this causes the engines to be starved for fuel and shut down.

Figure 7-3   *Set the Fuel Selector to Off to starve the engines of fuel and shut them down.*

4. Enter slew mode by pressing the Y key, and then press F4 to gain altitude to about 7000 feet AGL. This flight challenge requires the aircraft to be at 5000 feet, but after leaving slew mode the jet will be at an air speed of 0 knots and aerodynamically stalled, and you'll require the 2000 extra feet to get your speed up and recover from the stall.

5. After you recover from the stall, you'll be in a glide at 5000 feet, roughly above the runway. Now glide away from the runway, turn back, and land safely.

> **Note:** *You might want to raise the landing gear as soon as you exit slew mode to reduce drag as much as possible. However, don't forget to lower the gear before you land!*

Flight Tips

- Break the stall as quickly as possible and preserve the maximum amount of altitude by keeping the aircraft gliding at its best glide speed.
- Determine the altitude of the airport in advance so that you can judge exactly how far above the ground you are at all times.
- Tight turns with no power are a recipe for disaster. When you turn tightly, you lose lift and increase the chance of stalling the inside wing even if you keep the speed up. In a large jet with only a few thousand feet of precious altitude, it's best to make a large banking turn rather than a tight, heavily rudder-assisted turn.
- The choice of whether to fully extend the flaps depends on the altitude. If you're coming in high, extending the flaps can slow you down and bleed off the extra altitude. However, if the aircraft is low, you probably don't want to slow the jet down any more by extending the flaps too much (as the plane needs time to react to the change in configuration).

Flight Challenge 3: Visual Blackout

It's a dark and stormy night. You're flying a Cessna when all of a sudden you realize you're out of fuel. You have to land the plane—right now. With a sinking feeling, you look out the window and see that everything is dark. (See Figure 7-4.) No runway lights, no approach lighting, nothing to guide you except the instruments, your experience, and your smarts. All you can hope for is a little visit from Lady Luck.

This is the challenge: Can you take off, circle the airport, and land again using only the aircraft's instruments? To pull this off successfully, you need to know the field elevation at the airport you'll use, and you also need to be aware of any obstacles in the immediate area. If the airport has an instrument landing system (ILS), it might help guide you to the runway.

This challenge is an excellent way to practice landings because it forces you to concentrate on the relationships between throttle and altitude, and pitch and airspeed. If you are successful at this challenge, you should have no trouble landing a plane in fog or in other weather conditions where your visibility is reduced.

Setup

1. Select the Cessna Skylane 182S IFR.

2. Choose an airport with a flat area over which to practice to avoid hitting buildings, hills, and other obstacles. I suggest Edmonton International.

Figure 7-4 *If darkness is all you see, your heart gets stuck in your throat pretty quickly when the engine stops.*

3. On the Aircraft menu, click Realism Settings. In the Realism Settings dialog box, clear the Can Collide With Dynamic Scenery check box so that you don't run into other planes.

4. Set the visibility to zero so that you focus solely on the instruments to land the plane. There are two ways to do this. The first way is to click Weather on the World menu, and then click the Advanced Weather button. In the Advanced Weather dialog box, add a surface layer of stratus clouds starting at 326 feet, and then click the Visibility tab and change the visibility to $\frac{1}{16}$ mile. The other method is to click the simulation view and press the closed bracket ( ]) key to close the view.

5. Take off normally, level out, and make a 90-degree turn to the left. Fly the traffic pattern (the circling traffic flow for aircraft landing at and taking off from an airport) and return for a landing on the runway that you left in step 2.

6. If you closed the simulation view in step 4, on the Views menu, point to New View and then click Cockpit to see how close you are to the runway.

Flight Tips

- To help keep track of the altitude, set the altimeter to zero when the plane is on the runway by turning the knob at the bottom of the altimeter until the needle is at zero. The altimeter then displays the altitude AGL.
- Taking off is easy without a forward view. Landing is the tricky part. As you make your final approach, follow the same procedures that you would for a visual approach. In a nice, flat area, it won't matter if you miss the runway as long as you maintain a smooth, controlled descent rate at or below 500 feet per minute and a slightly nose-high attitude at touchdown. Don't overcorrect with the yoke; make small adjustments, and judge their effect by watching the vertical speed indicator (VSI). (See Figure 7-5.)

Figure 7-5 *Rely on the VSI to complete the visual blackout challenge.*

- While you fly, tune in the ILS system (if one is available for that runway) to help you stay on the proper glide path. If you're too high, decrease the throttle to lose some altitude. If you're too low, increase the throttle. Adjust the nose to maintain the proper airspeed, and extend the flaps to decrease the stall speed.
- You'll notice that the throttle and yoke have an immediate effect on the VSI, altimeter, and airspeed indicator. Watch carefully to see what effect your control inputs have.

Flight Challenge 4: Inverted Traffic Pattern

The Extra 300S is designed specifically for aerobatic flight. One of the Extra's advantages is its ability to quickly roll to inverted flight (upside down) and stay inverted with minimal manipulation of the controls. The challenge in this flight

is to take off, roll inverted, fly the traffic pattern inverted to about 200 feet on final approach, and then roll out (turn rightside up) and land. If you need to brush up on traffic patterns, refer to Rod Machado's excellent tutorial on take-offs, traffic patterns, and landings (Tutorial 8) in Microsoft Flight Simulator 2000 *Pilot's Handbook*.

Setup

> **Tip:** *If you've mastered this maneuver, you can add low visibility or winds to boost the challenge. Flying upside down with a crosswind is difficult for even the most experienced pilots.*

1. Select the Extra 300S.

2. Pick an airport where there are some visual reference points, such as Los Angeles International.

3. Make sure that the wind is light and the visibility is high. To set these options, on the World menu, click Weather. (See Figure 7-6.) In the Weather dialog box, adjust the Visibility and Wind Strength sliders.

Figure 7-6   *Adjust the weather to ensure high visibility and light winds.*

4. Decide before you take off whether you'll fly a right or left pattern (that is, whether you'll turn right or left after takeoff).

5. Take off, and at an altitude of 200 feet, roll inverted.

6. Fly the pattern at the correct height (1000 feet AGL on the downwind leg).

7. Roll out of inverted flight 200 feet above the runway for the landing.

Flight Tips

- Mentally outline the sequence of events before you try this challenge. It's easy to get disoriented when you fly inverted.
- Use the left and right views (left and right out of the pilot's seat) to judge where you are in the circuit.
- Watch the altitude. Visual flight rules (VFR) pilots are trained to judge an aircraft's attitude by looking at the visual "picture" outside the cockpit window, but when a plane is inverted, that visual picture is very different (as shown in Figure 7-7), so judging attitude (and altitude shifts) visually is difficult. Keep an eye on that altimeter, and don't rely solely on visual cues.
- Be careful with your control inputs as you roll out of inverted flight with only 200 feet of altitude before touchdown. If you overcontrol the Extra now, you're too low to correct it in time.

Figure 7-7   *The view from an inverted aircraft can be confusing.*

Flight Challenge 5: The Slot Machine

A true test of your flight skills is returning a tumbling aircraft to straight and level flight without using any sort of attitude indicator. In this challenge, you're flying instrument flight rules (IFR) when the attitude indicator fails. The next thing you know, you're tumbling out of control with no idea which way is up. Can you keep your cool and right the plane before it smashes into the ground?

Setup

1. Select the Cessna Skylane 182S IFR.

2. Choose an airport. A good one for this challenge is Boeing Field.

3. Increase the altitude to 5000 feet. A quick way to do this is to engage slew mode by pressing Y, and then press Q until you reach the desired altitude.

4. On the Aircraft menu, click System Failures, and then select the Failed check box for the Attitude Indicator. While you're still in slew mode, press the 0 key four times, the 7 key on the numeric keypad two times, and the 1 key on the keypad two times. This should get you tumbling across all three axes. (See Figure 7-8.)

Figure 7-8   *A tumbling Cessna is an unenviable place to be.*

5. Click the simulation view, and press the closed bracket ( ]) key to black it out. Let the plane tumble awhile, and then press Y to exit slew mode.

6. Try to get the plane straight and level again. You have 5000 feet to right the plane.

7. After you think you've got it, on the Views menu, point to New View, and then click Cockpit to see where you are. Good luck!

Flight Tips

- First you should correct the spin. Check the turn indicator, and bank the aircraft until the turn coordinator shows that you are level.
- Try to find the point at which the VSI starts to return toward zero, and then stop pushing or pulling on the yoke; if you wait until it reads zero, you will overcorrect in the opposite direction. After the altimeter stops changing, you are level.
- If you stall the aircraft, push forward on the yoke to recover. As the nose of the aircraft drops, the plane will come out of the stall; pull back gently on the yoke, and watch for the VSI to swing back up toward zero. At this point, it shouldn't be too difficult to stabilize the aircraft.
- Make large changes at first, and then make smaller, fine-tuning changes. When you try to level out, the airplane oscillates between stalling and picking up speed.

Note: *To recover from unusual attitudes when you have lost use of the attitude indicator and possibly also the heading indicator, you need to stop the turn with the turn coordinator and correct the pitch using the VSI and the altimeter.*

Flight Challenge 6: Himalayan Cessna

The Himalayan mountain range is the highest and most daunting in the world. The mountain climbing world often judges elite climbers by whether or not they've conquered such Himalayan peaks as K2 and Mount Everest, the highest point on earth. Some climbers pay more than $100,000 for a shot at reaching the summit with the help of professional climbers and guides.

In this challenge, you fly a Cessna 182S through the most treacherous part of the Himalayas, near Mount Everest. The challenge arises because the Cessna's maximum service ceiling is 18,100 feet, and the peak of Mount Everest sits at a towering 29,028 feet. Much of the basic terrain in this area is close to the service ceiling altitude of the 182S. Because the aircraft's performance above 18,000 feet is very limited, it takes plenty of skill and finesse to coax every last foot of altitude out of your plane. Make sure to look beyond the plane's instrument panel occasionally during this challenge; there's no better way to view the majestic Himalayas than in the cockpit of a small single-engine aircraft! (See Figure 7-9.) Good luck.

Figure 7-9 *The view of the Himalayas is spectacular, even if you are flying for your life!*

Setup

1. Choose the Cessna 182S as the aircraft for this challenge.

2. On the World menu, click Map View. Your destination is at 28 degrees north and 87 degrees east, so in the Latitude box, type **N28**, and in the Longitude box, type **E87**. (See Figure 7-10.) In the Altitude box, type **18,700** and set the initial airspeed to 120 knots. Click the check mark to apply your changes and take you to the Himalayas!

3. Press the P key to pause the simulator while you change the weather settings.

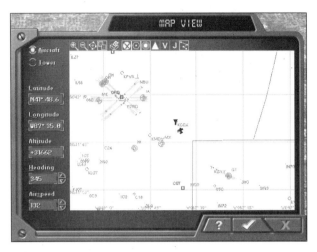

Figure 7-10   *Enter desired latitude and longitude.*

4. Before you resume the simulator, set the winds to heavy. On the World menu, click Weather. Use the Wind Strength slider to select Heavy winds. Press the P key to resume the simulation.

5. Fly as close as possible around Mount Everest.

6. After you're done touring the Himalayas (assuming you haven't become part of a mountain), land at the nearest major airport at Bharatpur.

Flight Tips

- Don't attempt to gain altitude quickly as you would if you were flying close to sea level. Any drastic attitude changes (pitching up) will induce a stall when you're this close to the Cessna's service ceiling.
- Use patience as you try to gain altitude. If you don't think you can clear a ridge, fly in gentle circles to try to gain more altitude before you cross the ridge.
- Don't fight the heavy winds too much. Let the aircraft ride the wind on its own or else you'll end up micromanaging and overcontrolling every little wind bump. Only correct to keep the aircraft on course.
- This challenge takes place among some spectacular vistas, so be sure to take the time to look around and enjoy the scenery.
- Use full power!

Flight Challenge 7: Washington Monument Race

Steve Barry is a commercial pilot with many years of experience in jets as well as an instructor and examiner for the Federal Aviation Administration (FAA). Much of his work takes place in a training facility using a large-scale flight simulator application. For fun, Steve suggests this race, which he flies using an MD-80. In this challenge you fly a 737-400 for a humbling experience. You take off from Washington Dulles International Airport in Washington, D.C., fly around the Washington Monument, and land at Washington National Airport. (See Figure 7-11.) Any flight time less than seven minutes is excellent.

Setup

1. Select the Boeing 737-400 for this challenge.

2. Take off from runway 19R at Washington Dulles International Airport in Washington, D.C.

3. On the Aircraft menu, click Realism Settings. Make sure the Aircraft Stress Causes Damage check box is clear.

Figure 7-11   *The National Mall, the U.S. Capitol, and the Washington Monument will help orient you in this challenging flight.*

4. Find the Washington Monument, fly around it, and prepare to land at Washington National Airport.

5. Try not to hit anything; in this race, it's considered especially bad form to destroy the Washington Monument.

Flight Tips

- Remember that you're not carrying any passengers, and the plane won't destruct from overstress, so the keys here are speed, speed, and speed. Make tight turns and use full throttle for most of the way to achieve the best time.

- On the left side of the instrument panel, above the clock, is a timer. Click it to start your time, and then take off. After you're airborne, re-tract the landing gear and turn to a heading of approximately 110 degrees to fly downtown and toward the Washington Monument.

- You might want to display the map view by pressing Shift+closed bracket ( ]). Press the plus sign (+) key to zoom in as you fly closer. The Washington Monument is at one end of the National Mall, with the U.S. Capitol at the other end.

- As you approach the Washington Monument, aim for a point just to the side of the monument because the 737's turn radius is fairly wide. The Washington Monument is only about 600 feet tall, so you might need to descend. The 737 turns slowly, so start your turn a little early, making a 60-degree bank turn for the tightest turn possible. Pull back slightly on the yoke to maintain altitude.

- After you round the monument, cut the throttle and get ready to land. You should be heading right for runway 18 at Washington National Airport.

- Fully extend the flaps and spoilers to slow down quickly for a good landing.

- This challenge is a lot of fun in multiplayer mode. (See Chapter 9.) Try flying it with a friend. It's also a fun challenge to use the Extra 300S.

Flight Challenge 8: "The Duke"
Heavy Landing at John Wayne Airport

It's always good to get a challenging suggestion from an experienced pilot who flies commercial airliners. In this case, I've enlisted the help of Captain Ron Hunt. Here's his suggestion for a flight challenge.

> *John Wayne Orange County is in a very noise-sensitive area and for that reason requires steep approaches and departures to keep the community happy. We affectionately refer to it as the USS Orange County because with a runway length of only 5700 feet, it appears more like an aircraft carrier rather than a commercial airport when you're lined up on final approach at night. [See Figure 7-12.] Landing to the south, the typical 757 will approach at around 130 knots. Precise control of the aircraft speed and descent rate is vital. Approaches are planned to touch down at the 1000-foot mark, no later! In cases like this you fly to touchdown and take the landing you get because at those speeds the remaining runway goes by pretty fast, leaving little room for error (or stopping distance for that matter). Add to that a good crosswind, a wet runway, and having shot an ILS approach to 300 feet and a mile visibility before you see the runway at night and you have yourself a good challenge providing a great deal of satisfaction once you're parked at the gate.*

Although there's no Boeing 757 in Flight Simulator 2000, much of this scenario can be duplicated. In this case, the challenge is to land a Boeing 777-300 at John Wayne Airport during the day while observing the noise-abatement criteria set by Orange County.

Figure 7-12   *The runway at John Wayne Airport in Orange County can look pretty darned small when you're approaching in a Boeing 777-300.*

Setup

1. Select the 777-300.

2. On the World menu, click Map View. Set the latitude to N33* 57.2' and the longitude to W117* 11.0'. Set the altitude to 10,000 feet, the heading to 290 degrees, and the airspeed to 250 knots. (See Figure 7-13.)

Figure 7-13   *Enter the map information in this dialog box to set up this challenge.*

3. On the Aircraft menu, point to Kneeboard, and then click Checklists. Complete the descent checklist.

4. Continue on a 290-degree heading and descend to 7000 feet. After you reach 7000 feet, slow to 190 knots. You have to cross a small mountain range, so 7000 feet is as low as you can go for now. This puts you on a high wide left approach, about 10 miles northeast of the airport.

5. After you are over the crest of the mountains, start a descent at 190 knots to 3000 feet. Plan to make a fairly square turn to a 7-mile final approach at 3000 feet while slowing to a speed of 160 knots.

6. At 2000 feet, lower the landing gear and adjust the flaps. Reduce the airspeed to the approach reference speed of about 130 knots.

Flight Tips

- Plan to touch down at about the 1000-foot mark on the runway. If you do this correctly, you can comfortably make the last turnoff prior to the end of the runway—quite an accomplishment for such a large aircraft!

- Start everything early so that nothing is missed. Tune ILS frequencies, complete checklists, and plan how to fly this approach. Slow the aircraft and configure it early to give yourself more time so that you avoid feeling rushed. For instance, flying the descent from 7000 feet at 140 knots can make a world of difference.

- Use flaps in the descent to keep on the desired descent path and on speed. Don't let the speed get away from you after the descent is started. You're going to be high; you don't want to be fast, too!

- Don't turn the corner to the airport from 7000 feet with a gentle slow turn to final approach; make it a tight turn. You need the room to get down and get the aircraft stabilized. Fly to a point where you can make a 30-degree bank turn to final approach. This gives you more ground to cover and more time to get down and stabilized. (See Figure 7-14.)

Figure 7-14   *The view of John Wayne Airport on final approach.*

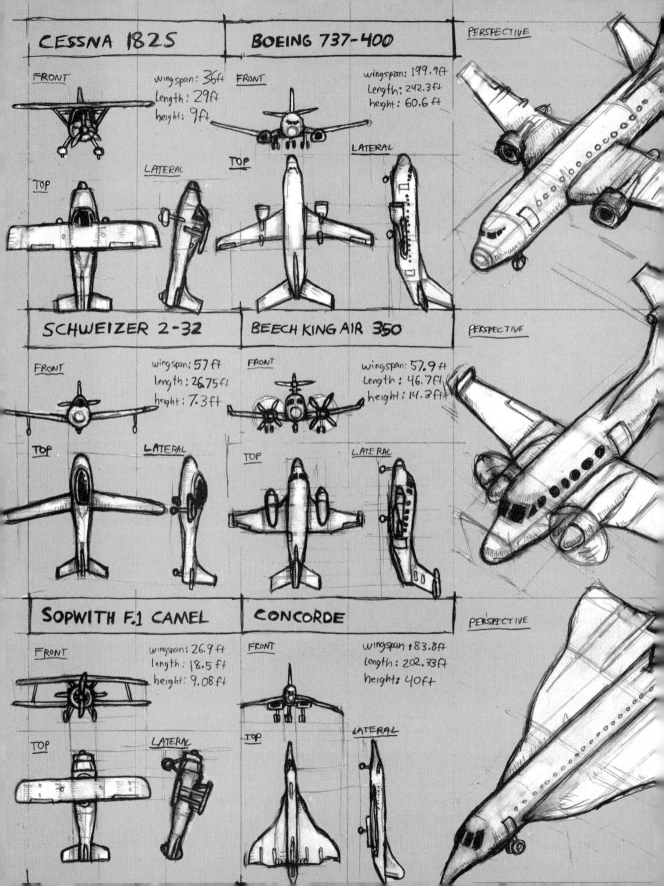

CESSNA 182S

FRONT

wingspan: 36ft
length: 29ft
height: 9ft

TOP

LATERAL

BOEING 737-400

FRONT

wingspan: 199.9ft
Length: 242.3ft
height: 60.6ft

LATERAL

TOP

PERSPECTIVE

SCHWEIZER 2-32

FRONT

wingspan: 57ft
length: 26.75ft
height: 7.3ft

TOP

LATERAL

BEECH KING AIR 350

FRONT

wingspan: 57.9ft
Length: 46.7ft
height: 14.3ft

TOP

LATERAL

PERSPECTIVE

SOPWITH F.1 CAMEL

FRONT

wingspan: 26.9ft
length: 18.5ft
height: 9.08ft

TOP

LATERAL

CONCORDE

FRONT

wingspan: 83.8ft
length: 202.33ft
height: 40ft

TOP

LATERAL

PERSPECTIVE

Chapter Eight

WORLD HIGHLIGHTS

With over 21,000 airports and an entire world of scenery in Microsoft Flight Simulator 2000, you could fly 24 hours a day every day for a month and still not see all that there is to see. (Yep, it's that big.) However, there are some very spectacular scenic flights that are worth singling out from the flights already provided in the Adventures and Select Flight dialog boxes. This chapter takes you to some famous cities, wonders of the world, and natural areas while providing some interesting background on what you're seeing. Each tour sets you up in just the right position for you to get the maximum viewing pleasure with minimal fuss.

Note: *Most of the tours in this chapter do not suggest an aircraft for the tour. It's assumed that you'll use the Cessna 182S or the 182 RG, but you can use whichever aircraft tickles your fancy. In many cases, the Bell JetRanger 206B helicopter is an excellent choice because of its ability to hover, but the choice of aircraft is entirely up to you. One caveat: The Schweizer 2-32 Sailplane is a poor choice in many cases because you'll need some power to maneuver through these tours.*

Grand Canyon Flyby

The Grand Canyon is truly one of the world's natural treasures. It took the Colorado River millions of years to carve it, and it is up to 1 mile deep and between 4 and 16 miles wide along its over 250-mile length. This is your chance to hop into the aircraft of your choice (although I suggest one of the Cessna aircraft) and tour this majestic canyon at your own pace.

Setup

1. Select Grand Canyon Natl Park as the airport.

2. Take off, and climb straight out on the runway heading (at 30 degrees).

3. Climb to an altitude of about 9000 feet above mean sea level (MSL). You'll see the canyon stretching out before you as shown in Figure 8-1.

4. Follow the canyon in either direction (30 degrees or 290 degrees). The 30-degree course is longer.

Figure 8-1   *The Grand Canyon lies before you. It winds away to the right and left of this position.*

Flight Tips

- After you reach the canyon, it's fun to drop down for some *nap of the earth flight*, or terrain flight. (See Chapter 7 for more details on this flight technique.) Winding through the canyon a few hundred feet off the ground is more exciting than soaring at a high altitude (for me, anyway).

- You can follow the canyon and the Colorado River for hundreds of miles, so you might not get to see it all in one visit.

• If you follow the canyon to the right, you'll pass over Marble Canyon Airport along the way. Feel free to do a stop-and-go landing there for practice.

> **Note:** *For more information about flying any of the aircraft in Flight Simulator 2000, see the Aircraft Information section of Help. For quick reference to checklists, procedures, and other information about an aircraft, press F10 to display the kneeboard.*

Mount Rushmore

Mount Rushmore National Memorial in South Dakota is one of the great American monuments to past leaders. Adorning the face of Mount Rushmore are the images of George Washington, Thomas Jefferson, Abraham Lincoln, and Theodore Roosevelt. These leaders' faces were carved into the face of Mount Rushmore

> **Tip:** *The story of how Mount Rushmore National Memorial was created is pretty interesting. For more information about it, check out the following site on the World Wide Web:* http://www. americanparknetwork.com/parkinfo/ru/.

by Gutzon Borglum in just over six years of total work between 1927 and 1941. This flight takes you on a head-on pass of this historic monument.

Setup

1. On the World menu, click Map View (as shown in Figure 8-2) to set your position directly in front of the monument.

2. In the Latitude box, type **N43* 52.23'**, and in the Longitude box, type **W103* 21.78'**.

3. In the altitude box, type **+7400**, and in the airspeed box, type 100 (unless you're flying in a jet that requires a higher speed).

4. In the Heading box, type **247**, and then click the check mark to apply your changes. You'll now be in flight heading straight for Mount Rushmore.

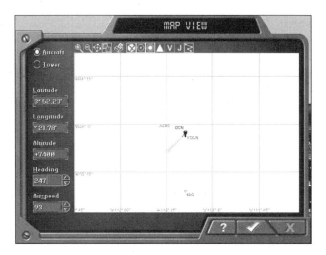

Figure 8-2 *Use Map View to set up this flight precisely.*

Flight Tips

- To get the best view of the monument, use a Cessna 182S. Lower the flaps to 20 degrees and keep your speed around 55 to 60 knots as you fly by. (See Figure 8-3.)

- Another way to get a good look is to point to Simulation Rate on the Options menu, and then click Half Speed. This will keep your flyby nice and slow so that you can enjoy the scenery.

Figure 8-3 *The faces of some of the great American presidents will stare back at you as you approach Mount Rushmore.*

New Orleans Riverboat Ride

Just the name "New Orleans" brings to mind images of the Superdome, riverboats, and Bourbon Street. In this flight you'll get two out of three. First you'll pass by a classic riverboat, and then it's on to the Louisiana Superdome. The Superdome, which opened in 1975, was one of the first great domed stadiums in the world. It has a seating capacity of 87,500! (See Figure 8-4.)

Figure 8-4   *The Superdome is large enough that the entire Houston Astrodome could fit inside it, but what do we care? We're just flying over it!*

Setup

1. Select New Orleans NAS as the airport.

2. Take off from the airport, and turn to a heading of about 345 degrees. This will take you to the downtown core where the riverboat and Superdome await. (See Figure 8-5.)

Figure 8-5 *The skyline of New Orleans looms ahead just after takeoff.*

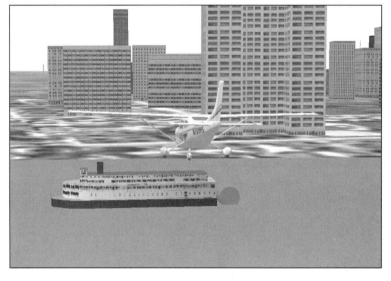

Figure 8-6 *It's worth slowing down to get a good look at the riverboat.*

Flight Tips

- On the way to the city, you might want to attempt to fly under the bridge to do a flyby of the riverboat.

Note: *In Flight Simulator, you can safely try maneuvers that you can't do in real life. Of course, you don't want to try these types of maneuvers in a real aircraft. They violate FAA regulations and can put your pilot's license (and your life) in jeapordy.*

- To get a better look at the riverboat (as shown in Figure 8-6), it's a good idea to reduce airspeed to about 65 knots and lower the flaps to about 20 degrees.

LAX to *Queen Mary*

The legendary Los Angeles International Airport (better known by its airport code, LAX) has been faithfully re-created, from high-detail runways right down to the famous spaceship-like restaurant (Encounter). (See Figure 8-7.) This flight takes you from LAX to the now permanently docked ocean liner, the *Queen Mary*, in Long Beach (a few miles away). The *Queen Mary* was launched as an ocean liner in 1936 and was used both as a luxury liner and for World War II troop transport. Today it is a floating tourist attraction that includes a hotel and several restaurants. For more information on the *Queen Mary*, visit its Web site at *http://www.queenmary.com.*

Figure 8-7   *This restaurant at LAX, Encounter (also known as the Theme Building), lets you know exactly which airport you're at (if you didn't already know).*

Setup

1. Select Los Angeles Int'l as the airport.

2. Take off from runway 07R, and then take some time to circle the airport to see the airport itself. During your takeoff run, the Theme Building is on the left.

3. After you've had your fill of the airport restaurant, fly a heading of 120 degrees to reach the *Queen Mary* in Long Beach.

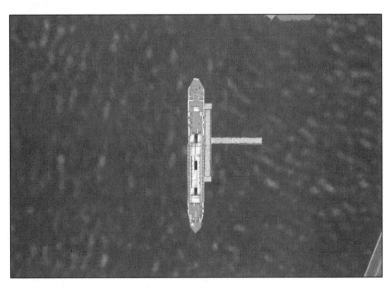

Figure 8-8   *A bird's-eye view of the* Queen Mary.

Flight Tips

- Try taking off from LAX at night; the lighting patterns are very impressive. Twilight is also an excellent time to fly around the Los Angeles area.

- Try using the Top Down view (point to New View on the Views menu and click Top Down) to get a look at the upper deck of the *Queen Mary* as you fly above it. (See Figure 8-8.)

The Hollywood Sign

The Hollywood sign in Los Angeles is an icon that represents all of the glitz and glamour of the movie business. This sign originally read *Hollywoodland* and was a real estate marketing ploy to attract residents to the area way back in 1923. In 1949, the suffix "land" was removed from the sign and the sign was repaired, and in 1973 the sign was declared a cultural landmark. If you've ever wanted to see this sign close up, this might be your best chance to get a look.

Setup

1. On the World menu, click Map View. Enter a latitude of N34* 8.98' and a longitude of W118* 15.74'.

2. Set the heading to 355 degrees, the altitude to 1500 feet MSL, and the airspeed to 100 knots.

3. Fly the 355-degree heading until you see the sign; it's only a few miles ahead of your starting position. (See Figure 8-9.)

Flight Tip

After you get close to the sign, press P to pause the simulator to make your view last a little longer.

Figure 8-9   *The Hollywood sign looms ahead of your starting position.*

The Taj Mahal

The Taj Mahal in Agra, India, is perhaps the most poignant example of a man's attempt to show his love of his wife. Shah Jahan, the Mogul emperor, lost his longtime companion and wife, Mumtaz Mahal, when she died during childbirth in 1630. As a monument to her, Shah Jahan had the Taj Mahal built. Completed in 1643, it still stands on the bank of the Tamuna River and is one of the most remarkable buildings ever constructed. Indeed, the Taj Mahal is one of the wonders of the world.

Setup

1. On the World menu, click Map View. Enter a latitude of N27* 8.99' and a longitude of E78* 1.84'.

2. Set the altitude to 1500 feet MSL, the heading to 022 degrees, and the airspeed to 80 knots (in the Cessna 182S).

3. Fly and descend toward the Taj Mahal.

Flight Tips

- Lower the flaps to 20 degrees and fly about 10 knots above the stall speed of the aircraft that you're flying (so that you can make your flyby as slow as possible to enjoy the view) because you'll be losing some altitude (and gaining speed) as you approach the Taj Mahal.
- For fun, try to land on the long stretch of green in front of the Taj Mahal. (See Figure 8-10.) You'll have plenty of motivation to stop before you run out of "runway."

The Parthenon in Athens

The Parthenon on the Acropolis in Athens still stands as a testimony to the skill and power of ancient Greek civilization. Built sometime between 500 and 400

B.C., the Parthenon is a temple for the goddess Athena, who was worshiped as the Greek goddess of wisdom, the practical arts, and warfare. The Parthenon is a massive structure punctuated by impressive relief and massive Doric columns, and it is well worth the virtual trip in Flight Simulator 2000.

Figure 8-10   *Land on the stretch of grass in front of the Taj Mahal to add some extra fun to your flight.*

Setup

1. On the World menu, click Go To Airport.

2. Select Europe in the Global Region list and Greece in the Country list. In the Airport Name box, type **Athens**, and then click the checkmark to apply your changes.

3. Take off and turn toward a heading of 360 degrees (north).

4. You won't need to climb much above an altitude of 2000 feet MSL to be able to see the Acropolis and the Parthenon rising from the surrounding terrain in front of you. (See Figure 8-11.)

Figure 8-11 *Head north from the airport to approach the Acropolis in Athens.*

Flight Tips

- Just southeast of the Acropolis is downtown Athens, where the Olympic Stadium sits. It can be worth a flyby to get a close-up look.
- Athens was an important part of the ancient world (as it is in the modern world), so it can be fun to fly high over the city to get an impressive overall viewpoint.

Chapter Nine

FLYING WITH OTHERS

By this point, you have probably experimented with Microsoft Flight Simulator 2000 a bit on your own. Perhaps you have honed your flying skills and, more important, your landing skills. Perhaps you have experimented with aerobatics, and now you're looking for an audience. Or maybe you've just installed Flight Simulator 2000, and the skies seem a little lonely up there without fellow pilots.

When you fly with other people in Flight Simulator 2000, you open up an enormous range of challenges, competitions, and fun activities limited only by your imagination. You and your fellow pilots can fly as a group from one city to the next. You can practice formation aerobatics as a team. You can fly coast to coast and experience real-life air traffic control as you go. You can join a virtual airline and receive route assignments, building your flight hours and the respect and admiration of your peers. Or you can receive interactive flight lessons from another person who can fly alongside you and offer helpful advice and suggestions. All of these scenarios and more are available by using the multiplayer feature in Flight Simulator 2000.

Getting Connected

There are a number of ways to fly with other people, depending on your system configuration. Perhaps the simplest way is to connect two computers with a null modem cable. You can also fly with other people on a local area network (LAN). If you and a friend both have a modem and a copy of Flight Simulator 2000, you can connect by calling him or her directly, or you can exchange Internet Protocol (IP) addresses and fly by using the Internet.

> **Tip:** *You can find more information about getting connected to the MSN Gaming Zone in Flight Simulator 2000's online Help. For more information about the Zone, refer to the Zone's online Help. Go to the Web site at* http://www.zone.com, *and then click the Services link at the top of the page.*

Finally, you can find other pilots to fly with on the MSN Gaming Zone.

Hosting a Game

The first step in flying with others is customizing the multiplayer options. When you host a game, you decide the details about it: how many people can join, what the object of the game is, and so on. As the host, you should be especially aware of lag, or *latency,* which occurs when the connection is degraded either because of a slow phone line or because of congestion on the Internet. In general, the player with the fastest, most reliable connection should host the game to ensure a smooth, lag-free game for everyone.

Tip: *For information on what a particular multiplayer setting does, click the yellow question mark at the bottom of the dialog box to access Flight Simulator 2000's online Help.*

Multiplayer Settings

To customize multiplayer settings, on the Flights menu, point to Multiplayer, and then click Settings. In the Multiplayer Settings dialog box, you can configure settings that will make it easier for players to find each other or speed up the frame rate by sending less visual detail of other aircraft. (See Figure 9-1.)

Host Options

After you have configured multiplayer settings for the game that you are hosting, on the Flights menu, point to Multiplayer, and then click Connect. Choose the appropriate connection protocol, and click the Host button to open the Host Options dialog box. (I'll go into more detail

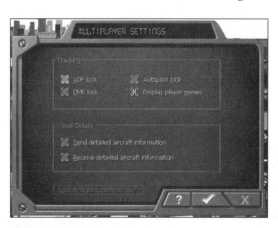

Figure 9-1   *Set up your multiplayer settings in this dialog box.*

on protocol choices later in this chapter.) In this dialog box, you can choose the maximum number of players who can join your game. You can also allow *observers* to join your game. Observers can switch to the point of view of any of the aircraft in the game, but they cannot fly their own aircraft.

Serial Connection

If you want to fly with just one other person and you both have a computer in the same room, you can use a serial cable, or null modem cable, to connect the two computers using a COM port on each computer. To host or join a multiplayer session in this way, on the Flights menu, point to Multiplayer, and then click Connect. (See Figure 9-2.) Click Serial in the Protocol list, and then

click the Host button to host a game. To join a game, click the Search button, select one of the found games, and then click the Join button.

LAN Connection

If you have access to a LAN, you can join or host a multiplayer session with other people. If you host the game, configure the multiplayer settings as described earlier in the Host Options section, and then click TCP/IP or IPX in the

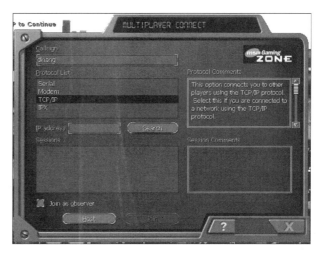

Figure 9-2   *Use the Multiplayer Connect dialog box to host or to join a game.*

Protocol list, depending on which protocol your network uses. If you're joining a LAN game, click the Search button to search for existing games. Consult online Help or your network administrator for more information on this.

Modem Connection

You can call a friend directly using a modem, or you can connect over the Internet if you both have Internet access, which might save you the cost of a long-distance call. To host a game using a modem, on the Flights menu, point to Multiplayer, and then click Connect. Click Modem in the Protocol list, and click the Host button. Specify the Host options, described earlier in the Host Options section, in the dialog box shown, and click the checkmark. The Modem Connection dialog box then appears. As the host, you're the one being called, so click the Answer button so that your modem will automatically answer incoming calls. If you are joining a game, you can dial your friend directly by using the Modem Connection dialog box. An advantage of dialing your friend directly is that neither of you needs Internet access. Some disadvantages are that a game that uses a modem allows only two players to fly together.

IP Address Connection

Another way to connect is by using your Internet connection and your IP address. All players will need to have Internet access through an Internet service provider (ISP). First connect to the Internet using your ISP, and then start Flight Simulator 2000. If you're hosting a game, configure the multiplayer settings as described earlier in the Host Options section, and select TCP/IP as the connection protocol. See the MSN Gaming Zone Web site for more information. Other players will need to know your IP address ahead of time to join the game. You can share your IP with prospective players by sending an e-mail message or even by using an Internet chat application.

Note: *Due to safety concerns many networks are protected with firewalls or proxy servers that don't allow two-way communication between the Internet and a specific computer. If your computer is protected with a firewall or proxy server, you might not be able to take advantage of Internet-based multiplayer gaming.*

Determining your IP address can be complicated. Try running IP Configuration by clicking Run on the Start menu and typing WinIPCfg.exe in the Open text box. Click the OK button to run IP Configuration and determine your IP. If IP Configuration is not installed on your machine, try checking your Internet configuration, the Internet status window, or

See the online Help area on the Zone for specific instructions on hosting a game.

There is also a chat window that appears in the lower half of the screen. Here, you might chat with other players about Flight Simulator 2000, say hello to old friends, or even discuss aviation-related issues in general.

To the right of the game room you'll see a list of the players in that game room, along with a graphic indicator of each player's latency rate, which reflects the speed that information travels from that player's computer to the server. The lower the latency, the less time it takes a computer to communicate with the server, and more bars appear. You can also check the color of the bars on the indicator: When there are more bars, they turn green. When there are fewer bars, they turn red. Make sure that you have a low latency rate if you plan to host a game; otherwise, the game will be slow for the other players. When you play with a group of people, the person with the lowest latency rate should be the host. If you're looking to join a game, try to find a host who has a low latency rate.

The Launch Pad

When you click a game's Join button in the game room, the *launch pad* for that game appears. (See Figure 9-5.) In this window, you can chat with other players while you wait for the host to launch the game. Sometimes the host writes a description of the game at the top of the launch pad window. You can also check the latency rate of the players and the host in this area. Click the Leave button to return to the game room.

Figure 9-5   *The launch pad.*

A Trip to the Zone

What follows (pages 190–94) is a factual account of one pilot's adventures while traveling on the MSN Gaming Zone. Some names have been changed to protect the guilty.

12:30 A.M.

I start up Flight Simulator 2000 and click Fly Now on the opening screen. Next, I go to the Flights menu, point to Multiplayer, and click Connect. In the Multiplayer Connect dialog box, I click the MSN Gaming Zone button, which automatically connects me to the Internet and opens my Web browser. I want to find other pilots to fly with on the MSN Gaming Zone, which is a special site set aside on the Internet where players can chat with each other and play multiplayer games. In a minute or so, I am in "the Zone," browsing the Flight Simulator 2000 Zone game page with Flight Simulator 2000 running in the background.

12:31 A.M.

The Zone is a busy place. There are over 80 players browsing through the chat rooms or flying online. Flight Simulator 2000 is popular worldwide; there are people from all different time zones here, at all hours of the day and night. Clicking the Free Flight game room, one of the Standard Rooms, I take a look at the multiplayer games that have players in them. These games all have their own names—some are descriptive, some are cryptic. Tonight I can choose among games such as "Choppers LasVeg," "RW mpla," "IP/RW Airliners," and "Beginners."

Note: *When you host a multiplayer game on the Zone, use names or abbreviations that will be meaningful to the players that you want to attract. Use the airport name or even the type of flying in the game's name. It also helps to write some details about the object of the game in the launch pad window.*

12:35 A.M.

I click the Join button for a game called Beginners, the launch pad window is displayed, and I wait for the game to start. There is a list of players at the top and a small symbol that indicates the quality of the Internet connection for each particular player. The slower or less reliable the player's connection is, the fewer colored bars are used in the symbol to the left of the player's name. The name of the host is the first in the list. Tonight the host has one red bar next to his or her name, which means that his or her connection isn't so great. Players often refer to this as the "latency rate."

I decide to give the game a try anyway, so I click the Join button. Nothing happens. After a few moments, I'm returned to the game room. This sometimes happens if the host has a troublesome connection. All you need to do is try to join the game again.

12:40 A.M.

I try another game, this one called "Fun at Meigs," and the launch pad window opens for that game. (See Figure 9-6.) This game has only one other player in it: N63207. He starts the game, and we're off!

"Hi," the other player calls out in the chat window once the game has started. (See Figure 9-7.)

"Hey, what's up?" I type back. We chat a little while, and I find out that player N63207 is actually Jon, from Florida. "Where are you flying?" I type.

Figure 9-6   *The launch pad for a game.*

Figure 9-7   *The chat window is where you communicate with other players during a game.*

Tip: *To move quickly in a multiplayer game, use slew mode, which you enter by typing Y on the keyboard. Entering slew mode affects only your flight, not that of the other players.*

Looking around, I am having a hard time locating him. Flight Simulator 2000 optionally displays the name of the player just above his aircraft, but without zooming in, it's difficult to tell how far away he is or if he is facing me.

"Hold on a sec," he types. I blink my eyes and see his enormous Boeing 737-400 just off my starboard wing. I jump.

12:42 A.M.

"Try this," N63207 suggests. He flies upside down and then proceeds to attempt to fly upside down above me, just like in the movies. We play around with different aerobatics for a while, and then we change aircraft and try flying helicopters in formation, but we both crash and burn. After a while, my flying companion needs to leave. I add N63207 to my ZoneFriends list, which will alert me the next time he's on the Zone so that we can fly together. I click the Leave button to leave the game and return to the game room.

1:05 A.M.

This time I decide to host my own game. I click room 9, which happens to be empty, and name the game "Multiplayer Racing." I then sit in the launch pad and wait for people to show up. After a little while, there are four people chatting with each other in my game's launch pad. I tell one of them how to set up her airplane so that it's invulnerable, and two other players tell me how to install "RW," which is short for Roger Wilco, a voice communication add-on that is currently very popular on the Zone. [See Appendix B, "Add-Ons."] One of the best things about the Zone is that it allows people to share their collective knowledge of Flight Simulator with each other. I've never been part of a multiplayer game where I didn't learn something new.

Note: *You can send a message in the chat window of the game room inviting people to come to your room. Be polite, however: send the invitation only a couple of times to avoid flooding the game room.*

1:15 A.M.

It's so much fun chatting with the other people in the launch pad that we never get around to starting the game! A few visitors drop by my room and invite me to join a race they're setting up in another room. I click Leave and head to another game with them.

1:17 A.M.

I try a game titled "Meigs to O'Hare" and place myself in a Cessna taking off from Meigs, with five other players somewhere in the air. "Hello!" the host broadcasts in the chat window. "Come on and join us!" "Thanks," I type back, but where exactly are they? To locate the others, I open the Map View dialog box by clicking Map View on the World menu. [See Figure 9-8.] After clicking the minus button a couple of

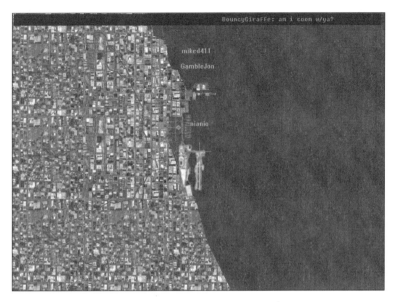

Figure 9-8   *The overhead Map View dialog box makes it easy to locate other players.*

times to zoom out, I spot the others flying as a caravan of aircraft already approaching O'Hare International Airport. To catch up quickly, I use the slew feature to place myself just behind the group of planes.

Just as I'm doing this, my name blinks in the chat window, and I see my friend N63207 from earlier in the evening, who has found me by using the ZoneFriends feature. "Hey, this is cool," he messages me. "I just found out you can click and drag your airplane in the Map View dialog box...it's much faster than slewing."

"Thanks," I type back, and I invite him to join our caravan.

1:21 A.M.

I can see O'Hare clearly in the distance as I approach. It also helps to follow a large group of aircraft toward the airport! As I get closer, I can see that the others in my group are flying a variety of aircraft: a 737-400, an Extra, a Bell

Tip: *To coordinate with the other players in a multiplayer game, use the Zone's chat window or talk using Roger Wilco, a separate add-on that allows you to talk with other players using a microphone. Talking with other pilots adds greatly to the feeling of immersion in the game. The more you communicate, the more fun it is!*

JetRanger, and another Cessna like mine. I line up the Cessna with an available runway and bring it in for a soft landing on the enormous stretch of tarmac. A chorus of salutations follows in the chat window. "Nice landing." "Dude, nice job." Turning onto the taxiway, I watch as the others line up their aircraft for a landing on the same runway. There's a burst of chatter in the chat window as we all get caught up in this shared adventure.

1:34 A.M.

"Where to now?" the other pilots ask. "How about Detroit?" one of them suggests. "Yeah, let's fly to Detroit!" comes the chorus, and everyone lines up along the taxiway to take off again. With so many planes in line, we have to wait our turns to take off. In addition to planes in our flight group, there are computer-controlled aircraft also patiently waiting their turn. I get in line behind the others and watch as, one by one, the other planes taxi smoothly into position on the runway and start their takeoff.

Usually, when I'm flying alone, I just head over to any runway and take off whenever I feel like it. I think it's fascinating how you have to adjust your flying style when you're in a multiplayer game. It gives you an appreciation for the complex, often personally inconvenient, yet vitally important, communication process that goes into coordinating ground and air traffic at a busy airport. Flying with other people adds a whole new sense of realism to the game.

Multiplayer Games

The number of multiplayer games you can play in Flight Simulator is limited only by imagination. This section shows several of the traditional multiplayer games, as well as a few new twists to whet your appetite for head-to-head simulations.

Kamikaze Tag

In World War II, the Japanese used a grave weapon known as the *kamikaze*, which literally means "divine wind." Japanese pilots attempted to crash their planes directly into enemy ships, causing considerable damage to their target if their aim was on. Of course, these pilots also lost their lives in this maneuver, but you're using a simulated plane, so you're perfectly safe. Give it a try!

With Flight Simulator, you can simulate the kamikaze flight—but hopefully not the often-deadly ending—with a game that I call Kamikaze Tag. This game is played with two players: one player is "it," and the other player is the kamikaze. The object of Kamikaze Tag is to run your plane into the other player's plane before the planes get more than 5 nautical miles (NM) apart.

1. To set up this challenge, you and your opponent should set your planes to display a distance measuring equipment (DME) lock to the other aircraft by selecting the DME Lock check box in the Multiplayer Settings dialog box. Click Select Aircraft on the Aircraft menu, and then select an aircraft. Start off at opposite ends of a runway, such as Merrill C. Meigs field in Chicago. Also make sure that you both set your aircraft to crash when you run into dynamic scenery: On the Aircraft menu, click Realism Settings. Select the Can Collide With Dynamic Scenery check box in the Realism Settings dialog box, and then click the green check mark.

2. After takeoff, the player who is the kamikaze tries to crash into the other player before he or she can get away. Use the digital clock that most aircraft have on the instrument panel to see how long the kamikaze player can keep the other player within 5 NM.

Playing Tips

- For a game that is evenly balanced, the kamikaze should be in a faster, more maneuverable plane, such as the Extra 300S, and the other player should be in a larger, slower plane such as the Boeing 737-400.
- When you play as the kamikaze, use a slow approach from the back rather than a high-speed head-on pass, in which the aircraft are flying directly toward each other. When the two aircraft are head-on, the closure rate is so high that it's extremely difficult to hit the other plane. Try to position yourself in the other aircraft's six-o'clock position, and then make your move.
- If you are "it," keep checking behind you by using the hat switch on your joystick or flight yoke or by using the numeric keys on the keypad. Try to face the kamikaze for a head-on pass, and then turn slightly

to one side or the other to avoid hitting the other plane. Once the ka-mikaze is past you, go to full throttle and try to fly as far away from the other plane as possible before it has time to turn around.

Multiplayer Race Courses

One of the most natural flight challenges is an all-out air race with another player. You can compete in a race in one of Flight Simulator's built-in aircraft or in a plane that you download. (See Appendix B, "Add-Ons." The Additional Aircraft section discusses aircraft in particular.) The truly committed even design and race their own airplanes, complete with custom paint jobs! This section focuses on racing the built-in aircraft in Flight Simulator 2000 and provides some ideas for ideal racing courses.

Race Course 1: Thread the Needle

The object of this course is to race around Seattle's Space Needle and back to any runway.

1. Take off from runway 31L at Boeing Field/King County International Airport, in Seattle, Washington.

2. After you're airborne, turn to a heading of 330 degrees and head straight for the Space Needle.

3. As you approach the Space Needle (as shown in Figure 9-9), decrease the throttle and bank hard to clear the top of the building.

4. After the turn is complete, increase the throttle and stay at a heading of 150 degrees until you can see the airport.

The Space Needle

Seattle's Space Needle is one of the most distinctive and recognizable structures in the United States. It was built to commemorate the 1962 World's Fair. It is 605 feet tall and has withstood all sorts of natural forces, including wind gusts of nearly 100 miles per hour and a 1965 earthquake of 6.5 on the Richter scale. During the earthquake, a radio show was being broadcast from the Needle; the record never even skipped a beat!

Race Course 2: Over Arch-iever

The object of this race is to pass under the Gateway Arch in St. Louis and then return for a landing at any runway. The

usual and sane way of completing this challenge is to perform an Immelmann maneuver (described below) as you pass under the Arch. However, to win the "Over Archiever" award, you must pass over the Arch, roll inverted, and then perform a split-S maneuver (described on the next page) to pass under the Arch from the opposite direction.

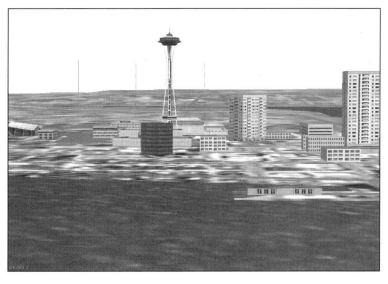

Figure 9-9   *The Space Needle.*

1. Choose the Extra 300S as the aircraft, and take off from runway 12R at Lambert-St. Louis International, in St. Louis, Missouri.

2. After you're airborne, remain on a heading of 120 degrees until you see the Gateway Arch.

3. As you approach the Arch, decide on one of two maneuvers.

   • For the Immelmann maneuver, climb to about 1500 feet to clear the buildings, and then dive toward the bottom of the Arch, where it's wider. The airspeed will increase to about 190 knots, which will carry you over the top of the Arch as you pull up and over. Keep pulling back on the yoke until you see the horizon again—at this point, you'll be flying inverted. Roll right side up again, and head back to the runway, maintaining a heading of 340 degrees.

- For the split-S maneuver, climb to about 2000 feet as you approach the Arch. Keep the nose level until you pass over the Arch. It helps if you press 5 on the numeric keypad to look directly beneath the plane. (See Figure 9-10.)

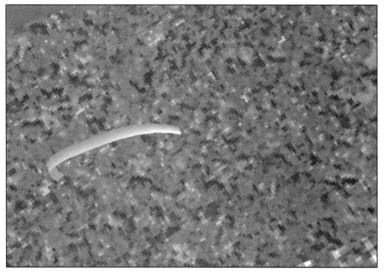

Figure 9-10   *Press Ctrl+5 on the keypad to look directly down at the Arch.*

As soon as you pass over the top of the Arch, cut the throttle, roll inverted, and pull back on the yoke, diving for the ground.

After the Arch comes back into view, correct the heading with the rudder, if necessary, and maintain backpressure on the yoke as you pass through the Arch.

Remember to increase power again and pull up immediately to avoid the buildings, because you'll be low and traveling very fast. Good luck.

Altitude and Speed Competitions

Other multiplayer pastimes that invariably show up in the Zone are altitude and speed competitions. These are usually informal competitions in which two or more pilots in the same type of aircraft try to push its performance to higher and higher limits. The goal is usually to see who can get the fastest indicated speed in straight and level flight or who can take an aircraft the farthest past its intended operational ceiling. In theory, the maximum air speed for two similar aircraft should always be the same, but pilot technique can also affect speed. Even a slight mistake with rudder control can affect speed, so this is where piloting really comes into play.

Follow the Leader

This is another relatively simple multiplayer diversion, but it can be a lot of fun. It's much harder than you might think to stay on another aircraft's "six" (tail), and if you get a crafty veteran pilot in front of you, it'll be a true challenge to stay close.

1. For a challenge, choose an airport in New York City as the starting point.

2. Set detail to high by pointing to Settings on the Options menu and clicking Display. Click the Image Quality tab, and adjust the Image Quality slider or individual settings to tune the image detail that best suits your computer hardware. Too much detail might make your simulation choppy on a slow computer.

3. Make sure that you'll see the effects of any crashes: On the Aircraft menu, click Realism Settings. Then select the Can Collide With Dynamic Scenery check box.

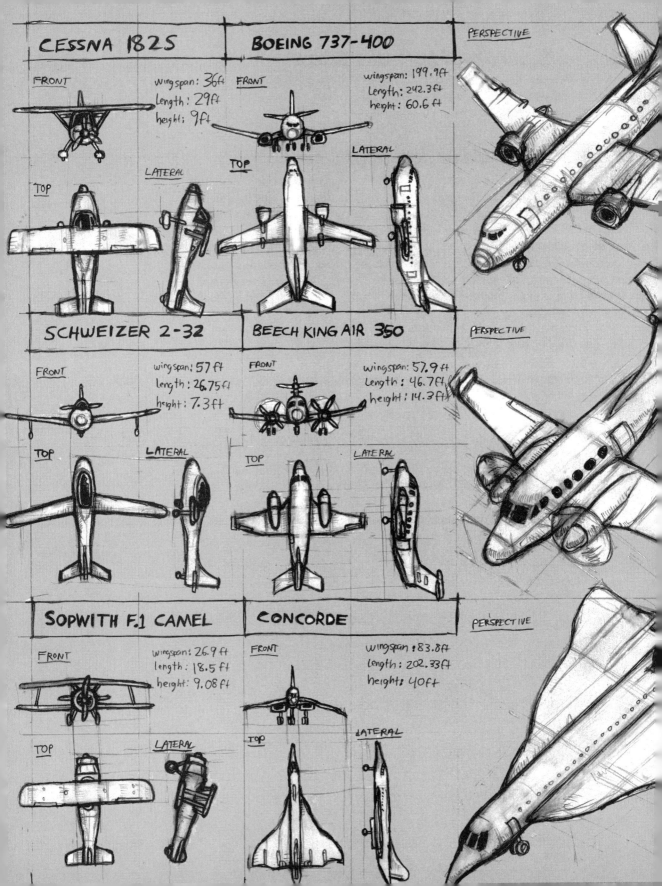

CESSNA 182S

FRONT

wingspan: 36ft
Length: 29ft
height: 9ft

TOP

LATERAL

BOEING 737-400

FRONT

wingspan: 199.9ft
Length: 242.3ft
height: 60.6ft

LATERAL

TOP

PERSPECTIVE

SCHWEIZER 2-32

FRONT

wingspan: 57ft
Length: 26.75ft
height: 7.3ft

TOP

LATERAL

BEECH KING AIR 350

FRONT

wingspan: 57.9ft
Length: 46.7ft
height: 14.3ft

TOP

LATERAL

PERSPECTIVE

SOPWITH F.1 CAMEL

FRONT

wingspan: 26.9ft
Length: 18.5ft
height: 9.08ft

TOP

LATERAL

CONCORDE

FRONT

wingspan: 83.8ft
Length: 202.33ft
height: 40ft

TOP

LATERAL

PERSPECTIVE

PART III

Microsoft Flight Simulator Professional

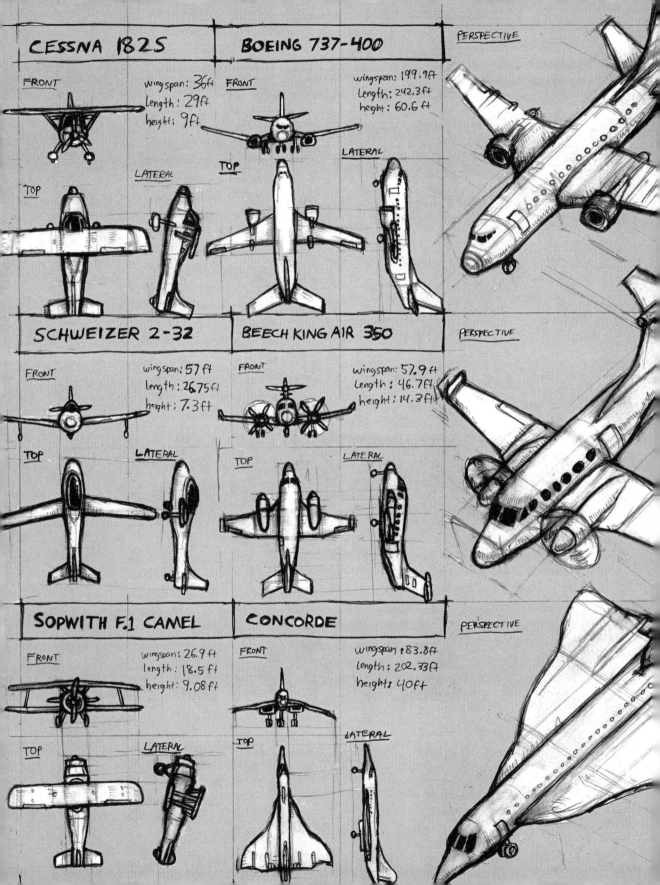

CESSNA 182S

FRONT

wingspan: 36ft
length: 29ft
height: 9ft

TOP

LATERAL

BOEING 737-400

FRONT

wingspan: 199.9ft
length: 242.3ft
height: 60.6ft

TOP

LATERAL

PERSPECTIVE

SCHWEIZER 2-32

FRONT

wingspan: 57ft
length: 26.75ft
height: 7.3ft

TOP

LATERAL

BEECH KING AIR 350

FRONT

wingspan: 57.9ft
length: 46.7ft
height: 14.3ft

TOP

LATERAL

PERSPECTIVE

SOPWITH F.1 CAMEL

FRONT

wingspan: 26.9ft
length: 18.5ft
height: 9.08ft

TOP

LATERAL

CONCORDE

FRONT

wingspan: 83.8ft
length: 202.33ft
height: 40ft

TOP

LATERAL

PERSPECTIVE

Chapter Ten

The Aircraft Editor

This chapter takes you on a brief tour of the Microsoft Flight Simulator 2000 Aircraft Editor, which is included with the Professional Edition of Flight Simulator 2000. The Aircraft Editor is a powerful tool that allows you to construct instrument panels and edit the flight dynamics of each aircraft. It also allows you to replace the textures of the aircraft, or the "skin," (see "Editing the Aircraft's Appearance" later in the chapter) and adjust the sounds the aircraft generates—from the way the aircraft sounds when the flaps are lowered to the way the engine sputters. You can even insert your own custom sounds. In short, the Aircraft Editor allows you to tinker with the aircraft in Flight Simulator 2000 in ways that would be impossible in real life.

Getting Started with the Aircraft Editor

The Aircraft Editor is a separate application, so Flight Simulator 2000 does not need to be running in order for you to use it. To get started click FS2000 Aircraft Editor from the Flight Simulator 2000 program folder on the Start menu.

Once in the editor, you can access the editing area of a particular aircraft by clicking its name in the Aircraft folder in the left-hand pane (as shown in Figure 10-1). In the Aircraft folder, you see a list of all the aircraft available to be edited (which is the entire roster of aircraft).

To customize one of the aircraft, double-click the one you'd like to work with (let's use the Cessna Skylane 182 RG). The selected aircraft will expand showing the four aircraft characteristics that can be customized: Panel, Sound, Texture, and Flight Dynamics. (See Figure 10-2.) Notice that each aircraft is marked "(read-only)" by default to prevent you from rendering the original planes unusable. The first thing you need to do is create your own plane using an existing plane as the starting point. With the Cessna Skylane 182 RG

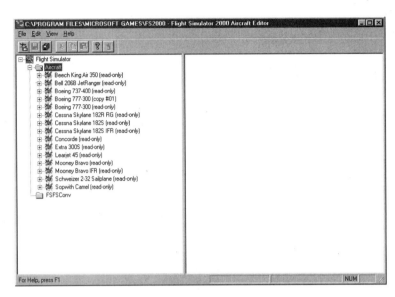

Figure 10-1 *By clicking the Aircraft folder in the Aircraft Editor you can see the list of aircraft that you can modify.*

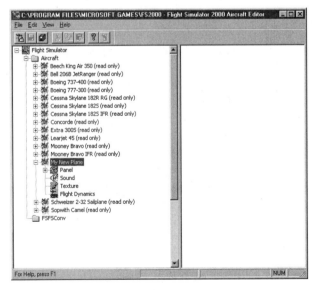

Figure 10-2 *In Aircraft Editor, you see aircraft characteristics you can edit: Panel, Sound, Texture, and Flight Dynamics.*

selected, click Save Copy As from the File menu and enter a new name for your aircraft in the Save Copy As dialog box. You should now have a new aircraft that you can customize, modeled after the Cessna Skylane 182 RG, in the left-hand pane.

Double-click your new aircraft in the left-hand pane to view the aircraft's characteristics. When you click Panel or one of the other aircraft characteristics, the right-hand pane of the Aircraft Editor will allow you to customize the settings for the selected characteristic. The remainder of this chapter will describe the details of customizing your new aircraft's characteristics.

Editing the Aircraft's Instrument Panel

When you click the Panel item in the left-hand pane of the Aircraft Editor, the right-hand pane allows you to customize the selected aircraft's instrument panel and to experiment with unusual and otherwise unattainable instrument setups. (See Figure 10-3.) The editor also allows you to

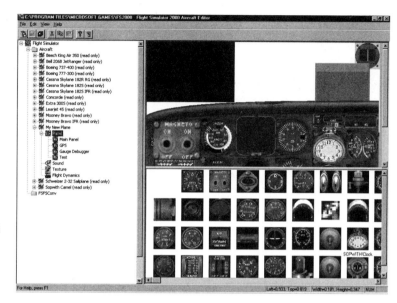

Figure 10-3　*The Aircraft Editor allows you to get creative with instrument panel designs.*

create special training panels, which you can use to practice flying using instrument flight rules (IFR) with limited instrumentation. This section takes a look at these two reasons for customizing an aircraft's instrument panel.

Making a Training Instrument Panel

You can set up training panels to create the experience of flying without certain instruments. Use this feature in the editor to configure your aircraft's instrument panel in a way that forces you to fly using instruments you are not otherwise accustomed to. Many pilots become dependent on one or more instruments to fly in instrument conditions rather than take advantage of the entire range of instruments before them. The most obvious abuse of this is trying to control the aircraft with just the altimeter and heading indicator rather than spending the majority of the time looking at the attitude indicator and checking the other instruments as needed. The attitude indicator will show a change in

Figure 10-4   *A Cessna Skylane 182 RG panel with the attitude indicator removed.*

pitch or bank long before the altimeter and heading indicator show any changes. However, if your aircraft experiences a failure of the vacuum pump, both the attitude indicator and the heading indicator will no longer function properly. It's good to practice flying "partial panel"— that is, flying without those two instruments—using the others (especially the turn coordinator and vertical speed indicator) to remain in control. Try creating a panel without the attitude and heading indicators (as shown in Figure 10-4) and see how you do!

Improving the Cessna's Instrument Panel

As an example of the kind of tasks you can perform with the Aircraft Editor, I'll show you how to replace the heading indicator in a Cessna Skylane 182 RG with the horizontal situation indicator (HSI) from a Beech King Air 350. By borrowing instruments from existing aircraft in Flight Simulator 2000, you can create your dream instrument panel in the aircraft you most enjoy flying. Here's how to go about changing the Cessna's heading indicator to an HSI:

1. Start the Aircraft Editor by clicking FS2000 Aircraft Editor from the Flight Simulator 2000 program folder on the Start menu.

2. If necessary double-click the Aircraft folder to expand it and then double-click the new aircraft you created in the Getting Started with the Aircraft Editor section.

3. Double-click your new aircraft's Panel item to expand it, and then select the Main Panel item in the left-hand pane. (See Figure 10-5.) When you select the Main Panel item in the left-hand pane, the editor will display the aircraft's instrument panel and a list of available instruments

to choose from. Simply click the instrument's picture in the list below to see its name.

4. Right-click the heading indicator on the instrument panel displayed in the right-hand pane, and click Delete in the menu that appears. (See Figure 10-6.) Note that some instruments like this heading indicator don't look the same in the editor as they do in the simulator.

5. Find the Beech King Air 350 HSI in the instrument list below and drag it up to the spot now vacated by the

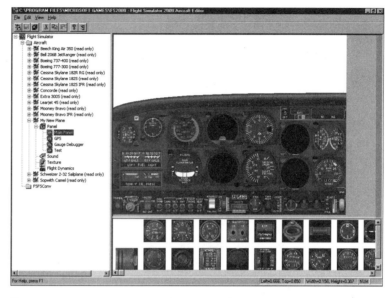

Figure 10-5   *You'll be making changes on the Main Panel.*

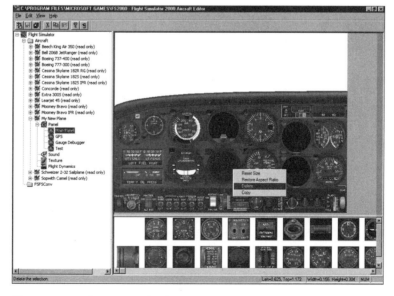

Figure 10-6   *Right-click the heading indicator and delete it.*

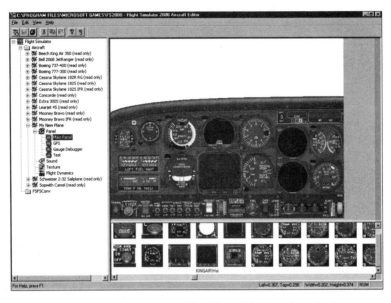

Figure 10-7 *Moving the Beech King Air 350 HSI up into the instrument panel is as easy as clicking and dragging.*

> **Note:** *Although customizing your instrument panel might make it more useful, it won't necessarily make it more attractive. The new gauges don't exactly fit like a glove.*

heading indicator. (See Figure 10-7.)

6. Now that the HSI is in place, you'll notice that it's too big for the spot. Use your mouse to resize the HSI window and place it where you like.

7. Save your work by clicking Save All on the File menu. Click Fly this Plane! on the File menu to launch Flight Simulator 2000 and try your new instrument panel (as shown in Figure 10-8).

Editing the Aircraft's Sound

This part of the editor allows you to modify the sounds made by the aircraft. Each aircraft has a set of predefined sounds for the various noises such as when the flaps are moved. Select the Sound item for your new aircraft in the left-hand pane of the editor, and use the right-hand pane to assign different sound files for any of the predefined sounds. (See Figure 10-9.) To modify a sound, simply right-click the sound you want to change and then click either Change Sound, Play Sound, or Remove Sound in the menu that appears.

Editing the Aircraft's Appearance

This part of the editor allows you to replace the textures (or visual skins) of an aircraft. (See Figure 10-10.) I wouldn't recommend this feature for anyone who isn't familiar with a graphics editing program, but there are no doubt many new textures (skins) available on the Internet that you can find to give your Boeing 777-300 (or any other aircraft) a new look.

Editing the Aircraft's Flight Dynamics

The Flight Dynamics Editor allows you to adjust different aspects of each aircraft's flight dynamics. Although each aspect can be

Figure 10-8   *Here it is, a Skylane 182 RG with a King Air 350 HSI.*

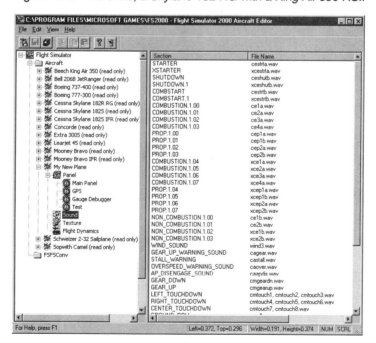

Figure 10-9   *The Aircraft Editor allows you to select your own .wav files to alter the sounds of an aircraft.*

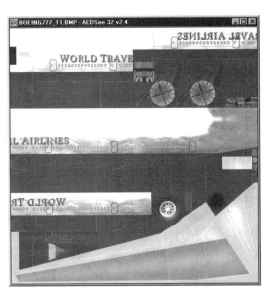

Figure 10-10   *Here's the .bmp file showing the skin of the Boeing 777-300.*

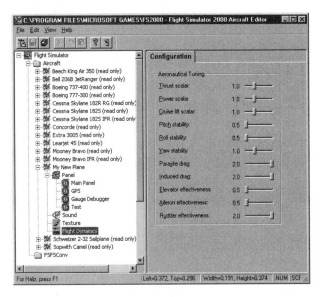

Figure 10-11   *The Aircraft Editor allows you to adjust the flight dynamics of an aircraft.*

modified, how each affects the individual aircraft varies. Rather than go into too much detail on the variations, I suggest you play around with these settings and have some fun with them. To modify flight dynamics, se-lect your new aircraft in the left-hand pane and expand it if necessary, and then select Flight Dynamics; a flight dynamics tuning area appears on the right-hand pane of the editor. (See Figure 10-11.) The follow-ing sections describe each of the flight dynamic aspects you can modify in the editor.

Thrust and Power Scalar

These two sliders are the main variables with which you can affect the aircraft's performance. The Thrust Scalar, when adjusted to the right (a value of 2.0), gives the Cessna an unbelievable punch on the takeoff run. You can literally double the thrust of your aircraft with this control.

The Power Scalar works in much the same way as thrust, except rather than giving your aircraft more acceleration "punch," it allows you to climb at a much faster rate (more feet per second). Of course, lowering these sliders will decrease your performance dramatically as well, so do so with caution.

Cruise Lift Scalar

This slider affects the amount of lift created in cruise flight. What this means is that if you set the value higher than normal, your engine won't have to work as hard as normal to maintain the same amount of altitude in cruise flight. By increasing the lift in this manner, you lower the stalling speed (usually a good thing), and the aircraft has a harder time losing altitude (which could be bad when you need to get down to land!).

Pitch, Roll, and Yaw Stability

With pitch, roll, and yaw, increased stability makes the aircraft more forgiving, whereas decreased stability tends to make these axes more temperamental, making them more difficult to hold steady. Pitch stability controls the stability of the pitch in the aircraft. The pitch is the movement of the aircraft about its lateral axis, which is also known as nose up or nose down as it relates to the horizon. The slider starts out at 1.0 and can be adjusted between 0.5 and 2.0. The higher the number, the more stable the pitch axis of the aircraft will be; the lower the number, the less stable it will be.

Roll stability controls the stability of the roll in the aircraft. Roll is the movement of the aircraft about its longitudinal axis, which is the bank of the wings. The slider starts out at 1.0 and can be adjusted between 0.5 and 2.0. The higher the number, the more stable the roll axis adjusted the aircraft will be; the lower the number, the less stable it will be.

Yaw stability is the movement of the aircraft about its vertical axis, that is to say, the movement of the nose to the left or right. For example, if you ran a steel pole right down through the top of the aircraft, the aircraft could only swivel left or right. This slider controls the Yaw stability; again, the slider starts out at 1.0 and can be adjusted between 0.5 and 2.0. The higher the number, the more stable the aircraft will be with regard to yaw; the lower the number, the less stable it will be.

Parasite and Induced Drag

Parasite drag is the inherent resistance to air flow over the aircraft's skin, landing gear, radio antennas, and other parts of the aircraft. In fact, any chips in the paint on the aircraft or insects that have stuck on the windshield add to parasite drag. Parasite drag can be adjusted between 0.5 and 2.0. The higher the number, the more parasite drag will affect your aircraft, which in turn can lower your top speed.

Induced drag is the drag that's created by lift. When a plane flies, there's a high-pressure area below the wing and a low-pressure area above the wing. (Creating lift makes flight possible.) The higher-pressure area beneath the wings wants to curl up around the ends of the wings up to the lower pressure area above the wing. This motion of air around the wingtips causes induced drag. Turning the slider up increases induced drag, which affects your stall speed and requires more engine power when you're flying very slowly.

Elevator, Aileron, and Rudder Effectiveness

The Elevator, Aileron, and Rudder sliders regulate the effectiveness of the various control surfaces. When the values are all set to 2.0 (the highest value), you can expect to get better performance out of your control surfaces. Being able to adjust the settings this high can be handy if you are flying a lot in slow flight, a time when the control surfaces are normally too sluggish to respond to control inputs. Likewise, you can reduce the effectiveness of the control surfaces to make slow flight (or any kind of flight for that matter) more challenging.

Chapter Eleven

Advanced Flight Techniques

Advanced techniques and challenges await you in Microsoft Flight Simulator 2000 as you progress in your flying abilities. Aerobatics take you beyond the realm of general aviation by putting the aircraft through trying and challenging maneuvers that require razor-sharp skills (and nerves) to perform properly. This chapter provides step-by-step flight instructions for some of the core aerobatic maneuvers. IFR flight, or instrument flight rules, is the natural progression for private pilots who are extending their training. IFR flight is, for lack of a better description, flying the aircraft using only the instruments rather than using visual cues from outside the cockpit. After touching on the intricacies of IFR and low-visibility flight, the chapter includes a short exercise that demonstrates the dangers of flying in marginal visual flight rules (VFR) conditions.

Aerobatics

For some pilots, flying is about having fun in the sky. It isn't about flying a traffic pattern or getting from point A to point B in the shortest amount of time; it's about strapping a 300-hp engine and a shiny, welded-steel airframe around your body and carving graceful figure eights in the sky. Aerobatic flying, for fun or competition, challenges pilots to fly a series of maneuvers that tests the limits of their airplanes, their flying ability, and even their physical limitations.

After getting a pilot's license, novice pilots might learn about aerobatics as a way of furthering their abilities. This is a great way to learn more about the capabilities of an aircraft, as well as how the various control inputs/surfaces (the rudder, ailerons, and elevator) affect the aircraft's flight. Most importantly, honing aerobatic skills can help pilots recognize when they are in dangerous situations, such as unintentional spins or stalls, and take the appropriate measures to get out of these situations safely.

The first maneuvers that a beginning aerobatics pilot learns are usually variations of the roll. Rolls require the pilot to use the rudder, ailerons, and elevator to smoothly roll along the longitudinal axis of the aircraft inverted and then upright again while maintaining the same heading. Pulling off a tight, clean roll looks very impressive from any view, and gaining confidence in coordinating these control inputs is a valuable skill in itself. When beginning pilots turn themselves flying inverted, the natural impulse for many is to pull on the yoke and execute a high-stress split-S maneuver to bring themselves upright again. But this maneuver can cause the aircraft to lose lots of altitude and can overstress the aircraft. After some aerobatics training, pilots feel comfortable performing a slow half-roll back to level flight, which is a much safer way of exiting inverted flight. Any aerobatics training pays off; it can lead to increased awareness of flight dynamics which leads to safer flying.

Example Aerobatic Stunts

The primary aerobatics plane in Flight Simulator 2000 is the Extra 300S. In real life, aerobatic flight in any aircraft that hasn't been rated for aerobatic maneuvers is courting disaster, as these maneuvers place the pilot in serious danger of overstressing the aircraft. One advantage that Microsoft Flight Simulator 2000 has over real life is that it gives pilots the opportunity to try things they would never do in a real aircraft. If you've already tried aerobatic maneuvers in the Extra or if you're curious about trying them in other aircraft, you can safely put other aircraft to the aerobatic test. The following step-by-step maneuvers use a variety of the aircraft available in Flight Simulator 2000.

To perform most of these maneuvers, the rudder needs to operate independently of the yoke, so click Realism Settings on the Aircraft menu, and in the dialog box that appears, clear the Auto-Rudder check box. You might want to clear the Aircraft Stress Causes Damage check box as well.

> **Note:** *All of the following example rolls are to the right. If you want to roll to the left, reverse the yoke and rudder directions.*

The Aileron Roll

The aileron roll is the easiest of the rolls to perform. The aircraft quickly rolls 360 degrees about its longitudinal axis in a corkscrew-like flight path. It isn't a competition maneuver, but mastering this basic roll is a good introduction to the slow roll and the snap roll, which you'll try later in this chapter. Here's how to do it in a Cessna 182S:

1. Pitch the nose up 20 to 30 degrees above the horizon.

2. Return the yoke to its center position, and then turn the yoke to the right to roll right. Maintain pressure on the yoke until the roll is completed.

3. Try not to let the nose drop much farther than 30 degrees. Pull back slightly on the yoke to return to level flight.

> **Note:** *At the end of this maneuver it is normal for the nose to be 20 to 30 degrees below the horizon.*

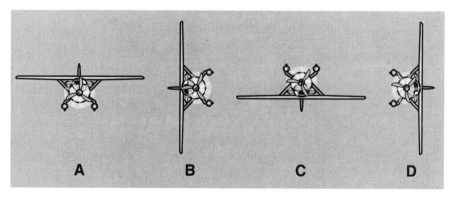

Here's a diagram of the aileron roll.

The Slow Roll

The slow roll can be challenging for the novice aerobatics pilot. It is a controlled maneuver in which you maintain a constant roll rate and continue along a straight line until the aircraft is level again. The maneuver provides valuable experience in coordinating the ailerons, elevator, and rudder to maintain control over the aircraft's heading and attitude. Try the Sopwith Camel for this maneuver.

1. Start out at 3000 feet. Pick a reference point on the horizon, or note the heading on the compass at the start of the maneuver.

2. Turn the yoke to bank the aircraft to the right, using a little bit of right rudder. As the bank angle increases past 45 degrees, start to add more and more left rudder to maintain altitude.

> **Tip:** *Some competitions require that the roll be stopped at various points so that the aircraft continues along its line of flight with the wings banked at 45 degrees, and then 90 degrees, and so on. Use rudder in the direction opposite of the bank to maintain your line of flight with the wings banked.*

3. As you roll inverted and continue until you're upright, you will have to constantly adjust the rudder and elevator to maintain your heading and altitude, although when you're sideways, the rudder will affect altitude and the elevator will affect heading.

4. The Sopwith Camel tends to drop its nose below the horizon in the final quarter of the roll, so watch the horizon and correct by using rudder in the direction of the bank.

The Snap Roll

The snap roll is a high-speed intermediate-level aerobatic maneuver that is a lot of fun to perform. In a snap roll, one wing of the aircraft is stalled (meaning it's not providing any lift, while the other wing is providing lift), and the aircraft

rotates about that wing while traveling along the same line of flight. The best plane to use for this maneuver is the Extra 300S; it rolls fast and it's specifically designed for aerobatics.

1. Start out in level flight at 5000 feet, at full throttle. Make note of the heading.

2. Pull back on the yoke while simultaneously applying full right aileron and full right rudder. The airplane should stall, flip over, and then return to level flight.

3. This flip and return to level flight can happen very quickly, so be ready to release pressure on the controls as soon as the plane performs one rotation and returns to level flight.

4. End the maneuver with the aircraft on the same heading.

The Immelmann

The Immelmann originated in World War I aerial combat as a way to trade speed for altitude. It's a great defensive maneuver in air combat because it turns the pursued into the pursuer. The aircraft starts out at high

The Loop

A loop is a basic aerobatic maneuver much like a loop on a rollercoaster. You fly the aircraft up, upside down, down, and then head back to where you started (all in a straight line—that is, without turning from left to right). Practice this with all the aircraft in Microsoft Flight Simulator 2000; this maneuver can get especially challenging in the Boeing 777-300!

speed and ends up several hundred feet higher, in the opposite direction, where you execute a climbing half-loop and then an aileron roll to return to level flight. The Sopwith Camel is the perfect aircraft in which to try this maneuver.

1. Increase the throttle to pick up some airspeed.

2. Bring your altitude to at least 3000 feet above ground level (AGL).

3. At 160 knots, pull back on the yoke to bring the nose above the horizon. The Sopwith Camel lacks an attitude indicator, so do your best to pull the yoke straight back to keep the plane from rolling. As the nose starts to drop toward the horizon, the aircraft will be inverted.

4. Perform a half-roll to return the plane to straight and level flight. This will require a little bit of rudder pressure in the direction opposite the ailerons until the plane gets close to 90 degrees from vertical. Pull back on the yoke as you complete the roll to keep the nose from dropping.

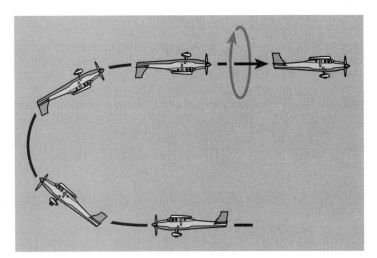

At the end of this maneuver, the plane will have gained about 300 to 500 feet in altitude and will be close to its stall speed. The temperamental flight characteristics of the Sopwith Camel will keep you more than busy trying to avoid flying out of control when attempting any maneuver.

Here's a diagram of the Immelmann maneuver.

The Split-S

This maneuver also has its origins in aerial combat. In contrast to the Immelmann, the split-S trades altitude for speed. The aircraft loses altitude and ends up facing the opposite direction by executing a half aileron roll to inverted and then a diving half-loop to return to level flight. In combat, the split-S can be used as an evasive tactic. It can also be used very effectively in a surprise attack; if the sun is directly behind an attacker's plane, the plane is much harder to spot, as it will blend into the sun. Try this with the Sopwith Camel.

> **Tip:** *The Sopwith Camel might go into a fast spin while you're trying various maneuvers. If this happens, cut the throttle, push forward on the yoke, and apply rudder in the direction opposite of the spin. As the spin begins to stop, center the rudder so that you don't start a spin in the opposite direction. Start the Immelmann above 3000 feet to give yourself a margin of safety.*

1. At the end of this maneuver, the plane will have lost about 500 feet of altitude, so start out above 3000 feet.

2. Turn the yoke to the right, and roll the plane inverted; you should add some right rudder as you start the roll. Try to keep the nose level with the horizon, using both the elevator and the rudder as needed.

3. After the aircraft is inverted, pull back on the yoke to start the dive, making sure the wings are level.

4. Maintain back pressure on the yoke as the nose drops, and smoothly relax your grip on the yoke as the nose comes back up toward the horizon.

5. End the maneuver facing 180 degrees from the original heading.

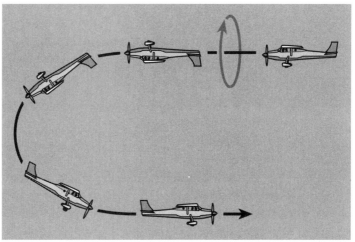

Diagram of the split-S.

The Wingover

The wingover is a competition maneuver in glider aerobatics. The glider starts out in level flight and then gradually starts a climbing turn with an increasing angle of bank until the aircraft is nearly perpendicular to the ground, at a 90-degree bank angle. The outside wing passes over the top as the glider's nose drops, and the aircraft returns to level flight, at the original altitude and heading but in the opposite direction. Try this maneuver in the Schweizer Sailplane.

1. Start out in level flight at 4500 feet.

2. Pull back on the yoke to pitch the nose above the horizon. At the same time, turn the yoke to the right to bank the aircraft.

Note: *As the bank angle exceeds 45 degrees, the nose will start to drop as the bank angle continues to increase. Halfway through the maneuver, the aircraft is 90 degrees from its original heading, the fuselage is level with the horizon, and the bank angle is 90 degrees.*

3. As the nose of the aircraft continues to drop below the horizon, decrease the pressure on the yoke to lessen the bank angle.

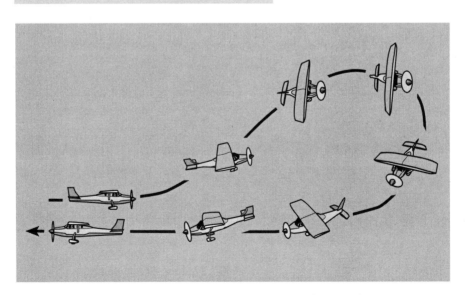

Diagram of the wingover maneuver.

4. When the bank drops below 45 degrees, pull back on the yoke to bring the nose back up toward the horizon.

5. At the end of the maneuver, return the aircraft to level flight, at its original altitude and 180 degrees from its original heading.

It might be difficult to judge the success of this maneuver, particularly if you are unfamiliar with how it's supposed to look. Try this maneuver over an airport so that you can see it close-up from the tower view. Add the tower view to the cockpit view by pointing to New View on the Views menu and then clicking Tower. Use the plus (+) and minus (–) keys to zoom in or out, respectively, to keep the sailplane in view.

> **Tip:** *If you try the wingover with a powered aircraft, pull the throttle to idle as you enter the maneuver.*

The Outside Loop

The outside loop is one of the most difficult and dangerous aerobatic maneuvers when performed in a large jet (as is any aerobatic maneuver). It's also a very exciting stunt to perform. In an outside loop, the pilot is on the outer rim of the loop, as opposed to on the inside as in an ordinary loop. The outside loop is an altitude-losing maneuver, made even more hazardous by our choice of aircraft: the Boeing 737-400 jet. Enter this maneuver by pointing the nose of the aircraft straight down and then continuing through the loop with you (the pilot) on the outside. The fact that you are diving straight down to start the loop makes it a little more dangerous.

1. To prevent the wings from being ripped off of your 737 (considered bad form, especially when carrying passengers) while performing this maneuver, make sure to clear the Aircraft Stress Causes Damage check box in the aircraft Realism Settings dialog box.

2. You need a lot of speed to carry the 737 through the loop. This maneuver also loses a lot of altitude, so start out at 40,000 feet. Increase the throttle to full, and dive to about 35,000 feet to build up the airspeed.

3. Start the maneuver at 480 to 500 knots to avoid stalling in the loop. A good indicator is the overstress warning. When the alarm sounds, start the dive by pushing the yoke forward.

4. Continue pushing forward on the yoke until the nose is straight down, and then maintain forward pressure on the yoke while the aircraft levels horizontally, on its back.

5. The remainder of the loop is the most difficult part because after the nose rises above the horizon, you lose your fixed reference point. Continue applying forward pressure on the yoke to bring the aircraft up over the top of the loop.

6. In the last quarter of the loop, the aircraft tends to roll onto its side. Try to keep the wings perfectly level; use the attitude indicator to judge how level your wings are. If you started the maneuver with enough airspeed, you should be able to return the plane to straight and level flight just above the stall speed.

The Inverted Outside Loop

If you thought the outside loop was difficult, try this even more challenging variation, which starts when the plane is inverted. Try the inverted outside loop in the Extra 300S. For this maneuver, the additional speed and maneuverability of the Extra 300S help power you through the loop, but it's still very challenging to keep the plane's wings level throughout the maneuver.

1. Instead of diving, start the inverted outside loop at about 3000 feet, and open the throttle all the way.

2. Perform a half-roll to inverted flight, and push forward on the yoke to bring the nose above the horizon.

3. As in the outside loop, in this quadrant it's easy to let the plane roll to one side or the other after the horizon is no longer in view. To avoid an unintentional roll, make sure that the wings are perfectly level at the start of the loop, and then push the yoke straight forward and use some rudder to counteract any torque-induced roll. Watch the attitude indicator to help keep the aircraft level.

4. At the top of the loop, the attitude indicator will flip over as the plane's nose descends toward the horizon. After the aircraft is upright and facing 180 degrees from the starting direction, continue putting forward pressure on the yoke to put the aircraft into a dive, again using rudder and ailerons, if necessary, to prevent any roll.

5. At the end of this maneuver, the aircraft will be inverted and facing the original heading. Perform a half-roll to return to straight and level flight.

IFR Flight

IFR flight and navigation are an important step in a pilot's progression in her craft. Instrument flight rules piloting and navigation are complicated because flying around without being able to see outside the window of your aircraft is a tall order for any pilot. Anything less than a 1000-foot ceiling and 3 miles of visibility is considered IFR flight, and you'll need a special rating on your pilot's license to be able to fly in such conditions. IFR flight also requires that you

> **Tip:** *For more in-depth information about IFR flight and IFR navigation, consult* Flight Simulator 2000's *Help system as well as tutorials by Rod Machado in the* Flight Simulator 2000 *Pilot's Handbook.*

have an aircraft with the proper instrumentation for IFR flight. This section looks at IFR flight in general and supplies some interesting and informative insights from an experienced commercial airline pilot, Captain Ron Hunt.

> *Aviation in itself is not inherently dangerous. But to an even greater degree than the sea, it is terribly unforgiving of any carelessness, incapacity or neglect.*
>
> *—Author unknown*

While this quotation can be applied to any aspect of aviation, it's extremely true of IFR flight. It is perhaps the best advice for any private pilot and for anyone who is learning to fly. Captain Ron Hunt says, "An instrument rating is the most important addition any pilot can add to their pilots' license. This you can bet your life on; without it you just might someday!"

IFR Flight and the Instrument Rating

Of all the requirements for flying IFR in any aircraft, perhaps the most important and most difficult to fulfill is the pilot's instrument rating, which is the rating on a pilot's license that allows you to fly in IFR conditions. But for a safe IFR flight, the instrument rating alone won't suffice. The pilot must consider a variety of issues before taking off in IFR conditions.

First, even though many single-engine aircraft are very well equipped to fly using just their instruments, the pilot must weigh the risks of flying IFR in a single-engine aircraft. (See Figure 11-1.) What is the terrain along the route of flight? Does the aircraft have the performance to safely handle or outclimb terrain that you can't see? What can you expect to see if you lose an engine when you come gliding out of the clouds? What are your options if your equipment or radio fails? Do these risks outweigh your abilities and the need to get to the destination? Only the pilot's experience and good judgment can address these issues. Luckily, Flight Simulator 2000 affords you the luxury of experimenting with IFR flight that new pilots in the real world don't have, so you can hone your instrument skills in the safety and comfort of your own home.

Weather

You might have heard the saying, "If you don't like the weather, just wait a little while; it'll change." This is especially true for flying, and now it's also true in Flight Simulator 2000. You can customize your own weather situation by selecting the World menu, clicking Weather, and then clicking the Advanced Weather button.

Figure 11-1   *The Cessna 182S IFR is well equipped for IFR flight.*

When you plan an IFR flight, you must consider every aspect of the current weather as well as forecasts and worst case "what if" scenarios.

- What if the ceiling and visibility drop below your personal comfort level?
- What is the freezing level? Is there a possibility of icing conditions?
- What alternate routes are available? How far will you have to fly to find better weather if you run into problems or unexpected changes in weather at your destination?
- How will the weather affect your ability to conduct the approach once you arrive at the destination?
- Will there be strong crosswinds or a possibility of windshear?

- Will the runway be wet and slippery?
- Will the wind allow you to use the approach you need to the runway in use?
- Will you arrive at night?
- Do you have all the necessary charts and airport information?

Flying IFR in Small vs. Large Aircraft

These are certainly considerations that need to be made by the newly rated instrument pilot, but all of these questions must be taken into account regardless of whether you're flying a single-engine Cessna 182S or a Boeing 777-300. The only real difference is the experience level of the pilot in command. How can that be true if the 777-300 is so much more sophisticated than the single-engine Cessna 182S? Consider the following scenario.

A Cessna 182S and a Boeing 777-300 arrive in the terminal area at a major international airport late at night. The weather is variable with a ceiling of 600 feet and 2 miles visibility. Because of maintenance and runway closures, the approach in use is a VOR (very high frequency omnidirectional radio range) approach to runway 9. The Cessna 182S and the 777-300 will fly the same approach in the same weather to the same runway with virtually the same minimums. (Minimums refer to the minimum visibility, cloud height off the ground, etc.) In this scenario, the 777-300 has no advantage. The only difference in handling this approach in these circumstances is the experience level of the pilot or pilots in command.

Note: *For more information on VOR, see the online Help and the VOR approach tutorial or the VOR navigation tutorial in the Flight Simulator 2000* Pilot's Handbook.

Most general aviation pilots will seldom fully (and the key word here is *fully*) use an instrument rating. By fully, I mean that it's not that common for general aviation pilots to be put in a situation in which they have to use every skill they learned when getting instrument rated.

But a pilot's instrument rating increases his ability to master the pursuit of aviation. Through the instruments, the pilot's vision is extended beyond what he can see out the windshield. The instruments might even make the difference between life and death if someday the weather quickly takes a turn for the worse.

Flying in Low-Visibility Conditions

When a small plane goes down in low-visibility conditions, the reasons are often much more shocking to the layperson than to pilots, most of whom have seen or heard of incidents like this far too often. "VFR into IMC," the investigative body often concludes about the cause of the crash. Flying under visual flight rules into IMC (instrument

Becoming an IFR Pilot

Getting an instrument rating requires many hours of instrument instruction, a written test, and a check ride with an inspector of the Federal Aviation Administration (FAA) or the equivalent, depending on what country you live in. Training is usually conducted in simulated instrument conditions by placing a hood over the student's head to restrict his or her view outside the aircraft. Instrument flight simulators can be used for some of the required training, and later an instructor might take advantage of actual instrument conditions (in a real plane), if the opportunity presents itself.

During this training the pilot learns to safely control the aircraft by using aircraft instruments, maps, and approach charts. Throughout all the instrument training, pilots are never alone in the airplane in instrument conditions. They are always with an experienced instructor, and usually they can quickly take off the instrument hood and look outside the window to gain their bearings. The first real instrument flight alone is a big step and can be very stressful. Flying the airplane, managing the radios, and navigating with the maps and charts require solid organization.

meteorological conditions, which in some countries is called IFR conditions) is one of the most common causes of small airplane crashes. Simply put, new or inexperienced pilots can very quickly get in over their heads when they try to fly in fog or other low-visibility conditions that demand instrument training.

IFR Troubles

One of my flight school instructors told us a story of several inexperienced student pilots who were put in simulators in IFR conditions. According to the instructor, it took on average less than a minute for each of the students to lose control of the aircraft. This account might seem unbelievable, but I can tell you from experience that what your body thinks is happening to the aircraft is usually not what's really happening. Such a disconnection happened when an experienced pilot was taking off in a jetliner at night with no visual cues such as the horizon. As the aircraft accelerated, he trimmed the aircraft nose-down because his body was telling him that the nose was going up (a common sensation when accelerating). In the end, he trimmed the aircraft so far nose-down that it flew into the ground before he could recover.

Why is it so disorienting to fly in IMC? First of all, it's easy to lose sight of the horizon. Without this very important visual cue, a VFR pilot can lose track of the plane's attitude and fail to realize that she is in a dangerous situation until it is too late. Compounding this problem is the fact that VFR pilots typically fly low, about 3000 to 4000 feet AGL, so that they can better spot land-marks on the terrain. A pilot might believe that the plane is in a climb, or a banking turn, even though the airplane's in-struments show that the plane is level. It is very difficult to ignore the signals that the in-ner ear sends to the brain and to concentrate solely on the instruments. If a pilot feels that the plane is climbing when it is in fact level, and she therefore pitches the nose down to correct it, the plane will enter a dive. If the plane is in a dive or a spiraling turn but the pilot believes that the plane is flying level, she might not take any action to correct the situation until it is too late.

Finally, VFR navigation involves looking for landmarks such as rivers, high-ways, and topographical features, and IMC makes it nearly impossible to navi-gate this way. The blurring of the terrain makes it much harder to pick up specific features such as trees or buildings that would help in judging altitude. The cockpit is a busy place. An instrument rating gives pilots an understanding

of the plane's instruments and teaches pilots how to interpret the readings. Pilots without an instrument rating and the flight hours to back it up might simply fail to notice crucial information on the instrument panel while they're trying to gain their bearings.

How can a pilot get into a dangerous situation like this in the first place? For VFR flight, FAA regulations state that visibility must be at least 3 miles and the cloud cover must be at least 1000 feet AGL. But these minimum conditions make VFR flight marginal at best. Sometimes pilots feel pressured to keep a certain schedule or to get to their destination that day. If a pilot has flown successfully in similar conditions a number of times in the past, he or she might feel he can handle these marginal conditions, even if the conditions are truly beyond the pilot's ability. If conditions are marginal, it doesn't take much of a change in weather to move from VFR conditions to IMC. It pays to be conservative on the ground. There's a common aviation saying: "It's better to be on the ground wishing you were up in the air than be in the air wishing you were on the ground."

Disorientation Exercise

To get a sense of how visually disorienting it is to fly in marginal VFR conditions, you can set up this situation in Microsoft Flight Simulator 2000:

1. Start out in Meigs Field, Chicago, or anywhere near a large body of water.

2. On the World menu, point to Weather, and then click Advanced. You can specify a low layer of stratus clouds from 1000 feet to 4000 feet. (These figures are AGL, so if you're not starting out at sea level, add the field elevation to these figures.)

3. Set the Visibility slider to specify a visibility of 1 km.

4. Set the precipitation to Very High.

5. Take off, climb to about 1000 feet, and try to follow the terrain.

6. After following the terrain for a few minutes, turn out to sea.

Figure 11-2 *Borderline VFR conditions can be downright scary, especially when you're already in the air and this is all you can see!*

You can now see what happens as the horizon disappears from view. (See Figure 11-2.) Also make the attitude indicator inoperative by clicking System Failures on the Aircraft menu and selecting the Failed check box for the Attitude Indicator. Can you keep the aircraft level by looking out the window or by relying on the altimeter and VSI (vertical speed indicator)? Can you tell if you are in a dive or a climb? Keep in mind that a large component of pilot disorientation occurs when your sense of balance conflicts with what your eyes are telling you, and this distortion can't be fully appreciated in a flight simulator.

PART IV

Appendixes

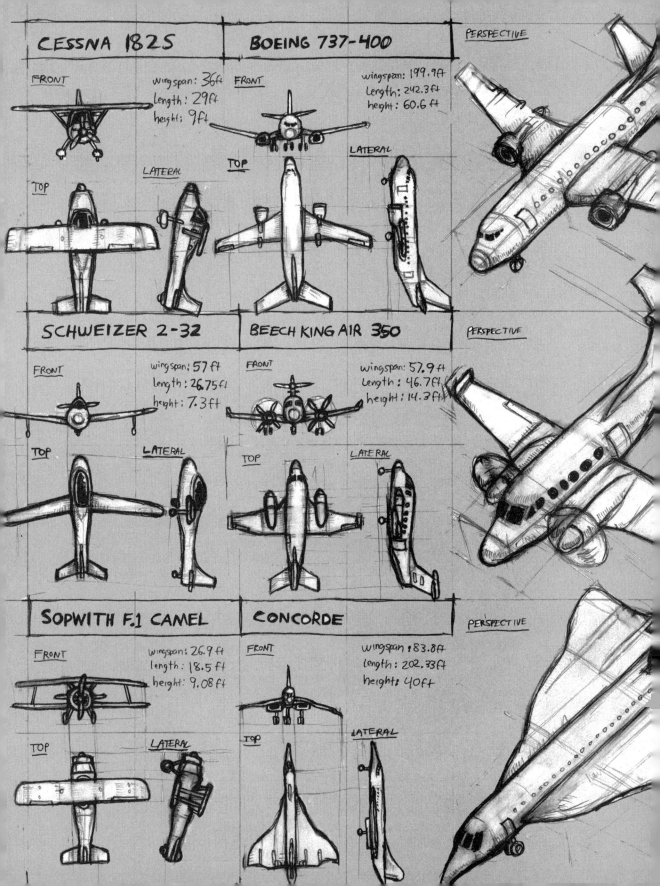

CESSNA 182S

FRONT

wingspan: 36ft
length: 29ft
height: 9ft

TOP

LATERAL

BOEING 737-400

FRONT

wingspan: 199.9ft
length: 242.3ft
height: 60.6ft

TOP

LATERAL

PERSPECTIVE

SCHWEIZER 2-32

FRONT

wingspan: 57ft
length: 26.75ft
height: 7.3ft

TOP

LATERAL

BEECH KING AIR 350

FRONT

wingspan: 57.9ft
length: 46.7ft
height: 14.3ft

TOP

LATERAL

PERSPECTIVE

SOPWITH F.1 CAMEL

FRONT

wingspan: 26.9ft
length: 18.5ft
height: 9.08ft

TOP

LATERAL

CONCORDE

FRONT

wingspan: 83.8ft
length: 202.33ft
height: 40ft

TOP

LATERAL

PERSPECTIVE

Appendix A

Controllers and Other Peripherals

Even though Microsoft Flight Simulator 2000 was developed to reproduce flight with the utmost realism, at the end of the day, flying a virtual aircraft with a keyboard and mouse can't capture the true flying experience. After all, you won't find a mouse near the left seat (or pilot's seat) of an aircraft! If you want the most realistic experience while using Flight Simulator, get a joystick, a flight yoke, or even rudder pedals. To guide you through the vast selection of controllers available, this appendix takes a look at flight yokes, joysticks, throttles, and rudder pedals. Each section highlights my selection of several of the products available and their main features. These are only suggestions and are certainly not meant to be an all-encompassing exploration of these products.

> **Note:** *If your third-party joystick or flight controller isn't working properly, the problem might lie with the driver for the controller. Make sure you have the latest software drivers for your controller. The best way to track down new drivers is to download them from the Internet. See the end of this appendix for a list of Web sites of game controller manufacturers.*

Flight Yokes

Using a flight yoke is the best way to make the flight simulator experience as realistic as possible. You can fly adequately using just the keyboard, but in real life pilots don't press keyboard keys to fly—they use a yoke or a flight stick. Fortunately, flight yokes are less expensive than they were a couple of years ago, while their selection and availability have

> **Note:** *Flight yokes are generally more expensive than joysticks; they usually cost from $80 up to several hundred dollars, whereas joysticks can be found as low as $20.*

USB: The Wave of the Future

The current trend in peripheral connectivity is to use universal serial bus (USB) devices. USB has several advantages over the old system of data transfer, which required plugging a joystick into the game port usually found on a sound card.

- *USB allows information to quickly travel between the joystick and the computer.*
- *A USB device can be hot swapped, or connected and disconnected while the computer is turned on.*
- *USB devices have cross-platform compatibility—that is, you can use the same joysticks on a Microsoft Windows–based computer or a Macintosh.*
- *The extra information that can be transferred across a USB interface means that USB devices can have more buttons and control axes available to them. This means that you can have a flight yoke that includes propeller pitch and fuel mixture knobs that work!*

Most new computers now come with a USB port, which can connect up to 127 peripherals. Because the USB interface allows for data to be exchanged between the peripheral and the PC at a faster rate, USB flight yokes more closely represent the yokes used in true flight.

increased, making for a windfall of great choices for the Flight Simulator enthusiast.

When shopping for a flight yoke, you should look for several qualities beyond the normal "look and feel" qualities (which are largely a matter of personal opinion). Look for a flight yoke that has many buttons and levers. With more controls to customize, you can control the aircraft more from the yoke than from the keyboard. You can perform basic tasks as well as fly the aircraft with a yoke that has many axes of control (slider switches such as the throttle and fuel mixture) and buttons and hat switches (fixed switches that move in four directions under your thumb). The following sections describe some of the controllers available, although this is not a comprehensive list of controllers. There are constantly new products on store shelves, so it's best to compare feature for feature and make your own decisions.

Virtual Pilot Pro

The Virtual Pilot Pro, by CH Products, has endured to become the granddaddy of flight yokes. The Virtual Pilot Pro revolutionized the flight simulator world by letting the user control a simulated aircraft with a yoke that is very similar to

the real thing. Although there are newer and fancier flight yokes, the Virtual Pilot Pro is still a solid choice. It features the following:

- Game port connection
- Three control axes, including throttle handle
- Six buttons
- Two 4-way hat switches
- Elevator and aileron trim controls

> **Note:** *In Flight Simulator, you can customize control on joysticks and yokes. Although many of the devices featured here come with special software (noted in each section) that allows you to reassign actions to buttons and other controls, keep in mind that you can do this from within Flight Simulator 2000 as well.*

Flight Sim Yoke PC

This is the current basic model of the Flight Sim Yoke, from CH Products. It connects to your computer via a game port. Released in March 1999, it is remarkably similar to the yoke used in real Cessna 172s and 182s, making it an outstanding addition for re-creating a more realistic flight experience. It features the following:

- Game port connection
- Three control axes
- Fourteen button functions, including separate flap controls and rocker switches (switches that are turned on or off in an up/down manner)
- Four-way hat switch
- Programmable in Windows
- Trim controls

Control Axes

When manufacturers mention the control axes of a particular controller, they refer to its sliding adjustable controls. For example, a two-axis controller will have a yoke that can turn the aircraft left and right and can pitch the aircraft up and down—hence, two axes. A controller with three axes might include a sliding control for the throttle, whereas a controller with five axes of control might also include levers for fuel mixture and propeller control. These axes are all independent of the various hat switches and buttons available on the controller. In general, the more axes, the greater the realism of the flight.

Microsoft
Flight Simulator 2000

Flight Sim Yoke USB

The USB version of the Flight Sim Yoke, from CH Products, sports the same design as the game port–driven Flight Sim Yoke PC, but the USB version adds a few more features, such as connectivity to many (of the newer) Macintosh computers and two extra axes of control. These extra axes control the propeller as well as the fuel mixture settings of the aircraft. A control axis for fuel mixture settings might seem unnecessary, but managing the fuel mixture of the engine is an important part of flying; it can make the flight more realistic. The Flight Sim Yoke USB features the following:

- USB connection
- Five axes of control
- Fourteen button functions, including flaps and rocker switches
- Four-way hat switch
- Programmable in Windows
- Trim controls

G-Force Plus

The G-Force Plus, from Suncom Technologies, Inc., is a hybrid device that can act as a flight yoke as well as a driving wheel. It offers three-axis control and is intended for use mostly with non-military flight simulators (right up our alley!). This yoke can be attached to a table or desk via clamps, but it also sports four solid suction cups for those who don't have a suitable surface for the clamping system. It features the following:

- Game port connection
- Three control axes
- Four buttons
- Programmable in Windows
- Trim controls
- Two mounting methods

Joysticks and Flightsticks

With the exception of the Schweizer Sailplane, the Sopwith Camel, the Bell JetRanger, and the Extra 300S, all of the aircraft in Flight Simulator 2000 are equipped with flight yokes. However, many modern large aircraft (such as the Airbus 320 and Airbus 340) use a similar fly-by-wire stick configuration, so in the absence of a flight yoke, a joystick (sometimes called a flightstick) will certainly suffice. There's a vast selection of suitable joysticks available, but only a few of the popular joysticks are highlighted here.

SideWinder 3D Pro

Microsoft's SideWinder 3D Pro is a great all-around joystick that is chock-full of features that work flawlessly with Flight Simulator 2000:

- Eight programmable buttons
- Eight-way hat switch
- Throttle
- Swivel stick for rudder control

Flightstick Pro

When a basic joystick is all that you need, the Flightstick Pro, from CH Products, is a great choice at a reasonable price. It has a solid and proven design that's been around for years. The Flightstick Pro features the following:

- Game port connection
- Three control axes
- Trigger with three single-fire buttons
- Four-way hat switch
- Trim controls
- Throttle control wheel

Top Gun

ThrustMaster has an extensive line of flight simulator joysticks, but for sheer value and functionality, the Top Gun is a solid choice. If you're looking for a higher-end stick with more functions, ThrustMaster's F-22 Pro would also be a good option, although the price of the F-22 Pro is considerably higher than the price of the Top Gun. The Top Gun offers the following:

- USB or game port connection
- Three control axes
- Three beveled buttons
- Four-way hat switch
- Programmable in Windows
- Weighted base
- Neoprene grip

SFS Flight Controller

The SFS Flight Controller, from Suncom Technologies, Inc., is designed primarily for military flight simulators, but it also performs well with Flight Simulator 2000. Although you will be using the SFS Flight Controller with a civilian flight simulator, joysticks like this are great to have if you use other flight simulator products, especially military simulators. The SFS Flight Controller features the following:

- Game port connection
- Three control axes
- Four buttons that can be triggered by one hand
- Four-way hat switch
- Programmable in Windows
- Trim controls

Saitek X36F

This joystick is sold on its own or in combination with the Saitek X35T throttle (seen later in this appendix). The X36F is also designed primarily as a combat simulator joystick,

but it works admirably in Flight Simulator 2000. Here's the feature set for the X36F:

- Game port connection
- Three control axes
- Four buttons
- Two 8-way hat switches
- Programmable in Windows

Force Feedback Joysticks

> ### The Stick Shaker
>
> *Commercial aircraft (like the large aircraft in Flight Simulator 2000) are equipped with a special stall warning system called a Stick Shaker. This mechanism literally shakes the yoke or stick (depending on the aircraft) when a stall is imminent. The Stick Shaker provides a quick, tactile warning that instantly conveys the seriousness of the situation to the pilot. In Flight Simulator 2000, force feedback joysticks duplicate this system very well.*

Two companies, Microsoft and CH Products, have led the way in the relatively new trend of "force feedback" controllers. Force feedback technology actually causes the joystick to move, making the simulation feel more lifelike. This means that when you perform a tight left turn in a Sopwith Camel, you'll really feel the resistance in the stick! Or when a 737's nose comes up too quickly and a stall is about to happen, the stick shaker mechanism will shimmy the joystick to indicate an impending stall. The tactile feedback is very impressive and adds yet another layer of realism to the simulation.

SideWinder Force Feedback Pro

The Microsoft SideWinder Force Feedback Pro offers fantastic abilities along with a design that lets you handle the stick in your lap rather than on a table. The previous version of Flight Simulator, Flight Simulator 98, took full advantage of this joystick's abilities, as does Flight Simulator 2000. The Force Feedback Pro features the following:

- Game port connection
- Three control axes
- Eight buttons
- Eight-way hat switch
- Trim controls
- Throttle controls
- Optical contacts (saves on wear and tear of internal mechanisms)

Force FX

The Force FX, from CH Products, was the first production force feedback joystick on the market, and it remains a popular alternative. According to CH Products, it has many force feedback effects, including jolt and vibration. Of course, each of the effects has various strengths and variations to enhance the flight simulator experience. The Force FX features the following:

- Game port connection
- Three control axes
- Six buttons
- Two 4-way hat switches.
- Programmable in Windows
- Trim controls
- A grip that is modeled after the control stick in the General Dynamics F-16 Fighting Falcon

Throttles

Many of the joysticks and yokes mentioned in this appendix include throttle controls. As a rule, separate throttles are used for military flight simulators, but if you use a plain-Jane joystick with Flight Simulator 2000, it might be worth getting the extra control and buttons that a separate throttle control can offer.

Pro Throttle

Besides offering the obvious action of throttle control, the Pro Throttle, from CH Products, has quite a few extra features and a solid feel. The Pro Throttle features the following:

- Game port connection
- Four single-fire buttons
- Four 4-way hat switches
- Programmable in Windows
- Sliding throttle action

F16 TQS Throttle

The F16 TQS Throttle, from ThrustMaster, is touted as a replica of the throttle of an F-16 Fighting Falcon. As with the Pro Throttle, the TQS is fully programmable and is designed to work in conjunction with ThrustMaster joysticks. It features the following:

- Two dials
- Two 3-position switches
- Four-way radio switch
- Afterburner and idle detents
- Authentic military design

Saitek X35T

The Saitek X35T is a feature-rich throttle that works best when coupled with the X36F joystick. Again, you can usually find it in a bundle with the X36F, but it can stand alone as well. The X35T has the following features:

- Game port connection
- Multiple standard buttons
- Rudder buttons for rudder control
- Three-position switch
- Four-way hat switch, eight-way hat switch
- Programmable in Windows
- Afterburner and idle detents

Rudder Pedals

To capture the true feel of flying and to execute aerobatics, you need to control the aircraft rudder yourself by turning off the Flight Simulator 2000 auto-rudder option and using a pair of rudder pedals. All aircraft except the Bell JetRanger use rudder pedals in pretty much the same way, and the Bell JetRanger makes use of a system very similar to rudder pedals. In short, if you want to fly the Bell JetRanger, do aerobatics in the Extra 300S, or have a more realistic experience flying the other aircraft in Flight Simulator, consider getting a set of rudder pedals.

When considering rudder controls, there are several features to look for. Make sure they have toe brakes. Toe brakes allow you to brake as you would in a real aircraft (where the brakes are applied by pushing toe-forward on the rudder pedals). The size of the base of the pedals is also important because when you press hard on the pedals, it produces a lot of force. Light rudder pedals might skid away from you when you apply pressure, whereas a heavy set of pedals or a set that anchors to the ground will stay put.

Elite Rudder Pedals

These rudder pedals from ThrustMaster provide solid performance in basic rudder control. Unlike a real aircraft's rudders, these rudders have no toe brakes, but for their cost, they're an excellent way to gain realistic rudder control. The Elite Rudder Pedals offer the following:

- True fore and aft movement (that is, not on a swivel base)
- Spring-loaded pivot that provides proportional spring tension
- Extra-large stable base
- Heavy-duty construction

Pro Pedals USB

This pedal set from CH Products is probably the most advanced rudder and pedal set available today. The motion is different from the motion in the ThrustMaster Rudder Pedals in that each pedal slides forward and backward inside the casing, rather than swinging on a moving arm, and the USB interface allows the Pro Pedals to incorporate toe brakes. Perhaps the biggest benefit of these pedals is that their price is very reasonable. Pro Pedals USB offers the following:

- Forward and backward motion for each pedal
- Three control axes
- Heal-to-toe motion for toe braking
- USB interface
- Large, heavy base

Headphones and Speakers

The visuals are only part of the flying experience; indeed, sound is also critical to achieve a quality level of realism. For this reason it's a good idea to get the best speakers you can afford. This usually means a set of speakers with an attached subwoofer (which greatly enhances sound quality). Fortunately the prices of these speaker sets have plummeted in recent years. Headphones are another good alternative, and in most cases they are cheaper (and for others in the room, quieter) than a speaker set.

Internet Resources

The following is a list of Internet addresses for companies that produce joysticks, flight yokes, speakers, and other accessories that can be used with Flight Simulator 2000.

Note: *The Internet is always changing. Web sites move, change their addresses, or disappear entirely. The addresses listed in this appendix were current at the time that this book was published, but in some cases you might have to use one of the major search engines to find a site's updated address.*

Joysticks and Flight Controls

- CH Products: *www.chproducts.com*
- Gravis: *www.gravis.com*
- Logitech: *www.logitech.com*
- Microsoft: *www.microsoft.com/hardware/sidewinder*
- Saitek USA: *www.saitekusa.com/home.html*
- Suncom Technologies, Inc.: *www.suncominc.com*
- ThrustMaster, Inc.: *www.thrustmaster.com*

Speakers and Headphones

- Altec Lansing: *www.alteclansing.com*
- Creative Technology Ltd.: *www.creative.com*
- Logitech: *www.logitech.com*
- Sony: *www.ita.sel.sony.com/*
- Yamaha: *www.yamaha.com*

The rudder pedals, joysticks, throttles, and flight yokes discussed in this appendix are only a small sampling of what is available for the flight simulator enthusiast. There are many products not mentioned here that also serve as great peripherals for use with Flight Simulator 2000.

Appendix B

ONLINE RESOURCES

There is a vast quantity of information, add-on products and adventures, and multiplayer resources on the Internet just waiting to take your Microsoft Flight Simulator 2000 experience to new heights. This appendix covers some of the Web sites and add-on products that are available to Flight Simulator 2000 enthusiasts.

Web Sites

Flight simulator enthusiasts make up a huge global community, and the Internet is their natural gathering place. This community includes a growing number of Web sites, which delve into every facet of flight simulators. The following Web sites are great places to find information on add-on aircraft, extra scenery, and gaming peripherals such as flight yokes and joysticks. These Web sites help you meet other people who share the same interests that you do; it's a great place to find flying partners. You'll also find the latest news in aviation, both simulated and real, as well as essential downloads such as patches and update files. Overall, the Internet provides you with many ways to share and build upon your flight simulator experience.

> **Note:** The Internet is always changing. Sites might move, change their addresses, or disappear entirely. The following Internet addresses were current at the time that this book was published, but in some cases you might have to use one of the major search engines to find a site's updated address.

The Official
Microsoft Games Web Site

One of the first Web sites that you'll want to look at is Microsoft's Web site Flight Simulator 2000 (*http://www.microsoft.com/games/fs2000/*). This site contains patches, technical support, controller profiles, links to other sites, and plenty of other Flight Simulator–related information.

AVSIM Online

The AVSIM Web site (*http://www.avsim.com*) is a great resource for news and current events of the flight simulator world. There are a number of forums in which you can discuss virtually any issue or question that comes to mind when you use Flight Simulator 2000. There is also an extensive file library with hundreds of aircraft to download, as well as detailed scenery files that you can add to the Scenery Library. AVSIM Online reviews freeware and commercial add-on products for Flight Simulator 2000, as well as peripherals and other products to enhance your enjoyment of the program. There's also an extensive online tutorial where you can learn the finer points of aircraft landing, instrument flying, scenery modification, and other advanced techniques.

Note: *New scenery and aircraft for Flight Simulator 2000 won't likely be available on line until after the SDK (Software Development Kit) is made public sometime after Flight Simulator 2000's release.*

FlightSim.Com

The FlightSim.Com Web site (*http://www.flightsim.com*) is a comprehensive site for simulation enthusiasts. It offers an enormous file library with many exclusive aircraft, and it also reviews add-on files and scenery. FlightSim.Com often features interviews with industry experts, scenery designers, and other professionals, and its online tutorials are very helpful for those just starting out in the world of flight simulators. Message forums, online contests, and industry news round out the offerings from this extensive Web site.

Landings

The Landings.com Web site (*http://www.landings.com*) is geared toward certified pilots. Its contents are so extensive that only a small portion can be mentioned here. Of particular interest to flight simulator enthusiasts are the news stories about significant events in aviation history, current industry news, safety reports, and links to aircraft manufacturers. You can also find many links to online stores that sell accessories such as maps, textbooks, flight logs, and aviator's sunglasses.

NTSB

The National Transportation Safety Board (NTSB) is the federal agency that investigates all civil aviation accidents (it's also responsible for safety in other modes of travel as well) in the United States and makes safety recommendations to prevent future accidents. At this Web site (*http://www.ntsb.gov/ aviation/aviation.htm*), you can access an online database of over 43,000 aviation accident descriptions that date back to 1983. Reading the accident reports is a powerful way to learn from past incidents.

FSGenesis

Justin Tyme is one of the world's premier add-on scenery developers for Flight Simulator 2000. His freeware and shareware scenery sets are so detailed that after installing his scenery, you can actually fly VFR (visual flight rules) in many areas of the country, even at night. (See Figure B-1.) The FSGenesis Web site (*http://www.fsgenesis.com*) offers screen shots (for previewing the scenery) and downloadable scenery sets to use with Flight Simulator 2000.

Figure B-1 *Some of the scenery from the PANJ scenery pack.*

MicroWINGS

MicroWINGS (*http://www.microwings.com*) is the site of the International Association for Aerospace Simulations. It provides a large number of links to other sites, add-ons, and the *MicroWINGS Magazine*. This is a great one-stop site for tons of great flight and flight simulator information.

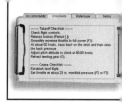

Horizon Group Software Publishing

This Web site (*http://www.fsaddon.com*) sells add-on scenery packs for flight simulator products. Products include a global scenery upgrade package and an Airbus package that includes hordes of various Airbus Industries aircraft in a wide variety of paint schemes.

Newsgroups

Usenet, another name for Internet newsgroups, is another area of the Internet where flight simulator enthusiasts gather to exchange information. You can browse the newsgroups using Microsoft Outlook Express or at *http:// www.deja.com*. The following newsgroups usually have pertinent, interesting information and discussions:

- *microsoft.public.simulators*
- *rec.aviation.simulators*
- *comp.sys.ibm.pc.games.flight-sim*
- *rec.aviation.piloting*
- *rec.aviation.misc*

Virtual Airlines

A virtual airline is another way to use online connections to add even more realism to Flight Simulator. A virtual airline is a group of flight simulator pilots who get together regularly to fly preassigned routes. A member of a virtual airline is assigned a particular flight route just as a commercial pilot is assigned a route for a real airline. The pilot must then fly that route, log his or her hours, and report back to the main office. Virtual airlines provide some structure and direction for flight simulator pilots who are looking for another way to direct their flight simulation activities.

There are two types of virtual airlines: fantasy virtual airlines and real world virtual airlines. Fantasy virtual airlines have fictitious names and logos, but their destinations are real airports in Flight Simulator 2000. Real world virtual airlines are modeled after actual airlines, and they fly the very same routes between the same cities that the real airlines serve.

Specific virtual airlines come and go. It wouldn't be very useful to list any of their Internet addresses here because new airlines sprout up as quickly as older ones retire or consolidate. The best place to find virtual airlines is by browsing a list of virtual airline links in a flight simulator Web site such as AVSIM Online (*http://www.avsim.com*) or FlightSim.Com (*http://www.flightsim.com*).

Add-Ons

This section covers a few popular add-ons in the vast number of add-on products available for Flight Simulator 2000. For an even more extensive and current listing of add-on products, consult the Web sites *http://www.avsim.com* and *http://www.flightsim.com*.

Roger Wilco

Roger Wilco is a product that adds real-time voice communication to Flight Simulator 2000, thus freeing you up from typing out your multiplayer messages by hand. (See *http://www.resounding.com*.) After you install Roger Wilco, all you need to do is find one or more flying partners, create a channel using your Internet Protocol (IP) address, and invite others to join you.

Note: *There's no scientific way to find users in the Microsoft Internet Gaming Zone who are using Roger Wilco. Often the best way to use this feature is to go online with a friend who you know is using Roger Wilco.*

You'll then be able to fly and talk to people at the same time. In some multiplayer games, one player acts as an air traffic controller and directs people around the traffic pattern. Nothing else approaches the feel of flying through controlled airspace when you're directed by the voice of ATC!

> **Tip:** *In the rooms on the MSN Gaming Zone, you might see people refer to "RW" in their room title. This means that the players in that room are using Roger Wilco to talk to one another while in flight. Contact someone in the chat room to find out the IP address of the host.*

Extra Aircraft

Have you ever wanted to fly a DeHavilland Twin Otter? How about a Piper Cub or an F-117 Stealth Fighter? Or a blimp, or even a UFO? One of Microsoft Flight Simulator's unique strengths has always been its support for third-party add-on aircraft files. There are literally hundreds of different aircraft, instrument panels, and sounds that have been created by other flight simulator enthusiasts, and you can download the majority of these files for free. All you need to do is copy the files into the appropriate Flight Simulator 2000 folder on your hard disk, following the installation instructions from the source, and then restart the game. The new aircraft will appear in the Select Aircraft dialog box.

There are many sources for add-on planes, but the best place to look is the file libraries at AVSIM Online and FlightSim.Com. You might also meet players through the Internet who will send you the files for a particular plane. Always make sure to scan files that you downloaded with a virus protection program, and follow the installation instructions exactly. It also doesn't hurt to make a backup copy of the Gauges folder if you're replacing anything in it. Some add-on aircraft must be installed directly in the Gauges folder, while others simply go in the aircraft folder.

One of the most meticulous, well-regarded aircraft developers is FlightSim Developers (*http://www.flightsim.com/flightsim-developers*). From this Web site you can download dozens of highly detailed aircraft, including the B-29

Stratofortress, the Lockheed Constellation, and the McDonnell Douglas MD-11. One of the nicest features of these aircraft is that FlightSim Developers makes up custom instrument panels for most of its planes, with instruments that work just like the real thing.

During multiplayer games, other players will be able to see the add-on planes only if they have also downloaded those particular planes. If you are flying on a local area network (LAN) or if you have a very fast connection to the Internet, such as with a cable modem or a Digital Subscriber Line (DSL), you can modify the FS2000.cfg file in the Microsoft Flight Simulator 2000 folder on your hard disk to send the plane data to other pilots in the area so that they'll be able to see your custom aircraft. Simply open the FS2000.cfg file in Notepad or some other text editor and look for the lines in the [MULTIPLAYER] section that read:

```
ALLOW_PLANE_MODEL_SEND = 0
ALLOW_PLANE_MODEL_RECEIVE = 0
ALLOW_TEXTURE_SEND = 0
ALLOW_TEXTURE_ RECEIVE = 0
```

Change all the 0s to 1s. Save and close the file. Now other pilots will be able to see your aircraft. This modification can slow down the simulation considerably, so make sure you have a fast connection to the Internet.

Extra Scenery

Installing extra scenery is an easy, inexpensive way to add more detail to your favorite flying areas in Flight Simulator 2000. Highly detailed, realistic terrain has been created for virtually every part of the United States and many areas around the world. Much of this work is done by flight simulator enthusiasts who have an interest in flying VFR around their own home state or an area about which they have personal knowledge. This additional scenery is often provided as a service to the flight simulator community, with no expectation of reimbursement beyond a few words of thanks or a postcard from those who use the scenery.

You can download scenery from the file libraries at AVSIM Online or FlightSim.Com. In most cases, you'll need to unzip the scenery into the Flight Simulator folder on your hard disk and then add the scenery as a scenery layer by clicking Scenery Library on the World menu. Most scenery sets come with detailed installation instructions, which you should follow exactly for best results.

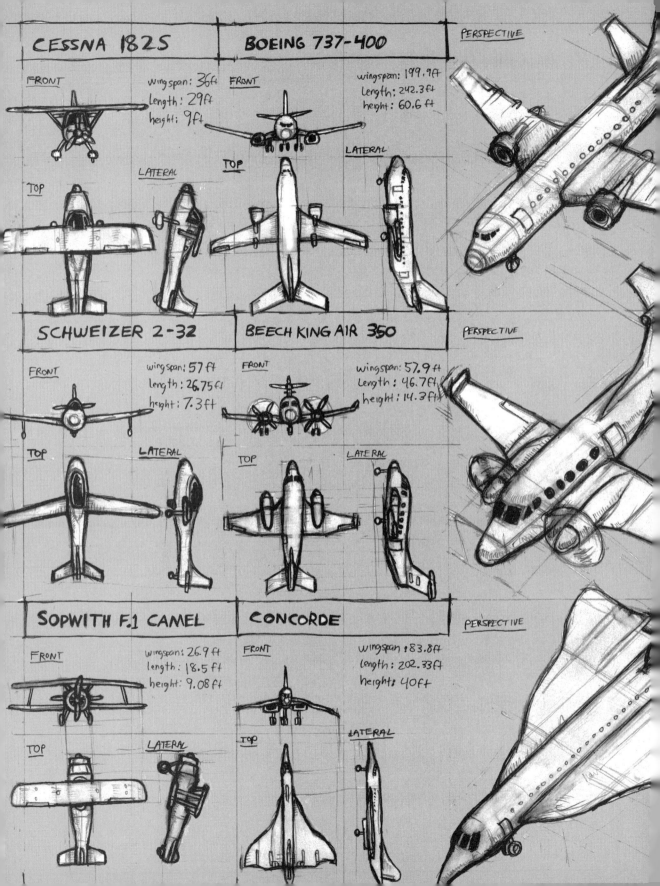

CESSNA 182S

FRONT

wingspan: 36ft
length: 29ft
height: 9ft

TOP

LATERAL

BOEING 737-400

FRONT

wingspan: 199.9ft
Length: 242.3ft
height: 60.6ft

TOP

LATERAL

PERSPECTIVE

SCHWEIZER 2-32

FRONT

wingspan: 57ft
length: 26.75ft
height: 7.3ft

TOP

LATERAL

BEECH KING AIR 350

FRONT

wingspan: 57.9ft
Length: 46.7ft
height: 14.3ft

TOP

LATERAL

PERSPECTIVE

SOPWITH F.1 CAMEL

FRONT

wingspan: 26.9ft
length: 18.5ft
height: 9.08ft

TOP

LATERAL

CONCORDE

FRONT

wingspan: 83.8ft
length: 202.33ft
height: 40ft

TOP

LATERAL

PERSPECTIVE

Index

·······························➤

Italicized page references indicate illustrations.

Bart Farkas

Bart Farkas is the author of over 25 books, including computer game strategy guides and help books. A relatively new pilot, Bart flies a (rented) Cessna 172 Skyhawk in and around the foothills of the Rocky Mountains. Bart lives with his wife, son, and two cats in the tropical climes of Calgary, Canada.

T he manuscript for this book was prepared and submitted to Microsoft Press in electronic form. Text files were prepared using Microsoft Word 2000. Pages were composed by Microsoft Press using Adobe PageMaker 6.52 for Windows, with text in Garamond and display type in Ultra Condensed Sans One and Helvetica Condensed Black. Composed pages were delivered to the printer as electronic prepress files.

Cover Graphic Designer

Tom Draper Design

Interior Graphic Artists

Rob Nance, Joel Panchot

Principal Compositor

Carl Diltz

Indexer

Bill Meyers

Sample Chapter from

inside moves

Microsoft®
AGE
of
EMPIRES® II
The Age of Kings™

Mark H. Walker

Want to learn how to conquer like a king? Read on to see a sample chapter from MICROSOFT AGE OF EMPIRES II: THE AGE OF KINGS: INSIDE MOVES—another winning game title from Microsoft Press.

Skill is good—but *knowledge* wins games. If you find MICROSOFT FLIGHT SIMULATOR 2000: INSIDE MOVES helpful, we'd like to suggest a title packed with inside tips, tricks, and tactics for mastering another exciting Microsoft game. The following chapter, excerpted directly from MICROSOFT AGE OF EMPIRES II: THE AGE OF KINGS: INSIDE MOVES, reveals strategic gambits and tactical maneuvers to help you triumph with the new version of Microsoft Age of Empires!

- Discover how to survive and thrive in the thousand years from the fall of Rome to the Middle Ages, when the destiny of humanity was at stake.
- Learn play-tested techniques for conquering enemy states, accumulating wealth, and creating and defending wonders of the world.
- Execute a winning strategy: Should you build a barracks before a farm, or a marketplace before a temple? INSIDE MOVES can guide you through questions like these—helping you build a tiny tribe into a mighty civilization!

About the Author:
Mark H. Walker is a former naval officer who has written and published nearly 75 articles and books about computer technology and game strategy. And when he's not writing, running, scuba diving, or playing computer games, he's racing cars.

Contents

AGE
of
EMPIRES II

Contents

PART I

Civilization-Specific Strategies and Backgrounds for *The Age of Kings*

AGE
of
EMPIRES II

Microsoft Age of Empires II: The Age of Kings picks up where the first game's expansion pack left off. Rome has fallen, marking the beginning of the Middle Ages. The result is a group of warring tribes and civilizations striving to build an empire of their own. Some of the more notable kingdoms include those of Genghis Khan's Mongols, Justinian's Byzantines, Sultan Osman's Turks, and the Chinese T'ang Dynasty. Overall, 13 different civilizations are featured:

- Britons
- Byzantines
- Celts
- Chinese
- Franks
- Goths
- Japanese
- Mongols
- Persians
- Saracens
- Teutons
- Turks
- Vikings

Each civilization uses similar weaponry; however, available technologies and units depend on each empire's unique history. For example, Persians have a strong cavalry of War Elephants, Vikings sail in Longboats, and the Japanese commission their famed Samurai warriors for battle. Other historical characteristics taken into account include China's large population and the Ottoman Empire's (Turks') heavy use of gunpowder units. To better acquaint you with these diverse features, the following chapters contain strategies and information for all 13 civilizations.

Chapter One

THE BRITONS

Like much of Europe during the early Middle Ages, Britain was besieged with countless invasions and battles. In fact, Attila's Huns were driving through the continental mainland at about the same time that Germanic and Danish tribes migrated to the British Isles. By the ninth century, Britain was composed primarily of Angles, Saxons, Jutes, and Celts. The southern part of Britain, settled by Anglo-Saxons, came to be called "Angle Land" (or England), while the northern part of the island was named after the Scotti, a Celtic tribe inhabiting the area. A distinct culture with its roots in the north soon emerged in southern Britain—the Britons. As missionaries brought Christianity to many of these new inhabitants, others entertained themselves with stories of adventure and valor, primarily in the form of the Arthurian legends and Beowulf tales.

Britain itself offered plenty of sword-wielding adventures in the latter part of the Middle Ages. Vikings began attacking the coast in the ninth century. Nearly 200 years later, William the Conqueror and the Normans captured the crown of England. The Crusades followed some time later, with Britain's own Richard the Lionhearted demonstrating his bravery and strength in the Holy Land. The Hundred Years War then ensued in France. The advent of the English Longbow contributed to major victories in the early stages of the war. Inevitably, though, the Franks (with the inspiration of Joan of Arc) were able to beat back the Britons from France.

Maximizing Strengths and Minimizing Weaknesses

At first glance, it might seem that the Britons should be the offensive power-house of *Age of Empires II* (as shown in Figure 1-1). Such a notion is to be expected since England is the "land of kings," known worldwide for its royalty

Figure 1-1   *The Britons harbor a classic hack-and-fling army.*

and castles. No doubt, the Britons are a strong civilization; however, they lack some of the more decisive abilities and heavy hitting units offered to other civilizations. For instance, British Monks do not have the ability to convert buildings or other Monks. The English also lack gunpowder-based units; in fact, they are the only civilization that doesn't use the Cannon Galleon. The unavailability of certain Imperial Age siege weapons, too, can create problems late in a game.

Despite such deficiencies in technology, the Britons, needless to say, still field quite an army and have many other strengths. For starters, the English put lots of emphasis on using archery in combat. When the Britons are engaged in team play, their Archery Ranges train Archers faster than any other in the game. Furthermore, the Blacksmith upgrades and increased range advantages in the Castle and Imperial Ages encourage you to continue creating Crossbowmen and Arbalests. (See Figure 1-2.) Their superiority to rival Archers is obvious.

Tip: *Create more than one Archery Range on a map to use all of your archery advantages to the fullest. Use the foot Archers for defense and offense. Place them on hilltops to attack enemy Villagers parading by.*

Additionally, the Briton's special unit is the Longbowmen, who are foot archers with extended range—think Robin Hood on steroids. These guys were especially influential in battles against the Franks and Celts. Stationed bdwlind a line of melee units, Longbowmen can do serious damage to an opponent's Knights and Cavaliers. I recommend using

them in all of your land attacks. Their range and attack strength are un-matched by any other medieval Archer.

The Infantry and Cavalry are no slouches either. They do not have special skills, but the plentitude of units and technologies available makes them formidable comple-ments to the Long-bowmen. They are especially great at injuring an opponent during the Castle Age—before any of your foes have a chance to use gunpowder technology.

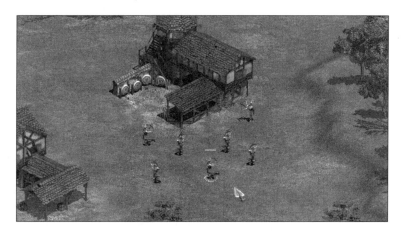

Figure 1-2 *British Arbalests hone their skills at the Archery Range.*

How Changes Through the Ages Affect Tactics

The Britons are a strong civilization in any age, whether it's Dark or Imperial. They do, however, change form as they march through time. The following sections will show how to make the best of the metamorphosis and march them to victory.

Dark Age

At the beginning of the Dark Age, your Town Center should produce 10 to 20 Villagers, and the first ones should build Houses. Meanwhile, send your Scout Cavalry over the terrain to search for resources and the enemy's location. Keep an eye out for Sheep. For each herd of Sheep you find, send a Villager to that area to shepherd them back to the Town Center. Have your Villagers collect Wood as well.

> **Note:** *Conserving resources is important, especially in the beginning of the Dark Age. British Shepherds work faster than those from other civilizations, so it's advantageous to keep Sheep for food. Besides, whereas Farms require a Mill and Wood to keep them running, resources such as Sheep and Deer only need a Villager to look after them.*

Send some Militia in to battle enemy Villagers. If you can, destroy their Barracks first. Disrupt the enemy's economic progress, military progress, or both as much as possible. However, don't recklessly send your units into a well-defended village to be massacred. After all, "discretion is the better part of valor," as Shakespeare once wrote. Build a Mill and some Farms to stockpile enough food for progression into the next Age. Upgrade to the next level as soon as possible.

Feudal Age

Build a Blacksmith and then an Archery Range while upgrading your Militia to Men-at-Arms. Send some Archers and Skirmishers to guard Gold and Stone sites near the enemy settlement. While they're protecting the sites, order several Villagers to mine the area. Construct some Watch Towers nearby if you encounter frequent opposition.

Figure 1-3 *Coordinate Galley attacks upon enemy Fishing Ships to cripple the opponent's economy in seafaring missions.*

Invest in the upgrades provided at the Blacksmith. Next, send some Men-at-Arms and Archers to destroy enemy sites such as Mining Camps. If you are playing on a map with a significant amount of water, send Galleys to attack enemy Fishing Ships (as shown in Figure 1-3). Place Stone Walls around your

island or location. These structures will buy you time if enemy Transport Ships try to establish a beachhead near your settlement. If you find enemy excursions a problem, just wait until the next Age when you can direct Heated Shots from your Towers at the ships.

> **Tip:** *Construct a Market if you are playing on a map with limited resources. In those cases, buying and selling goods is the quickest way to advance to the next Age.*

Castle Age

This is the period of the game where things usually get interesting. Not only do you have more resources, but you also have a greater and more diverse number of units at your disposal. In general, these two advantages can require or lead to two things: research and battles. Don't skimp on either; otherwise, you'll be out of the picture by the time you enter the Imperial Age.

Continue with upgrades at the Mill and Blacksmith. Erect a University, Stable, and Siege Workshop. Produce a group of Light Cavalry and Crossbowmen. Next, build a Castle and Town Center near the enemy's settlement, using the Light Cavalry and Crossbowmen to defend the builders. Train some Longbowmen at the Castle. It's time to begin your attack on the enemy's village.

Set up a group of Longbowmen and Knights, place them in Flank Formation, and send them into the opponent's camp. Attacking the same target from different directions "sandwiches" enemy units, enabling you to effectively thin out enemy units. While enemy mobile units are distracted, concentrate Mangonel firepower upon your foe's Castle Age buildings, in particular the University.

> **Tip:** *Build a University. Although Chemistry isn't much help at this point, Ballistics can improve the accuracy of your Archers—another step toward creating the perfect warrior. Unfortunately, many enemies can use Chemistry research to create gunpowder units in the next Age. That's why you need to destroy as many enemy Universities as possible.*

Imperial Age

The Britons are not as well equipped for battle in this Age as in previous ones. They lack the big guns—the Cannon Galleon and Bombard Cannon—that medieval enemies such as the Franks and Saracens have. The key to taking down civilizations with such technology is either to prevent them from building a University or to utilize your strength in numbers by executing lots of attacks with Cavaliers and Longbowmen (as shown in Figure 1-4).

Figure 1-4   *Continue to emphasize your strength in numbers in the final stages of a game.*

Fortunately for the Britons, other enemies—such as the Celts and Vikings— lack Bombard Cannons and Bombard Towers. The Vikings, however, do have a strong navy capable of building Cannon Galleons. When playing against the Vikings in seafaring battles, concentrate in the Feudal and Castle Ages on dominating the water with many War Galleys and Fire Ships. Because of their firing speed and maneuverability, Fire Ships are also the best British naval vessel for battling enemy Cannon Galleons. (See Figure 1-5.)

Figure 1-5   *Fire Ships are best suited for sinking Cannon Galleons.*

Unique Unit Tactics: Longbowman

> **Note:** *The Longbowman's range is longer than that of the typical Archer, while still yielding about the same attack points as the Man-at-Arms.*

British Longbowmen are perhaps one of the best unique units in the game, as they can shoot farther than any archery unit in *Age of Empires II*. With that advantage, they can stand far away from the battle, sparing them from enemy Crossbowmen's fire. Using them in Flank Formation (as shown in Figure 1-6) allows gamers to surround enemy units with a barrage of firepower, improving accuracy and decreasing the damage done to the melee units.

Stationing a horde of Longbowmen on ledges or hills gives them free reign to attack unsuspecting enemies while awarding them the game's height bonus.

Just make sure that you place them in Stand Ground mode so that they do not rush into a situation they cannot handle. For protection, use a couple of melee units to guard the Longbowmen. You can also garrison several Longbowmen in one of your Towers to increase the structure's attack points.

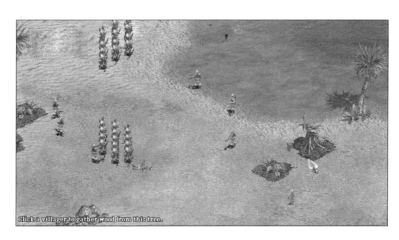

Figure 1-6   *Placing Longbowmen in Flank Formation has obvious advantages.*

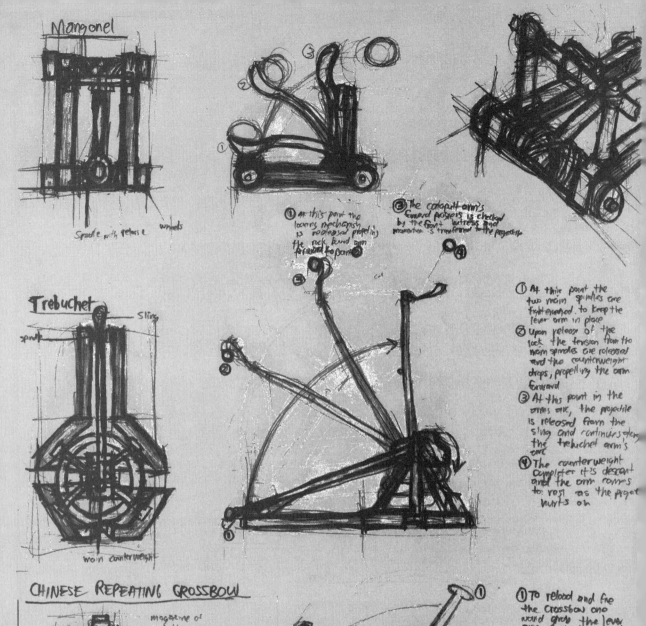

Mangonel

Spindle with release   wheels

① At this point the loading mechanism is released propelling the rock bound arm forward to point

② The catapult arm's forward progress is checked by the front buttress and momentum is transferred to the projectile

① At this point the two main spindles are tightened/loosened to keep the lever arm in place

② Upon release of the lock the tension from the main spindles are released and the counterweight drops, propelling the arm forward

③ At this point in the arm's arc, the projectile is released from the sling and continues along the trebuchet arm's arc

④ The counterweight completes its descent and the arm comes to rest as the projectile hurls on

Trebuchet

Sling   spindle   main counterweight

CHINESE REPEATING CROSSBOW

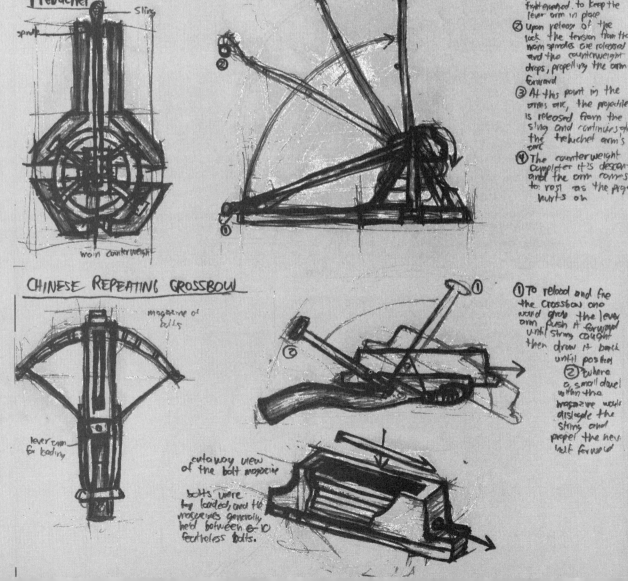

magazine of bolts

lever arm for loading

① To reload and fire the crossbow one would grab the lever arm push it forward until string caught then draw it back until position

② where a small dowel within the magazine would dislodge the string and propel the next bolt forward

cutaway view of the bolt magazine

bolts were top loaded, and the magazines generally held between 8-10 featherless bolts.

Expert *advice!*

Master the expert tips, tricks, tactics, and strategies for popular Microsoft games with the Microsoft Press® INSIDE MOVES series. Most of this inside information comes straight from the game developers and isn't available anywhere else. So to get the most fun from the game, get the book!

- MICROSOFT® AGE OF EMPIRES® II: THE AGE OF KINGS™: INSIDE MOVES. ISBN: 0-7356-0513-0

- MICROSOFT FLIGHT SIMULATOR 2000: INSIDE MOVES. ISBN: 0-7356-0547-5

- MICROSOFT COMBAT FLIGHT SIMULATOR: INSIDE MOVES. ISBN: 1-57231-592-X

- MICROSOFT URBAN ASSAULT™: INSIDE MOVES. ISBN: 1-57231-861-9

Microsoft®

mspress.microsoft.com

It's your move.

Sharpen every facet of your game with these readable, entertaining, and brilliantly insightful books—the Microsoft Press® WINNING CHESS series, written by Yasser Seirawan, one of the world's top-ranked chess players.

PLAY WINNING CHESS is a valuable introduction to the moves, strategies, and philosophy of chess, with clear explanations of the game's fundamentals, instructive examples, question-and-answer sections, sample games, and psychological hints.
ISBN: 0-7356-0919-5

WINNING CHESS ENDINGS is a gripping guide to what you need to know to prevail consistently in chess endings. You'll master strategies for all basic endgame patterns and learn to march relentlessly to the checkmate with common and uncommon combinations of pieces.
ISBN: 0-7356-0791-5

WINNING CHESS TACTICS is the essential guide to the use of tactics—the watchdogs of strategy that take advantage of short-term opportunities to trap or ambush an opponent and change the course of a game in a single move.
ISBN: 0-7356-0917-9

WINNING CHESS STRATEGIES is a complete overview of proven chess principles that teaches you how to deploy your pieces using the right moves at the right time to build small advantages into effective, long-range strategies.
ISBN: 0-7356-0916-0

WINNING CHESS OPENINGS shows beginning players how to survive the game's opening phase and how to choose appropriate attack and defense formations in the process.
ISBN: 0-7356-0915-2

WINNING CHESS BRILLIANCIES is a scintillating, move-by-move account of the best chess games of the last 25 years, played by the world's greatest Grandmasters. These awe-inspiring and controversial games are made enjoyable and easy to understand.
ISBN: 0-7356-0918-7

Recommended price for each title in the series:

U.S.A.	$19.99
U.K.	£14.99
Canada	$30.99

Microsoft Press products are available worldwide wherever quality computer books are sold. For more information, contact your book or computer retailer, software reseller, or local Microsoft® Sales Office, or visit our Web site at mspress.microsoft.com. To locate your nearest source for Microsoft Press products, or to order directly, call 1-800-MSPRESS in the U.S. (in Canada, call 1-800-268-2222).

Prices and availability dates are subject to change.

Microsoft®

mspress.microsoft.com

OWNER REGISTRATION CARD

Register Today!

0-7356-0547-5

Return the bottom portion of this card to register today.

Microsoft® Flight Simulator 2000: Inside Moves

FIRST NAME   MIDDLE INITIAL   LAST NAME

INSTITUTION OR COMPANY NAME

ADDRESS

CITY   STATE   ZIP

(   )

E-MAIL ADDRESS   PHONE NUMBER

U.S. and Canada addresses only. Fill in information above and mail postage-free.
Please mail only the bottom half of this page.

For information about Microsoft Press®
products, visit our Web site at
mspress.microsoft.com

Microsoft·Press